The Art of
EVALUATION

The Art of
EVALUATION

A Resource for Educators and Trainers

Second Edition

TARA J. FENWICK
University of British Columbia

JIM PARSONS
University of Alberta

THOMPSON EDUCATIONAL PUBLISHING, INC.
Toronto

Information on how to obtain copies of this book is available at:

Website: www.thompsonbooks.com
E-mail: publisher@thompsonbooks.com
Phone: 416-766-2763
Fax: 416-766-0398

Library and Archives Canada Cataloguing in Publication

Fenwick, Tara J
     The art of evaluation : a resource for educators and trainers /
Tara J. Fenwick and Jim Parsons. — 2nd ed.

Includes bibliographical references and index.
ISBN 978-1-55077-166-4

     1. Adult education—Evaluation--Textbooks. 2. Educational tests and measurements—Textbooks. I. Parsons, Jim, 1948– II. Title.

LB3051.F46 2008   374'.126   C2008-905184-X

Publisher: Keith Thompson
Acquisitions Editor: Michael Valerio
Project Editor: Rachel Stuckey
Proofreading: Gillian Urbankiewicz
Design: Christine Kwan

Formatting: Tibor Choleva and Christine Kwan

Thompson Educational Publishing, Inc.
20 Ripley Avenue, Toronto, Ontario, Canada, M6S 3N9

We acknowledge the financial support of the Government of Canada through the Book Publishing Industry Development Program (BPIDP) for our publishing activities.

Printed in Canada.

2 3 4 5 6 7 8   16 15 14 13

Contents

Preface

Evaluation is an integral part of learning. In this age of accountability, assessment of learning outcomes has become a critical, albeit daunting, responsibility for many educators. We are supposed to develop clear criteria for learner capacities that are frequently emergent, unclear, and constantly changing. We are supposed to report comprehensive and realistic measurements of highly complex and often invisible human understandings and abilities. Above all, presumably, we hope to honour learners and their individual processes and to keep their growth and their own understanding of their development at the centre of our evaluation purposes.

This book is intended as a practical introduction to learner evaluation in various contexts of adult education. We have attempted to address issues and provide examples that would fit the interests of students of adult education, new college and university teachers, trainers in business and government, and consultants whose work involves learner evaluation. Every educator works within a unique context of learners, purposes, structures, and cultures. Every reader, therefore, needs to be critical and selective when choosing among the materials offered in this book. Some of it will suit you, some of it may not fit your philosophy or your situation, and some of it will need adaptation to be useful in your work. We hope that the book becomes a useful reference for beginning educators and trainers, and perhaps even for experienced instructors looking for some new strategies and perspectives.

Our focus here is the learner and the instructor, rather than the program. Of course, all evaluation of learning must be considered within the total context of the program and institution, but program evaluation seeks different purposes, resolving different questions than learner evaluation.

> "Celebrate what you want to see more of."
> – Tom Peters

Features of the New Edition

Each chapter begins with an introductory statement to focus the reader on the key issues. A new, engaging design helps identify the interactive forms and models throughout, and includes margin boxes, full-page features, and a variety of lists and examples. As modes and methods of learning develop, so to must assessment and evaluation; for example, since the publication of the first edition, the role of internet-based curriculum has greatly expanded. To help the reader understand how new developments in education impact assessment and evaluation, two new chapters have been added. Chapter 15: Assessment for Learning explains the principles of assessment for learning and gives examples of how it can be used to raise learner achievement. Chapter 16: Assessing Online Distance Learning discusses the impact of online learning and provides tools and strategies to promote dynamic assessment and evaluation. The Toolbox section offers twelve self-contained pullouts on topics ranging from portfolio assessment to using objective tests. Finally, this new edition includes key terms with margin definitions.

Contents

We start with the basics. In Chapters 1 through 5 we encourage readers to carefully examine fundamental issues in evaluation purposes and planning, criteria development, and evaluation strategies. In Chapters 6 through 10 we explore different evaluation approaches for assessing conceptual growth, technical skill mastery, and relational skills. For instructors working within an institution, we have included a chapter about the meaning of grades and grading practices. You will see our bias towards integration of authentic assessment into all parts of learning and life in Chapters 11 to 16. These are crucial chapters for us, offering arguments and suggestions for making assessment "dynamic," and for focusing mostly on learners' self-assessment and continuous assessment as an ongoing, integral part of education, even when one must assign a "grade." Chapter 17 ends the way it begins: encouraging readers to reflect deeply upon their own practice and philosophy in evaluating learners. Finally, to further emphasize the practical nature of evaluation, this text ends with the Toolbox section, which offers additional strategies for evaluation to complement those found throughout each chapter.

We believe that the richest growth opportunities for us as educators are embedded in our own dilemmas of everyday practice and the selves that emerge from them. When we are able to confront these dilemmas knowledgeably, lovingly, critically, and courageously, we can begin to work through them. Only then do we begin doing what this book suggests that we help learners to do—integrate self-evaluation into the fabric of our lives.

1

The Purpose of Evaluation

Is Anybody Learning Anything Out There?

Evaluation is shot through with issues of power, responsibility, sensitivity, and even personal taste. You already know a great deal about evaluation because you make judgments every day. However, everyone who wishes to study evaluation must first grapple with important and fundamental questions about teaching, learning, and evaluation.

> "Our perceptions of people and events shape the reality we then end up struggling with so much... Every time we go to measure something, we interfere."
>
> – Margaret Wheatley

Educational evaluation is becoming more important every day. Resources are scarce, budgets are tight, and quality is the bottom line. People need to know they are getting good value for their educational dollar. Accountability is the rallying cry of today's organizations, and continuous measurement of individuals, teams, businesses, and institutions is considered to be the vehicle. In simple terms, accountability means measuring how well people or programs keep their promises. Yet a recent survey found that, of all the training conducted by private and public organizations, less than 25 percent of the trainers used any form of evaluation of the learning besides learner satisfaction surveys, or "smile sheets."

The Importance of Authentic Evaluation

Accountability asks three questions: Who is responsible? What are they responsible for? To whom are they responsible? To evaluate for accountability you need to know the objectives or goals of the person or program. You must also determine what you will use as evidence of learner improvement. The more accurate and defensible your criteria, the more confident you can be that your evaluation is authentic. In other words, you usually can't find what you don't know you are looking for.

Note that when we use the term measurement, we use it broadly. Some teachers believe that what gets measured is what gets learned. But measurement can restrict learning. For example, if we equate measurement only with the use of the numbers on a metre stick, we limit measurement to spatial arrangements and physical things. But, because learning involves more than just the physical, using only numbers is limiting.

Many teachers or program developers believe that measurement should be physical or scientific. But counting doesn't tell the whole story. For example, if you are trying to teach a second language to adult learners, you might be inclined to base the evaluation of your teaching on a count of new vocabulary words your students know at the end of the week. To measure these words, you could give your adult students a test on Monday (a pre-test) before teaching the vocabulary and another test on Friday after five days of teaching (a post-test). You would probably find that your students know more words on Friday than they did at the beginning of the week. And you would be pleased with yourself as a teacher, your students, and your curriculum program.

But research shows that the pre-test/post-test design is an unreliable indicator of program effectiveness, because so many unmeasurable influences besides the educational program affect learner achievement. For example, how might you evaluate the work of a second teacher whose chief talents lie in making learning comfortable for students and inspiring them to learn? The test scores of that teacher's students may fall below those of the teacher who drills vocabulary on short-term numerical evaluations; however, in the long run, the second teacher's students may have distinct advantages that would only show up after six months of learning. Plus, the second teacher's students might have more fun in class. Is fun important to learning, even if there are no immediate numerical advantages? That's a question you have to answer for yourself. The point is that knowing what to evaluate is not always easy. You must always be aware of what you are selecting to evaluate—and what you are omitting.

Evaluation provides critical feedback that we all know is essential to the learning process. Yet for many adults the very thought of having their performance evaluated causes anxiety and defensiveness, especially if they feel vulnerable in the learning situation. Their self-esteem is on the line. Most adults can point to painful personal memories of what they remember as brutal evaluation practices. Sadly, to many adults the word *evaluation* still means "a test." The word test itself has all sorts of negative connotations, especially around the issue of power. Teachers know what is going to be on the test; students must guess how to shape what they know to fit the teacher's frameworks. When evaluating student work, teachers assume powerful roles as controllers of knowledge; what the teacher decides is important may or may not fit what students see as important or what students need.

Evaluation is the systematic collection and analysis of data needed to make decisions, a process in which most well-run programs engage from the outset.

Nine Purposes of Evaluation

To better understand how to evaluate, we must ask what we are doing and why we are doing it. Listed below are nine different reasons for evaluating learners.

1. To compare actual learner performance to the goals of the instruction

The most common purpose of evaluation is to compare learning progress to learning goals. A complementary purpose is to give learners information about their learning.

To See a Learner Is To See Possibility

A *Peanuts* cartoon shows Sally at school, ruefully studying a mangled, shapeless piece of wire that has been graded and returned to her by her teacher, with a "C." "How could anyone get a 'C' in coat-hanger sculpture?" she asks herself.

She finally puts up her hand and launches into a veritable treatise on the subject of evaluation: "Was I judged on the piece of sculpture itself? If so, is it not true that time alone can judge a work of art? Or was I judged on my talent? If so, is it right that I be judged on a part of life over which I have no control?"

Soon Sally finds herself on a roll and raves on to the entire class. "If I was judged on my effort, then I was judged unfairly for I tried as hard as I could! Was I judged on what I had learned about this project? If so, then were you, my teacher, not also being judged on your ability to transmit your knowledge to me? Are you willing to share my 'C'?"

"Perhaps I was being judged on the quality of the coat hanger itself out of which my creation was made. Is this not also unfair? Am I to be judged by the quality of coat-hangers that are used by the dry-cleaning establishment that returns our garments? Is that not the responsibility of my parents? Should they not share my 'C'?"

Settling back in her desk, she concludes smugly to the reader, "The squeaky wheel gets the grease!"

Who and what is linked to the progress of the learners you work with?

2. To help learners make decisions about their next action

A second, related, purpose of evaluation is to help students (and teachers) make decisions about how they should proceed (more study, practice, remedial help, or further instruction). Used in this way, evaluation can increase student motivation.

3. To monitor students' ongoing progress

A third purpose of evaluation is to monitor an individual student's progress along the learning journey. Some goals are long-term, complex, or incremental. The best way to evaluate these complex goals is to break them into parts—to think of learning as a series of actions instead of a single, one time event. Unless there is a single bit of content to learn, learning is more like a journey than a destination.

4. To assess the teaching methods

A fourth purpose of evaluation is to determine how effective teaching has been. Is there a high correlation between what students are learning and what the teacher is teaching? How do the teacher's actions affect how the students are learning?

5. To revise the program

A fifth linked purpose of evaluation is to review and revise the teacher's or the learner's program plan. Evaluation can be used to make decisions about changes to the program.

6. To provide information for other stakeholders

A sixth purpose of evaluation, and one that is growing in importance, is to provide quantitative data that will satisfy the public interest. In other words, governments use evaluation to support public decisions. The idea is simple: before government commits money to education, it needs to know whether the money is being well spent.

7. To assess a learner's background knowledge

A seventh purpose of evaluation is to assess a student's prior knowledge, skill, or experience before beginning a new learning experience. In times of rapid change in society and the workplace, people change jobs often. Evaluation helps institutions or employers provide satisfactory and efficient instruction. Good teaching is efficient. It is not helpful to teach content that students have already learned or that is far beyond their maturity level.

8. To determine learner satisfaction

An eighth purpose of evaluation is to discover whether learners are satisfied with the instruction they have been given. Central to democratic teaching is the belief that students should have input into the content and the *methodologies* of their learning. Evaluation can help students make their feelings about the learning process known to those who are in charge of their instruction.

9. To develop self-assessment in learners

Finally, a ninth purpose for evaluation is to help learners evaluate themselves. In these cases the evaluation becomes instructional. New knowledge and habits of behaviour are only incorporated into long-term changes when learners develop strategies and criteria for monitoring their own ongoing performance.

Although the specific ways of evaluating may seem scientific or complex, the idea of evaluation is simple. Good evaluation is all about making wise judgments. When we evaluate anything we are placing value on it as part of the judging process. Some view evaluation as a way of collecting information about learners or programs, but evaluation is not just data gathering and data analysis. To be effective—to accomplish what evaluation is supposed to accomplish—evaluation must help you, the evaluator, make decisions about what you are doing.

When evaluating anything—curriculum programs; learners' performances before, during, after, and later; learners' understandings; program deliverers; the value of curriculum programs; learner achievement—there are many considerations. Some of these considerations include the documents used in learning, the live and unfolding action in the classroom, the amount of learner achievement that includes participation, the growth of positive attitudes, and the general satisfaction of the learners when they have completed their work. The physical measurement of the learners' or the program's performance may also be important, but these are not the only things to measure. Any complete evaluation requires the use of multiple methods, with multiple samplings, multiple input from the stakeholders, across multiple dimensions of the learning experience, at multiple times, and in multiple contexts. In other words, although the idea of evaluation is not complex, evaluating what you want to know and evaluating it correctly and completely may present some practical difficulties.

Traditional Training Model for Evaluation

A traditional approach to evaluation is rational and sequential, using objectives as the foundation for the learning process and for grounding the evaluation. The steps are appealing because they make logical sense and convey the impression that learning is an input-output process. As you read, think about a work-related skill you have mastered through a learning process. Compare your process with the one below (Laird, 1985). Does the measurement model here correspond to your own experience?

❑ Determine a base line: someone counts incidents of performance by a group or individual to determine that a situation exists, and that it exists to a degree that is serious or intolerable. This is BASELINE NUMBER ONE.

❑ Establish learner objectives, ensuring measurable criteria.

❑ Conduct the learning, changing the program according to the measurement of learners during training.

❑ Give a "terminal test"—a job tryout—to see if the learner can perform all objectives.

❑ Conduct on-the-job measurement: observe learner performance over long periods, assessing frequency and standard of performance.

❑ Measure and evaluate: someone counts on-the-job performance and calculates a new baseline. This is BASELINE NUMBER TWO.

The final evaluation asks if the situation improved enough to justify the training costs. What kinds of important human changes would be invisible under this measurement system?

Principles of Authentic Evaluation

The goal is to create authentic learning experiences for adults, where people are honest, learning is relevant, and evaluative feedback is helpful. Like any other instructional act, evaluating involves making choices. Every time you make a choice you take a philosophical stand. When the choices are consistent, when the methods and judgments of the evaluation process are congruent with your learning philosophy, you have authentic evaluation. Authentic evaluation, like the best of any kind of instruction, is thoughtful, reflective, and considered. It is also specific to circumstance. In other words, one type of evaluation may be right for one setting or situation, but it may be wrong for another. Two useful books for further exploration of authentic assessment are Lauren Leslie's *Authentic Literacy Assessment* (1997) and Martin Tombari's *Authentic Assessment in the Classroom* (1999).

Even though authentic evaluation changes to meet specific circumstances, some general philosophical principles hold true for all evaluation. Although following these principles in every circumstance can be difficult, they provide targets teachers can shoot for when creating student evaluations.

1. Authentic evaluation is ongoing

Evaluation should take place many times during the instructional process. If adults receive feedback or assessment only at the very end, they have no opportunity to use that guidance to grow in their learning. Instructors need to collect information throughout a learning experience to accurately judge a learner's progress in different areas. And when assessment occurs frequently as an integrated, natural part of the learning process, the fear of evaluation is eased considerably. Adults can be directly involved as partners with instructors in evaluating their own learning and performance when evaluation is ongoing.

2. Authentic evaluation is valid and reliable

Evaluation is valid if it measures what it's supposed to measure. As an example, too often adult learners are subjected to paper-pencil tests asking them to report isolated facts related to a particular topic of instruction, when the actual instructional goals focus on developing broad conceptual understandings in the learners. Such tests are not valid measures of the learning. Evaluation is reliable if it measures the same information consistently. For instance, many instruments used to evaluate people's learning styles have been found to be unreliable because different people interpret the terms differently, or answer questions differently depending on their mood or most recent experiences.

Validity and reliability go beyond simple correlations between objectives and results. First, some goals cannot be stated easily or measured well. Learners have individual tastes, different learning styles and personal needs, and build upon their own past and present experiences when they are learning. General goal or objective statements cannot and should not try to measure these more personal goals (Joint Committee, 1994). Second, some wonderful, unplanned things happen during any learning activity. While these cannot be planned for, they should be nurtured and fed. One problem of working from specific objectives, stated before learning takes place and measured by behaviour, is that serendipitous experiences are undervalued. Remember: what is measured often becomes what is learned. Authentic evaluation provides learners with a chance to show what they have learned—everything, not just what the instructor planned.

3. Authentic evaluation is comprehensive

Evaluation should measure the full range of skills, attitudes, and concepts the instruction intends to develop. To be authentic, evaluation should also address considerations affecting the learning process beyond the learner's own effort and ability: the teaching methods, the program design, the relation of the content to the learner's background, the long-term influence of the instruction on the learner, the learning community, and other environmental considerations, such as the institution sponsoring the learning. Authentic evaluation also includes different perspectives in the judgment process: the learner's own perspective, workplace perspectives, other learners, as well as the instructor.

4. Authentic evaluation is communicated

Any judgments made about an adult learner's progress belong first and foremost to that learner. The rationale for any methods used to evaluate learners should be clearly explained, and the criteria used for making judgments should be explicitly outlined. All evaluation results, including explanations about how these results were achieved, must be communicated clearly to the adult learner. Good evaluation also involves the learner either in deriving criteria or choosing appropriate methods for evaluating, with the ultimate goal of helping the learner to self-evaluate.

5. Authentic evaluation uses a variety of methods

Human beings are too complex to be judged using only one particular instrument. Some people can tell but not write what they know; others can only show. Still others understand something but haven't yet integrated it into their behaviour well enough to show an evaluator. To be authentic, evaluation tries different techniques to capture learner performance and requires multiple sources of information. This information can be quantitative (counting amounts) or it can be qualitative (describing and interpreting quality). Sometimes both quantitative and qualitative information are used at the same time—observation, learner self-reports, peer reports, testing, writing, projects, learner presentations and demonstrations of newly learned skills or knowledge, and indirect outcomes of behaviour can all be used together. (For instance, a bank counts client uses of the automatic teller to evaluate a recent training program to help personal banking representatives educate clients about the machine's uses.) In short, authentic evaluation is made up of a number of different types of activities—each useful in its own way in its own time.

Four Traps in Evaluation

It's easy to get so preoccupied in daily issues of planning and coordinating activities, or meeting demands for quantifiable data, that we get mired in poor evaluation practices. Here are four traps to watch out for: measuring what's easy, underestimating the learning embedded in evaluation, unexamined power, and reductionism.

Measuring What's Easiest to Measure

Be careful not to make the cardinal error of measuring what is easiest to measure, instead of measuring what is most important. It may be easy to measure and rank numbers, but can numbers represent what you really want students to learn and which programs to focus on? What you evaluate tells the learner what they should learn. Almost anyone who reads this book can recount how, as learners, they crammed isolated facts before school tests. Post-secondary students complain about having to write papers to demonstrate knowledge so remote from their own interests that it will never be integrated into their personal learning. Trainees despair at having to demonstrate skill learning in such artificial conditions that there is little chance of transferring the new learning to the workplace. Focus your evaluation only on what truly is most important. The best instructors help focus themselves by determining the two or three things they really want learners to understand or be able to do at the end of each learning experience.

Underestimating the Learning Embedded in Evaluation

How you choose to evaluate becomes an integral part of your program. A project or observation or test of learners is sometimes the most vital, permanent part of their learning experience, not only with respect to the content but also the processes of thinking and behaviour. The reason is twofold. First, learners are at heightened points of emotional, physical, and cognitive awareness during evaluation, and thus very susceptible to learning. The way a test is structured, the wording, format, and sequence of the questions, causes learners to synthesize information in a particular way. Second, the evaluation is often the last part of the learning process that is mediated by an instructor. Cognitive psychology shows that learners retain the first and last parts of any experience the most vividly. Thus, the criteria used to observe a performance, and the personal approach of the instructor in applying the criteria and giving the feedback, often

Towards a Community of Learners

The way you evaluate shapes the learning process and the whole learning experience. Evaluation doesn't have to be a reductionist exercise in getting grades.

The following are goals of an evaluation that strives towards learner self-assessment.

◆ Help learners move away from reliance on external evaluation and approval, so they are motivated to monitor their own learning and make adjustments.

◆ Help learners establish their own realistic benchmarks and measure their behaviour against these.

◆ Help learners see standards different from their own, and appreciate the behavioural and conceptual expectations of the community they aspire to join.

◆ Give learners new perspectives on themselves, so they can better judge their own behaviours in the context of the community's expectations.

◆ Help learners become more open to feedback even when this feedback is painful to confront, and to help them learn to use this feedback to further their learning and make decisions.

◆ Help learners become more comfortable giving honest feedback to others in helpful ways.

You have the power to make evaluation instructional, not destructional. Learners really want to know how they are doing. All you need to do is to care enough to be thoughtful, comprehensive, and discerning when designing and implementing your evaluation.

results in the most significant learning. Evaluation isn't simply measurement: it shapes knowledge.

Unexamined Power

The evaluator carries the power in the learning situation. Learners know it, and their relationship to the instructor is influenced by this dynamic. Two implications are worth noting here. First, if adult learners are used to wielding control and enjoying autonomy, they may resent being thrust into a situation where someone else has power and authority over them. This resentment may be acted out in questioning the instructor's expertise and resisting directives, or it may be expressed in learner satisfaction forms commonly filled out after a learning experience. The situation becomes more complicated when learners are asked to engage in activities that make them uncomfortable or are confronted with ideas that challenge their values and beliefs. Learners must surrender their own knowledge structures and sometimes their sense of self to enter an unknown realm of learning—and they must trust the instructor or mentor who leads them there. Such learning can be threatening, and it reinforces the power position of the instructor.

The second issue of power is that evaluators sometimes take their own authority so much for granted that they may forget to examine their own assumptions and choices. They need to ask themselves: Who says this performance or project is better than that one? Why is this concept more important than that one? Who am I to judge—and who do I allow to be my judge?

Reductionism

A fourth problem is that the curriculum can be reduced to only what is being evaluated. For example, a written curriculum program may be innovative and exciting, but antiquated evaluation can rob it of its vibrancy. Many teachers and business people lament that, in their curriculum programs or jobs, the tail wags the dog.

One government agency evaluated its employees' performances according to how many new jobs they created each year. This "bottom line" measure was short-term—meaning that their bosses wanted to see results right away. The employees had given up even trying high-risk projects, or long-term projects that would build the infrastructures to enable job creation over the years. Instead, they settled for short-term, highly visible activities (called "deliverables" in many organizations) that they knew were less effective ways of meeting their key organizational goal of sustainable employment. In this way, the evaluation had reduced the way they viewed and worked at their jobs.

A Final Thought...

Evaluating is not easy. An instructor can know all there is to know about evaluation and still have a difficult time evaluating students well. Our philosophy is that, with adult learners, the goal is to make evaluation an important thread woven throughout learning, developing continuous self-assessment in learners as a way of inspiring lifelong learning.

2 Evaluating Your Philosophy

The Foundation for Planning Evaluation

How you think about adult learners—your philosophy of learning and teaching—has a major impact on the evaluations you create. This chapter asks you to look at your own history and experiences and to consider how what you already know affects what you will, and should, do.

Effective evaluation is intricately woven into the teaching-learning process. When evaluation is incongruent with the philosophy of teaching, learners are more likely to be confused or angry than helped by it. To bring your evaluation and teaching practices into line with your ideas, you need to reassess your philosophy of teaching and ask yourself if your methods and criteria for evaluation match your beliefs about what and how adults should learn. There are many examples of incongruent evaluation and teaching methods. No doubt you have stories you could add to this chapter. Below are four examples that illustrate how ideas and actions can contradict each other. As you read each case, ask yourself how the instructor could have avoided the disgruntlement of students. What evaluation procedures would you have designed that would be more closely aligned with the teaching-learning philosophy and methods?

"You can't depend on your judgment when your imagination is out of focus." – Mark Twain

Story 1:
Apparent teaching–learning philosophy: *self-directed learning*
Evaluation: *graded presentations*

A college instructor teaching a graduate course entitled "Adult Learning and Development" had informed students that the class was to be democratic, based on students' self-directed learning. The culminating project was a self-directed research study, and learners were invited to share their results with the whole class. But the presentation itself was graded by the instructor, using criteria the instructor had developed and failed to share with students until the final grades were in their hands. Even though the grades were relatively high, many students felt betrayed, and the instructor's evaluative comments were largely distrusted or ignored altogether. Two students lodged complaints with the department chair.

Story 2:
Apparent teaching–learning philosophy: *exploratory process-oriented dialogue*
Evaluation: *graded essay examinations*

A seminar course called "Issues in North American Adult Education" was taught using collaborative dialogue among students. The instructor presented herself as a nurturing, guiding facilitator of learning, rather than an authority. Students were encouraged to question the instructor's statements, and to explore and appreciate multiple perspectives on various issues. To calculate final grades, students were given a single essay-type examination. The grade for the whole course was based on the instructor's unilateral judgments of the written exams. Many learners concluded that the notion of process-based exploratory learning was a fraud.

Story 3:
Apparent teaching–learning philosophy: *collaborative learning*
Evaluation: *individual achievement*

In a course entitled "Leadership and Change" collaborative learning was touted as the philosophy of choice in adult learning situations. Learners were encouraged to share learning in cooperative groups, to explore concepts together, to teach each other skills, and to work as hard developing the group dynamics and the group process as they did contributing to the group's product. However, the instructors graded students on their individual performance at the end of each unit. Learners understood that the collaboration to which they devoted so much effort was not valued as much as their individual achievement. An interesting dimension of competition and cynicism crept into the group work.

Story 4:
Apparent teaching–learning philosophy: *technical skill performance*
Evaluation: *paper–pencil standardized tests*

In a course to certify river-rafting guides, the trainees' ability to perform particular motor skills with precision and control was to be evaluated. To pass the course, trainees had to perform these skills consistently on the particular stretch of white water where they would be working, in various situations of stress and hazard. But a large part of the certification requirement was based on trainees' grades achieved on paper-and-pencil, multiple-choice, standardized certification examinations. Trainees treated the test as a necessary albeit time-wasting evil, memorizing information just to get through it. Meanwhile, skills like responsibility and quick thinking, the ability to interact well with and train all ages of tourists, control under pressure, and ability to make the river-rafting trip fun and safe were never evaluated.

Examining Your Own Beliefs

Spend some time honestly reviewing your teaching and instructional planning practice. To determine the **beliefs** that are evident in what you do, try asking yourself the following:

- What are the most essential things learners should know and do at the end of the program? Should learners be helped to create their own knowledge, or to master the knowledge that you and others deliver to them?

- Which is more important: collaborative or individualized learning?

- Should the instructor control the content and process of learning, or should learners have more control?

- Does learning happen mostly in systematic steps, mastering one skill or understanding one piece of knowledge before moving to the next? Or is learning mostly holistic, unpredictable, complex, and idiosyncratic (unique to each learner)?

- Does learning happen more in "Ah-ha!" insights, or through gradual evolutionary change?

- Should learners be able to demonstrate what they have learned in your program upon its conclusion, or will much of the learning be visible only at a later time?

Of course many of these questions can be answered with, "It depends on the situation." Different course content, learners, and learning contexts will guide instructor choices. As well, these questions may seem to imply that beliefs are either/or matters, when in fact they are complex and multi-layered. But such questions are useful starting points for an honest review of how we understand the learning process as it unfolds in our own teaching. Review your answers. What implications do your answers have on how you proceed as an evaluator?

Before going on, think back over the last educational program you delivered. What kinds of learning activities did you set up? How much did you speak, and how much did the learners speak? How many learner activities took place in your program? What kinds of control did you exert, and how much did learners control the activities? In collaborative activities, to what extent did you encourage learners to develop effective group processes? How much did you trust the learners to guide their own discoveries?

Beliefs are the fundamental values you hold that motivate your actions. These beliefs, for mature learners, seldom change.

Compare these memories of yourself in practice with your responses to the previous questions. Are your beliefs and practices congruent?

See the checklist below to examine your practices of evaluation.

Aligning Philosophy with Practice in Evaluation

❑ Do your methods for evaluating learners really show whether they have mastered the essentials they need in order to develop?

❑ Does your evaluation process allow students to reveal the knowledge they have personally constructed, or does it mostly compel students to display knowledge that you have constructed and they have memorized?

❑ Does the type of activity students must use during final evaluation match the type of activity they have learned during the instruction? (Does your evaluation ever use procedures that learners have not been taught how to use?)

❑ Does the language of the evaluation match the language used during instruction?

❑ Do your final evaluation procedures provide opportunities for students to really show what they know?

❑ How much do learners participate in the evaluation methods of your program?

❑ Do your evaluation methods match your instructional methods?

❑ Do your evaluation methods embody your deepest beliefs about teaching and learning?

❑ Could you justify each assignment or method of evaluation you use as a valid way of assessing your learners' progress towards developing the most important elements in your program?

How did you do? What could you do to better align your evaluation practices with your educational philosophy?

_____

_____

_____

Maintaining Trust and Positive Self-Esteem During Evaluation

Brookfield's "Characteristics of Helpful Evaluation"

Stephen Brookfield (1990) emphasizes the threat of evaluation to adults' fragile egos, and the responsibility of the evaluator to be sensitive to adult learners' feelings. He points out the tension between the relationship of trust that most facilitators work hard to establish with adult learners, and the critical final judgments of evaluation that can damage this trust. Ultimately, if learners are angry or hurt or made defensive by evaluation, they may not be able to deal with the evaluative information. Thus progress is not enhanced when evaluation does not attend to learners' feelings.

Brookfield suggests that an evaluation process should have the following ten characteristics. These characteristics will ensure that the evaluation process is honest and helpful, while being as sensitive as possible to adult learner needs and the delicate learner–teacher relationship.

1. **Clarity**: teachers must make criteria and methods for evaluation crystal-clear to learners, and use terms and language that people understand.

2. **Immediacy**: teachers should make evaluation immediate. Learners look for feedback immediately after performing a skill, and are able to remember and incorporate suggestions into their performance while the memory of the last trial is still fresh in their minds. The sooner evaluation occurs, the more helpful it will be.

3. **Regularity**: teachers should incorporate evaluation as a regular part of instruction, rather than save it for end-of-unit periods. When evaluation is more frequent, it becomes less threatening, and learners are less apt to be surprised by the results. More regular evaluation also delivers more information more immediately to learners, which maximizes its effect on improving learning.

4. **Accessibility**: teachers should be as available as possible to learners during and after the evaluative information is delivered. Learners often want to seek clarification, respond to the feedback, discuss concerns, or sometimes just get a little comfort.

5. **Individualized**: teachers should personalize the detail, but focus on the learners' actions. Help learners avoid interpreting the evaluative feedback as judgments about them personally.

6. **Affirming**: teachers should acknowledge whatever the learner has achieved before delivering the critical feedback. Critical feedback itself needs to be embedded in a basic attitude of respect for the learners' effort towards accomplishing the task.

7. **Future-Oriented**: teachers should provide clear and specific suggestions to learners about future actions they could take to improve their performance or understandings.

8. **Justifiable**: teachers should show learners the reasons for the criticism, matching learner performance to the criteria required, as well as showing how criticisms spring from a basic concern for the students' learning and a desire to assist them in reaching their own goals.

9. **Educative**: teachers need to ultimately remember their responsibility to help learners learn. Comments that are warm and sympathetic may make learners feel better, but are they educative?

10. **Selective**: teachers need to avoid overwhelming learners with too much evaluative information. Focus only on a few areas that learners can work on. Learners can't improve everything at once.

Reflecting on Your Own Learning and Teaching Biography

There is probably no more valuable way to slip into the shoes that are worn by the learner during evaluation experiences than to remember being evaluated as a learner. Below are some starting points for re-creating memories of incidents in your learning and teaching biography, and considering the lessons they teach you about evaluation. We call them **think-backs**.

Set 1: Remembering as a Learner

Think-back 1: to a product you created as a learner that you were proud of—an essay, a piece of art, or a project. Do you remember the evaluative comments? Were they helpful or harmful? Was the process of creating the project more vivid in your memory than the evaluation?

Think-back 2: to grades or comments you've received that were negative and critical of your performance as a learner. How was the feedback delivered? How did you respond? Why do you think you responded the way you did? From today's vantage point, how helpful was the feedback in your long-term progress as a learner?

Think-back 3: to an evaluative experience you learned a great deal from. What took place? What made it valuable to you as a learner?

Set 2: Remembering as a Teacher

Think-back 1: to a method of evaluation you tried once and swore not to do again. What went wrong? Did the problem lie with the method itself? Were there other underlying issues at stake—such as the difference between the expectations of the learners and the evaluation process and results, the lack of match between the evaluation methods and the teaching methods, or the way you used the method or reported the results to learners?

Think-back 2: to an assignment you gave that learners enjoyed and learned a great deal from, and that encouraged high degrees of effort and excellence. What elements made this assignment a successful learning and evaluation tool?

Think-back 3: to an evaluation experience you directed where the general learner performance was unusually low. Assuming for a moment

Think-backs are critical reflections on prior experiences, with the intention of seeking insights that will help you improve your practice or learning.

that the learners honestly tried their best, where did the fault lie? Was there a problem in the method of evaluation or the preparation of the learners? What would you do differently if you could repeat the exercise?

Thinking back can be very instructive. Our experiences are treasures, waiting to be explored in powerful ways. But simply remembering critical incidents doesn't always further insight. As you remember incidents involving evaluation and constructive feedback, either giving it or receiving it, ask yourself specific questions. What happened? Why did it happen? What did I feel? Why did I feel this way? What can I learn about what works and what doesn't from this memory? What should I do to improve?

The Dilemma of Evaluating Other Adults

Adults have rather fragile egos. We protect our self-esteem and tend to instinctively respond to criticism by being defensive. Protective walls go up when we feel attacks on our sense of self and our feeling of control.

Children, too, are extremely vulnerable to criticism. Someone once said that it takes a hundred positive praising comments to wipe out the effect of one harsh negative comment given to any child. Children learn more when responding to praise rather than to denigration and criticism. Think of a child learning to walk—a tremendous achievement in balance and coordination. What parent would stand apart from the wobbly child, pointing out her errors or punishing her for failing as she experiments, stepping this way and that? Instead, most parents are as excited as the child with each new bit of progress. We smile and encourage the child as she pulls herself up to the coffee table, comfort her when she falls, guide her patiently as she clings to an extended finger trying again and again. But in formal education—from elementary school to adult learning—learners are often required to measure up to standardized benchmarks and age-graded outcomes, or suffer the humiliation of being judged unsatisfactory. In this system people often learn to be competitive, to seek external approval rather than trust their own creative instincts, and to avoid making mistakes at all costs. Many learn that tests are traps, tricking them into failing.

This picture may be bleak, but many of us do remember the educational world of childhood as a realm of fear, submission, and boredom. By contrast, in adulthood, we usually take control of our own lives. Most

To better understand the values and assumptions you bring to evaluation, consider the following questions.

Who are the learners?

When answering this question, consider the interplay between adults, learning, and evaluation; diversity and individual needs; and the pain of honest evaluation.

What is the context for evaluating the learners?

When answering this question, consider why context matters to evaluation; the relationship of teacher to learners; and the nature of the learning community.

Whose interests are controlling the learning content and desired outcomes?

When answering this question, consider who requires what information, and why; who will be using the information, and for what; and the politics of the evaluation context.

adults believe they are competent. We pose our own questions, solve our own problems, and learn to deal with messes and mistakes as best we can. Most of all, we learn to trust ourselves as the most reliable judges of what is worthwhile, and what isn't. This includes judging our own worth.

As instructors, we need to remember what happens when adults who consider themselves competent, self-reliant, and self-directing are once again in a learning situation. First, we lead people who like to be in control on a journey which is, by definition, a trek into the uncontrollable and the unfamiliar. Second, we require people who are accustomed to independence to surrender to the authority of another adult or an institution. Third, we encourage people who believe that mastery brings power and respect, and who have learned to hide their weaknesses and sell their strengths, to now risk making mistakes. We subject them to situations where their weaknesses are on public display, where they will likely fail, and where they may not compare favourably to other adults. Fourth, we expect people who have learned to protect their status and sense of self in order to succeed in a competitive world to accept criticism from another adult. No wonder many adults have difficulty being evaluated.

A Final Thought…

Evaluation tools may be complex; but, for the most part, evaluation is quite simple. You already know a great deal about evaluation and the environment of evaluation. If you are a teacher, you were a learner. As a learner, you learned content—plus. You learned about power and control—who had it, when it could and would be used, and what it felt like to be on the weak side of the power relationship. If you are like us, you sometimes resisted that position; and, if you are like us, you probably vowed as a teacher not to treat others as you had been treated.

Now's your chance to make changes. We hope that this chapter has helped you recall some of the good and bad points of evaluation. But simply remembering isn't enough. If evaluation is to improve, instructors must work to improve it. You are an instructor. Now's your time.

3

Planning for Evaluation

What Do You Want Learners to Know?

Before you begin planning, there are three questions you should ask yourself. Why should evaluation take place? What should be evaluated? How should the evaluation be done? If you can answer them, you will know what to look for and how to make sense of what you see when you are evaluating the learner's progress.

> "The major
> contribution
> of evaluation
> is a heightened
> awareness of the
> qualities of life
> so that people
> can become more
> intelligent within it."
>
> – Elliot Eisner

Valid, reliable, and authentic evaluation does not just happen. It must be carefully planned. A hastily thrown-together test or a quick look at learners will probably yield some sort of information, but it may not reveal what you really want to know—the progress your learners have made or how effective your program or teaching has been.

Evaluation is not a single step; it is a process that involves many activities. These activities don't necessarily unfold in a particular sequence, and some take more time than others. Some happen simultaneously, and some may be so intuitive that you're not aware you're doing them. But whenever you conduct an evaluation, you will need to consider the following in your planning:

- Why should the evaluation take place?
- What should be evaluated?
- What do you want learners to know?
- What do you want to know?
- What does the institution want to know?
- What approaches should be used?
- What about validity and reliability?
- How much time and other resources do you have?
- What do learners need to know that will help alleviate their anxiety?

Why Should the Evaluation Take Place?

To answer this question, first ask another question. What are your real reasons for evaluating? Be honest with yourself.

There are many reasons for evaluating. Getting scores for your final grades—if you have such things as final grades—is only one of them. For example, you might want a quick indicator to decide what further help a learner needs. Or you might want learners to know how they have progressed since the beginning of the learning experience, or to celebrate their own growth. Perhaps you want to find out if learners are ready to move to more advanced levels, or assume responsibility for doing certain tasks. You may have to report how well the learner is doing to your supervisor or institution. Finally, you might want to know how well particular teaching methods are working. All these reasons are valid.

Summative or Formative Evaluation

Summative evaluation occurs at the end of a unit or course of study. Its purpose is to summarize what the learner has accomplished and the growth that has taken place. Usually the results of summative evaluation are shared beyond the learning situation, reported to the institution or corporation sponsoring the learning, and used by this agent to determine what happens next.

Formative evaluation occurs during the learning activities. Its purpose is to give feedback to learners about their progress or growth. Usually the results of formative evaluation are shared only with the learners in order to help them decide what they need to work on as their learning progresses.

Summative evaluation occurs at the end of a unit or course of study. Its purpose is to summarize accomplishment and growth.

Formative evaluation occurs during the learning activities. Its purpose is to give feedback about progress or growth.

What Should Be Evaluated?

To answer this question, begin at the beginning. Do you have a clear vision of what the learning outcomes will be, or do you want the vision to evolve according to the path you and the learners take together? The evaluation approaches you use will depend on your answer to this question. But how do you know which of these very different approaches to choose? This depends on the particular situation. Whether or not you know it, you already have a preference. The next step is to determine what your preference is.

Making Sense of Your Preferences

Read through the approaches outlined below. Ask yourself which one most closely matches your way of planning courses. Put a checkmark in front of the approach most like yours.

_____ **Approach 1:**

You prefer to plan your course according to pre-determined goals and learner objectives. When you plan, you note what learners will know and do by the end of the course. Your curriculum prepares learners to demonstrate particular competencies so they can pass the course.

What Do You Want to Know?

Be as honest as you can be. In the checklist that follows, write yes (Y) or no (N) in the space in front of each question. This information is not a test, so you may want to substitute your own phrases—such as sometimes (S), not really (NR), or usually(U)—for yes or no.

___ 1. Do you want to know what the learners are thinking or feeling about what happens in class?

___ 2. Do you want to know whether learners remembered what you said in the last class?

___ 3. Do you want to know how adept learners are at test-taking and essay-writing, using techniques learned in grade school?

___ 4. Do you want to know what questions learners have or which parts of the content are confusing for them?

___ 5. Do you want to know what kinds of associations learners are making between class experiences and their own life experiences?

___ 6. Do you want to know how much time and effort learners are putting into course work outside of class?

___ 7. Do you want to understand how the learner thinks?

___ 8. Do you want to know whether learners can perform a particular skill effectively by themselves?

___ 9. Do you want to know if the learner did the assigned class work?

___10. Do you want to know what activity to do next that will be most helpful?

___11. Do you want to know what learners think about the learning activities?

What else do you want to know?

_____

_____

_____

_____

_____ **Approach 2:**

You keep goals and objectives flexible. You like it best when outcomes emerge as you listen to learner concerns. You tend to see each unique learner as different, and you try to learn new ways of doing things or change old thinking patterns. You prefer to outline a few general goals that set the boundaries of the course. However, you encourage each learner to develop a direction of inquiry according to individual interest and concern.

Did you check Approach 1 or 2? Maybe you use both types of evaluating, and fall into one camp or another at different times. The purpose is not to encourage one choice or another, but to emphasize that your evaluation methods should be in line with your evaluation purposes. Sometimes teachers feel they just don't have enough time to design and carry out truly effective systems of evaluation. When you do not have as much time as you would like, focus on your bottom-line purpose for the evaluation. Define precisely what you want to know before setting up an evaluation activity.

What Do You Want Learners to Know?

If you are designing evaluation activities with only your questions and the institution's needs for progress reports in mind, we think you have forgotten the most important people in the enterprise. Learners need to know what you hope they are learning. If you assume that everyone is working towards attaining the highest possible scores, then don't blame learners if they focus on grades instead of learning. They will find themselves competing with others, comparing their test scores with other people's and wondering why theirs was higher or lower. It is as true of adults as it is of younger students; learners respond to the norms you set out as the instructor.

What do you want learners to know? Whatever you choose to evaluate will signal your answers to these questions. Do you want learners to understand your logic and your rationale for applying criteria to assess their performance? When you make a suggestion, do you want the learner to understand why you are offering this feedback? Do you want them to understand their own learning process? Do you want learners to change the way they do things? Do you want them to understand how you, as the instructor, feel about the way they behave and think in the course? Thinking about these questions with an eye towards turning your answers into practical activities may help you become a better evaluator.

What Does the Institution Want to Know?

If you are teaching in a formal setting, you are likely responsible for reporting and justifying a quantitative grade for each student to an administrative office. The grade you report can represent different things. Usually it is supposed to summarize the degree to which a particular student has mastered whatever knowledge and skills your course is supposed to teach. This traditional approach implies that the student's main task is to soak up information and that the appropriate thinking abilities have already been determined.

Keep in mind why institutions require such information. Some justify their operation to public stakeholders by showing how high a grade level their students achieve. Others demonstrate their rigorous standards by showing generally low-to-average grade levels. Some institutions work from general models of evaluation, such as "total quality management." They need to establish an institutional life that can be assessed and tracked over time, and be compared to other institutions using visible measures, such as key performance indicators. If you teach in a business or industry, you are likely responsible for reporting and justifying how training has contributed to the business. You probably need to show how the training "adds value" to the company by increasing productivity or by saving money or time.

Two things are worth remembering. First, you may work for the institution, but you also work for the learners. Sometimes this dual role can be difficult. If you consider only the needs of the institution, there is a price to pay. You may come to equate the institution's need for certain information with your own purpose for evaluating student progress. You might end up thinking of evaluation as a series of assignments or tests (usually concrete paper-and-pencil products) that can be translated into numbers, which then yield a grade.

Consider the logic of such an approach. If you evaluate a student's essay, looking for coherence and quality of writing, originality, and logic of thinking, are you assessing what the student has learned in your course? You may simply be taking a reading of the ways the student is applying former learning: how to develop an argument, how to find and select useful information to support that argument, or how to write in a clear and inviting way. When you assign a number to that essay, then weight the essay as a percentage of the student's overall grade for the course, are you confident that this number corresponds to the percentage of the course content that the student has mastered?

What Approaches Should Be Used?

Your answer to what you, your learners, and your institution want to know will help determine the methods you use to gather and interpret data to evaluate learners. There are two different approaches to evaluation: qualitative and quantitative.

Quantitative Measures of Outcomes

Quantitative information is usually conveyed through numbers. But, more important, quantitative information is concerned with "counts and amounts" that can be conveyed through words. For example, after a career-search skills program for low-income women offered by a social services agency, quantitative assessment might report that 15 of the 25 women contacted by the agency participated in the program, that 12 women completed the program and demonstrated satisfactory understanding of the concepts taught, and that five found employment after the program. In the learning context, quantitative measures translate human endeavour into quantities that can be added, averaged, and compared. Whenever human effort or human change is counted or measured in terms of amounts, the evaluation is quantitative.

> **Quantitative information** is usually generated by measuring counts and amounts so choices can be made between two or more options.

Although the use of quantitative measures is declining in evaluating adult learning, quantitative depictions still tend to be regarded in North American education as more reliable, more factual, or more empirical than qualitative depictions. Quantities can be graphed and charted, can be changed into money and percentages, or can reduce entire populations of complex people and their messy learning processes into clean and easy-to-deal-with numbers. Quantities are seen as objective, unquestionable, and immutable. Often when a number or a percentage is used to support an argument, it will be perceived as a cold, hard fact. As a result, institutions and businesses often present learner development to the public using quantitative measures of achievement.

Qualitative Approaches to Evaluation

Qualitative information
is usually conveyed through
words and tries to describe a
situation rather than count its
parts; it also explores human
qualities and meanings, often
digging below the surface and
asking why.

Qualitative information is usually conveyed through words and tries to describe a situation rather than count its parts. Qualitative information explores human qualities and meanings, often digging below the surface and asking why. In the realm of quality, there are no absolutes, no definitive criteria, no value-free statements. The subjectivity of the evaluator is clearly evident; as a result, qualitative assessment appears to be more fallible and less reliable than quantitative information.

In the learning context, qualitative description does not try to measure human change. Measurement does not exist in the qualitative paradigm. Instead, the quality (characteristics, attributes, features, traits, or distinctiveness) of a skill, or the kinds of knowledge the learner has developed, is described. Qualitative descriptions, if they are good descriptions, are careful not to generalize or force different things together for the sake of producing manipulable "averages." In the example of the career-search skills program for low-income women, a qualitative assessment might report the barriers to the program cited by the ten non-participants, the reasons why three women dropped out, the kinds of experiences reported by those who finished the program, the perceptions of the program facilitators regarding the kinds of non-measurable growth and problems evident throughout the program, and the actual satisfaction of the employed graduates with their jobs.

Qualitative description also begs all kinds of questions about who is doing the describing, what sorts of values it is based on, what kinds of conditions it takes place in, and the environmental context (power dynamics, history of the relationship, or motives and interests involved). Of course, quantitative measures are also riddled with these issues. But to many people, slippery questions of value are more apparent in qualitative descriptions.

What About Validity and Reliability?

Validity and reliability are important constructs, but only for certain evaluation methods. Some approaches to evaluation, such as self-referenced evaluation or evaluation that uses criteria that emerge as the learning unfolds, are more concerned with individual, personal criteria. In these cases, the evaluator is more concerned with what data mean rather than validity and reliability. For instance, pre-determined criteria can shape what the evaluator sees. The learner and the instructor may hold different perspectives about what is most important to learn and what the learner understands.

However, if you approach evaluation as a process of measuring what a person has learned, using an evaluation instrument to compare what he or she can do against pre-determined criteria, you need to be sure your evaluation methods are valid and reliable. In simple terms, an evaluative instrument is valid when it measures what it is supposed to measure. *Validity* refers to congruency between the assessment process and its purpose. An evaluative instrument is reliable when it measures what it is supposed to measure over and over again, each time you use it. *Reliability* refers to consistency.

Validity

There are three kinds of **validity** to check for.

- **Content Validity**

  Does the assessment measure the assigned content of the instructional program? Assignments, tests, student performance of tasks, and other methods of evaluation should match the articulated course objectives. One way to check content validity is to correlate different items on a test with your specific course objectives. Some teachers create test items by working straight from course objectives.

- **Criterion-Referenced Validity**

  Does the performance of the student on Task A yield results similar to the performance of the student on Task B for the same skill? If your criteria and indicators have validity, you should be able to apply them to various activities and achieve similar results. As you observe the student participating in each activity, you should be able to rate the student's skill using your chosen criteria. If the ratings are dissimilar, there may be contextual factors that you need to consider. If you're trying to decide the validity of two tests, administer both to the same group of students and compare the scores. If students consistently score higher on one test, you can assume the two tests vary in difficulty. We will discuss criterion-referenced evaluation in further detail in Chapter 4. For a good illustration of criterion-referenced validity in performance observation, refer to the Royal Roads University example on page 43.

> **Validity** refers to congruency between the assessment process and its purpose. An evaluative instrument is said to be valid when it measures what it is supposed to measure.

■ **Construct Validity**

Does the task being evaluated measure what it is supposed to measure? When you're teaching a technical skill, you can evaluate by sampling directly from the learners' performance of that skill. For example, you can assess how well a person can keyboard 60 wpm while facing a deadline simply by watching them perform the task. But a task set for evaluation purposes can't always conform directly to the skill you're trying to measure. Sometimes student learning cannot be demonstrated by a behaviour you can sample. When the objective is to develop individual creativity, problem-solving skills, an appreciation of others' points of view, or a willingness to take risks, indirect means must be found to measure learners' growth.

Does a student really demonstrate creativity by listing a hundred uses for a paper clip? Does a learner really show increased listening skills by not interrupting conversations? To determine construct validity you need to think carefully about what the learners are showing when they perform a task. Be careful not to make inferential leaps which link learning to particular behaviours.

One way to determine construct validity with adult learners is to talk with them after they perform a task. Why did they make the choices they made? What was running through their minds when they performed the task? What do they want to work on next? Another way is to compare learners' evaluation of their performance with your own assessment.

Reliability

Reliability is consistency. An evaluative instrument is said to be reliable when it measures what it is supposed to measure each and every time you use it.

There are three types of test **reliability** that you should be looking for as a teacher.

■ **Test–Retest Reliability**

Does a test yield consistent results when it is administered several times? Test-retest reliability can be determined by giving the same group of students the same test that they took some time ago and correlating the results. Unless outside variables influence the results, students should achieve results similar to their first tests. If results are similar, the test can be said to be reliable.

Notice we use the phrase "similar to." Many things come to play in testing a test for reliability. No two testing circumstances are ever alike. Even weather patterns affect student scores. Students might learn from the first test and thus do better on the second. Different test conditions change how students will do on each test.

- **Internal Reliability**

  Are the different items on the test consistent in difficulty? Certainly, some test questions are more difficult than others; but a group of very difficult questions, especially when put near the front of an exam, can have a profound influence on those taking the test. Teachers, often without knowing it, can create a test that is so difficult that even students who know the answers cannot do well.

  One way to determine internal reliability is to give the exam to a group of students, then score the odd-numbered items (group A) separately from the even-numbered items (group B). Students' score results for groups A and B should be roughly the same.

- **Inter-Rater Reliability**

  Will test results be consistent when graded by different raters or scorers? Most written, oral, or skill tests require a subjective judgment on the part of the person assessing the students' test performance. Starch and Elliott's (1912) classic study of English teachers pointed out the difficulty of achieving inter-rater reliability. In this study, two compositions rated by 142 English teachers were given scores ranging 47 points on a 100-point scale. One composition was failed by 15 percent of the raters and graded at over 90 percent by another 12 percent of the raters.

  Although not perfect, inter-rater reliability can be developed and enhanced by having small groups of raters discuss criteria for scoring tests, then compare their own scoring. Usually sample tests are scored by each rater in the small group using criteria the group has established, then the group compares everyone's scores.

How Much Time and Other Resources Do You Have?

Although other resources (e.g., pre-made tests and assignments) are important to consider in choosing types of evaluation, time is usually the most significant consideration. Even the hardest-working teacher in the world must have a personal life outside the classroom in order to retain

Establishing Inter-Rater Reliability

Sandy, James, Hasim, and Laurel all teach a general introduction to business writing at a community college. To mark students' final papers, they first established criteria and indicators for holistic scoring, assigning a number from 1 to 5 to each paper in four categories: thought and detail, organization, style, and mechanics of writing.

They next went through the essays looking for sample papers that demonstrated the different indicators. Each then marked three papers individually, applying the criteria they had agreed on.

When they compared their results and discussed their reasons for awarding marks, Sandy found that her grading was on the low side. She consistently scored a 3 to signify the same sort of judgment for which the others were awarding a 4. After discussing their original indicators, Sandy decided she needed to adjust her scoring to match what others were seeing.

The group then marked essays individually for an hour, and reconvened for another session of checking inter-rater reliability. Again, they each marked three student essays, then compared their judgments.

This time, their consistency was very close.

Here is a system that has been used in some training programs:

Step 1

Identify the discrepancies: needs, problems, "what is wrong," deviations from the expected standard, level of performance, or goal.

Step 2

Develop goals from the discrepancies (a goal is a statement of intent to correct the problem or meet the need).

Step 3

Develop an activity or program to accomplish the goals (show when and how things will be done, and by whom).

Step 4

List evaluation techniques matched to the goals that show how well you have accomplished them.

This system of evaluation is linear, and treats "learning" as solving a problem or removing a discrepancy.

Many instructors would dismiss Discrepancy- Based Evaluation as mechanistic and too simplistic to be useful in complex, change-oriented class or work situations.

What do you think?

---

vigour. Be realistic about how much out-of-class time you can commit to assessing work relative to the benefits yielded to the learner. And carefully estimate how much time will be absorbed by activities designed to evaluate learner progress, process, and feelings. Planning ahead helps avoid time crunches. Explore approaches other than marking assignments; for example, you could try peer evaluation, learner self-evaluation, focus-group sessions, or class presentations. Check out some of the Toolboxes at the end of the text for practical details.

Alleviating the Anxiety—What Do the Learners Want to Know?

Adults are, by nature, wary of evaluation. However, a good instructor can help alleviate anxiety by working to create an atmosphere where honest evaluation is welcomed as an aid, instead of a threat; where evaluation is ongoing rather than a fearful one-shot event; and where the flow of evaluation is not uni-directional from instructor to learners, but flows back and forth between learners and instructor. The following are some techniques to help create a favourable climate for evaluation. Refer to Chapter 13: Integrating Ongoing Evaluation into the Learning Process, for more ideas.

Key Evaluation Checklist for Program Evaluation

Program evaluation includes learner evaluation, but is broader-based and serves different goals. The focus of this book is evaluation of learners and learning. However, for those interested in program evaluation, the following from Michael Scriven (1991) is provided as an introductory overview.

Start with a problem statement. This should state what is to be evaluated, why it should be evaluated, and what the findings will be used for. (Note: In the examples below, the evaluand—or subject of the evaluation—is an educational program offered at a college.)

❏ Description

The nature and operation of the evaluand; its function (what does the program try to do?); the delivery system (how does the program do it?); and the support system (what helps the program to continue operations?).

❏ Client

The person/agency for whom an evaluation is formally done and other interested stakeholders.

Key Evaluation Checklist for Program Evaluation cont.

☐ **Background and content**

Circumstances that do or may influence the outcome of the evaluand (such as the past history of the program, the reputation of the course, instructor qualifications).

☐ **Resources**

Sources of support available to both deliver the program and to conduct the evaluation (such as instructor time, student time, books, guest speakers, field placements, support staff to duplicate materials, student feedback, workplace supervisors).

☐ **Consumers**

All people who use the program, and people indirectly affected by it (such as students, their spouses, other faculty, workplace supervisors, administrators of the agency).

☐ **Values**

Criteria for deciding the worth of the evaluand, and whose criteria these are (such as consumer needs, consumer wants, program goals/objectives, professional standards).

☐ **Process**

Aspects of the evaluand's operation that you will include in the evaluation (such as attendance, timing/pacing of the course, adequacy of facilities, fit with other courses, student satisfaction).

☐ **Outcome**

Post-program effects, both intended and unintended, long-term and short-term (such as student knowledge of the course content, student's ability to apply concepts on the job six months later, contacts students make, research opportunities for instructors).

☐ **Generalizability**

How well the program would work in other circumstances (such as at other times, other places, or with different people).

☐ **Costs**

Who incurs the cost, what kind of costs and when they are incurred; monetary costs (such as student tuition, books, transportation, and so on); non-monetary costs (i.e., student time and energy, enthusiasm, self-esteem); opportunity costs of the program (what else could the student's money or time have been spent on?).

☐ **Comparisons**

Other options that could produce similar or better effects for less cost or better results (such as on-line delivery, a mentorship program, or field-based coaching).

Key Evaluation Checklist for Program Evaluation cont.

❏ **Significance**

Synthesize the preceding considerations to make an overall judgment; list each of the above points, show the relative importance of each, judge the merit of each (with numeric score or written description), then weight the performance of each.

❏ **Recommendations**

List actions to be taken towards improvement if there is sufficient information to make recommendations (such as reducing the total number of readings for students, developing supervised practice activities on job sites, developing follow-up trouble-shooting debriefings at three-month intervals, and so on).

❏ **Report**

List all audiences (clients and stakeholders) to whom findings will be reported; for each, consider which findings will be of greatest relevance; for each, decide what report vehicle is most effective (such as formal technical report with charts and tables for client, written summary in student newspaper for student information, oral presentation to general faculty council for colleagues, article in scholarly journal reporting methodology for professional community).

❏ **Meta-evaluation**

Evaluate the evaluation plan and process: apply the key evaluation checklist to the evaluation you have just described.

  ❏ Describe the evaluation process from a meta-evaluative perspective.

  ❏ Identify the client or audience for whom the meta-evaluation is being prepared.

  ❏ Identify the background and context of the evaluation process.

  ❏ Identify the resources available to the evaluation.

  ❏ State the consumers of the evaluation, show the values underlying the evaluation.

  ❏ Assess the evaluation process, state the conclusions about the results of the evaluation.

  ❏ Show how these results can be generalizable.

  ❏ List the costs of the evaluation.

  ❏ Compare alternative types of evaluation that might have served, state the overall significance of the evaluation.

  ❏ State some overall recommendations about this evaluation process.

  ❏ Report the meta-evaluation.

Introduce Evaluation in the First Session

Have learners try a pre-test or problem that assesses their own efforts, but don't make the same mistake one psychology professor made: this prof gave his students a 30-minute exam in the first class, overwhelming and frightening many of them into thinking that the class was oriented around failure. Instead, try a lively "evaluation-teaser" like a ten-question true-or-false quiz. Or give partners two or three problems to solve, then allow the pairs to share their results with other pairs. Or facilitate a discussion based on an open-ended question or short case study.

In a formal course, try giving learners a short assignment that is worth a small portion of their final grade early in the course. It could be a one- or two-page article review, a description of a case problem in their own experience related to course content, a letter, a sample product to design, a problem to solve, or a list of ideas to brainstorm. Give very specific instructions and models. Skim the completed assignments quickly, and provide each learner with one comment pointing out a strength and one comment offering a suggestion. Then give a holistic grade. This kind of ice-breaker helps learners get past the initial barrier of getting something on paper, gives the instructor a good first indication of students' skill levels, and gives learners an early look at how an instructor grades.

Begin giving corrective feedback early in the course. Starting this practice early helps learners become comfortable with feedback as a natural flow of the instruction. It also helps familiarize them with your assessment criteria and your delivery style.

Circulate often among learners as they attempt new skills, work on problems, or discuss issues. Be selective: focus on only two aspects of the learner's performance. Use the "bouquets and beefs" approach: point out one thing that is strong in a learner's performance, and make one suggestion. Focus on the learner's observable actions, and avoid "you" statements that can be taken as personal criticism.

An instructor with a pleasant, straightforward approach in constructive feedback is often more welcome than an instructor who seems afraid to say anything critical. If the instructor's attitude towards feedback is fearful, the message to learners might be that teacher-learner rapport is more important than helpful feedback or that learner feelings are so delicate that any comments other than praise might damage the self-esteem.

Invite Learners to Evaluate the Learning Experience

Ask learners to evaluate the instruction as frequently as you think is appropriate for the instructional context and content. Quick and simple evaluations are often the best. For example, Stephen Brookfield, in *The Skillful Teacher* (1990), suggests you might ask learners midway through a class session to take out a sheet of paper and, without putting their names on the papers, jot down their responses to questions like the following:

- Which part of this class today was the high point for you? Which part of this class was rewarding or interesting?

- Which part of this class today was a low point for you? Which part of this class made you feel confused or bored?

- Name two things you learned in this class that interest you.

- Write two questions about parts of the content that you would like to know better.

Collect the responses and read them quickly outside the class, then report what you have discovered at the next class meeting.

Invite learners to submit suggestions for improving the instructional methods or program plan. Either distribute slips of paper, asking each person to write down one suggestion and hand it in, or use a suggestion box. Refer to Chapter 17: Evaluating Your Practice, for more ideas.

Teach Learners How to Give Constructive Feedback to One Another

Start by sharing a list of the criteria being used to evaluate a particular skill. Using this list, ask learners to brainstorm the kinds of errors or problems they have observed or anticipate observing as the skill is performed. Then, together, find ways to describe both the desired and the less-desired practice of the skill in a precise, straightforward, and non-hurtful manner. Have learners observe one another and apply these descriptive statements to what they see.

Give learners a protocol to use when giving feedback. Students are often asked to respond to each other's writings. This sort of response is usually delicate, given the personal nature of writing and the fragility of the writer's confidence. Our technique was to write the following four questions on a flip-chart. Students asked each other these questions one at a time.

- What part do you like best?

- What part would you want to change or modify, and how would you change it?

- Which part do you want to hear my feedback about?

- The part I liked best is … because ….

Don't just teach learners how to evaluate themselves. Allow time during instruction for evaluation and follow-up discussion. Refer to Toolbox 11: Evaluation Through Peer Assessment, for more ideas.

Integrate continuous evaluation with regular instruction. Make evaluation something learners understand and expect to be linked directly to continuous improvement. If a technical skill is below standard, make sure the evaluative feedback is followed by practice and further evaluation until the skill can be performed correctly. Feedback on assignments should always be directed towards a further step the learner can take.

A Final Thought…

In *Planning Responsibly for Adult Education* (1994), Ron Cervero and Arthur Wilson argue that adult educators need to consider the politics of making choices about other people's learning. Those who plan education for adults determine which knowledge counts and how skills should be developed. When we evaluate others' learning, we choose what is important enough to evaluate, and the standards. The choices we make fundamentally shape what a learner comes to know, believe, and do. The evaluation we do is a form of world-making.

Good evaluation doesn't just happen. It must be well-planned if it is to be effective and worthwhile. Make evaluation a natural part of your instruction, just like other parts of your lesson plan. Above all, evaluation should be fair—if you tell learners something, you should follow through—and evaluation should be a continual pursuit of answers to the questions that matter most to you, the learners, and others who have a stake in learner progress.

4

Developing Criteria for Evaluation

Choosing a Frame of Reference

Evaluation involves making judgments. Making judgments involves making comparisons, and this is where criteria come into play. The purpose of this chapter is to look at the criteria you will use as you develop your own approach to evaluation.

L et's take a personal example to illustrate the main theme of this chapter. Tara is an accomplished classical pianist; Jim collects hockey cards, using the activity as a way to relax at the end of a hectic day. While these activities seem quite disparate, they have one thing in common: each is governed by specific rules. Tara reads the music she plays; in her head she hears an interpretation based on years of listening to performances, studying scores, and music criticism. This is the standard she uses to judge her playing. If Jim buys or trades a special hockey card, he checks the wear of its edges to judge its shape and evaluates if it is a good buy or not. This activity also has certain rules or standards.

In evaluating learning, the criteria (rules or standards) should be stated as explicitly as possible, and they should be congruent with the intents of the learner and the purposes of the program or instructor. The criteria should also be applied equally to every learner in the group over the period of learning. Even in programs using emergent criteria (such as personal-growth courses where neither outcomes nor criteria should be pre-determined), facilitators and learners need to work hard to name the criteria or benchmarks as they evolve.

In selecting criteria, there are other important considerations. Priorities among criteria must be established clearly: it is easy to generate too many criteria or criteria that are difficult to apply thoughtfully when marking an assignment or observing a single learner performance. Some criteria are idealistic but impractical: they can't be realistically used to compare learner performances. Politics are involved: criteria often must be negotiated with stakeholders besides the learners. Finally, criteria must be fitted into the big picture: time, environment, learners, resources, and history will shape and are shaped by the criteria.

> "Man's judgment of value follow directly his wishes for happiness— they are an attempt to support his illusions with arguments."
> – Sigmund Freud

Criterion-, Normative-, and Self-Referenced Evaluation

You can use three different frames of reference to make judgments about the learner's progress: criterion, normative, and self-reference. Each represents a very different perspective of what learning counts most, and each sets up a different authority on which judge the learner's progress.

Criterion-referenced evaluation compares a learner's performance to an absolute, external standard or criterion. Teachers or institutions

Criterion-referenced evaluation compares a learner's performance to an absolute, external standard or criterion.

use criterion-referenced evaluations when they believe a source external to the learner (such as standards compiled through consensus among subject-matter experts, or job competencies stipulated by a professional association) has the authority and expertise to state what the learner should know and be able to do. This external agent sets the criteria. All learners' progress is compared to these criteria.

An example of appropriate criterion-referenced evaluation is training for specialized technical skills in trades or professions, where learners must demonstrate that they can perform tasks essential to an occupation. An overused, yet effective, example to illustrate how important criterion-referenced evaluation can be is to consider putting your life in the hands of a surgeon whose hand-eye coordination and motor skills are suspect. Often criteria are set by the industry that will hire learners, in conjunction with the professional or trade associations of the occupation that sets standards. But it is possible for teachers and students to set their own standards.

Normative-referenced evaluation compares one learner's performance to others in the same group and is governed by the belief that a "normal" standard of particular skills, understandings, or attitudes will emerge for a particular group.

Normative-referenced evaluation compares one learner's performance to others in the same group and is governed by the belief that a "normal" standard of particular skills, understandings, or attitudes will emerge for a particular group. All members of the group are compared to this "norm" to determine whether they are in line with the norm, below it, or above it.

An example of appropriate normative-referenced evaluation is when a teacher experiments with a new assignment or facilitates a developmental course of instruction where outcomes are unpredictable. But the most common use of normative-referenced evaluation is when institutions require instructors to grade students according to the "bell curve." This is called "normalizing" student grades.

Self-referenced evaluation compares what the learner understands or can do today to what he or she understood or could do in the past.

Self-referenced evaluation compares what the learner understands or can do today to what he or she understood or could do in the past. The overall philosophy guiding self-referenced evaluation is the belief that each learner's growth is idiosyncratic and unfolds in personal ways. As a result, at least some kinds of learning should be assessed without reference to other people or external standards. An example of a time when self-referenced evaluation is appropriate is in personal development programs, where learners shape their study according to their own needs and desired directions for change.

Choosing a Frame of Reference

Each frame of reference (self-referenced, norm-referenced, criterion-referenced) represents a very different perspective. Be clear in your own head which you are using. Match it to the purposes of the program and your philosophy about learning. If you know that learners must pass a standardized exam at the end of your course, don't lead them to believe that their own pace and personal development is what counts. If you know you must mark according to the bell curve at the end of a course, ask yourself why you would set external criteria to assess learners' performances during the program. If you know that the learning during your training program on "Managing Change" must be converted to return-on-investment performance outcomes, think carefully about how you will reconcile the corporate criteria with learner growth.

The Source for Criteria in Criterion-Referenced Evaluation

There are no universal standards understood and accepted by everyone. No instructor can assume that everyone shares a common vision of what makes good writing or what constitutes a mistake. Criteria derive from a particular source. It may be inside or outside the learners, but it must be identified. The source could be a specific group of people, such as a group of architectural engineers or psychological therapists, who set standards governing all who are certified to practise in that occupation. Or the source and motivation for evaluative criteria could be a competitor, whose performance sets standards that the learners must meet and exceed. Sometimes the source of criteria could be an overall developmental curriculum of which a course is but a part. See page 42 for further discussion on sources of criteria.

Some learning skills take a considerable amount of time to master, and the standards for judging the learner's efforts are different at various points in the overall process. The source for learning criteria could sometimes be the goals of an organization. For example, Taco Bell implemented a system to train all of its people to give more personal attention to each customer, which significantly increased sales according to the corporation.

Sources of Criterion-Based Reference

Different contexts for growth and change require different sources of criteria. Here are examples where evaluation is based on criterion drawn from a curriculum, job task requirements, personal vision, professional community or other competitors.

Curriculum

A psychology degree program in a particular university requires learners to understand and remember certain foundational concepts of the discipline and its research methods. The mastery of these concepts determines the criteria for evaluating students in Introductory Psychology 151. Whether or not students can write a clear and fluent article or deliver a crisp, informative speech is beside the point. Students are required to show reasonably good grades on the multiple-choice exams that are the hallmarks of Psych 151. Thus the source of criteria is the entry-level understandings required by further courses of study.

Job Task Requirements

A new package of federal programs for funding training and development initiatives in private and non-profit agencies requires the project officers delivering the programs to fully understand the rules and regulations, and to be enthusiastic, but sensitive, marketing agents for the new programs. The source of criteria for evaluating the project officers at the conclusion of their own training is derived from the task requirements of the work itself.

Personal Vision

A group of people are attending a course in hopes of improving their relationships with their adolescent children. All have different problems to solve and skills they want to learn. Each will evaluate his or her own learning in and through their developing relationships with their children. The criteria by which each will judge his or her own improved choices and parenting behaviours will evolve according to the situations they cope with at home. The source for criteria is the personal vision that each parent holds of family relationships. Of course, this vision and criteria is subject to change as the parents learn to appreciate other ways of viewing parenting, including their own teenagers' views.

Professional Community

To become a certified management accountant, learners must demonstrate in an examination that they have memorized quantities of specific regulations, and that they can suggest appropriate solutions to accounting problems. They must also show their effectiveness in handling accounting tasks and people issues on a daily basis in a firm where they are supervised while articling.

Competitors

Athletes break world records by using their competitors' performance as a standard-setting challenge for their own. Businesses locate "best practices" among their competitors, which function as benchmarks for their own performance. Criteria is thus determined by the most recent standard of achievement set among a community of competitors pursuing a common goal.

Who Owns the Criteria?

"Who owns the criteria?" is an important question to ask after determining what or who will be the sources of the standards for evaluating learners. Part of the criteria of any learning must be externally determined. If they were not, most people would never break free from their personal limits, beliefs, and behaviours. If learners are expected simply to grow according to internal objectives and standards, they might not develop the necessary skills to gain entry into the knowledge community of their choice, whether it be a culture that speaks a different language or an occupational group that knows how to solve particular problems.

When learners come to own the criteria for judging themselves, they take responsibility for creating their own knowledge. People are inspired and aspire most to meet and exceed the criteria that they design for themselves. Conversely, people who are pushed, pulled, or dragged to meet someone else's criteria may adopt a passive or defensive response to the learning process. Some may resist. Some may engage passively in the procedures of learning without internalizing the knowledge.

When there are specific, externally prescribed standards that must be attained in a particular course of study, the instructor needs to help learners find ways to make these personally meaningful, as well as to help them develop their own criteria for assessing their performance.

Criterion-Referenced Competencies in Graduate Education

Royal Roads University in Victoria, British Columbia, Canada, has adopted a criterion-referenced evaluation system for its programs. The Masters of Arts in Leadership and Training (MALT) program specifies several leadership competencies that learners must demonstrate in a variety of settings: team problem-solving activities, presentations, papers written to complete online courses, leadership in the community of learners during the summer residency phases of the program, and a major research project.

Indicators have been developed for each competency as it might appear in the different settings. There are two sets of indicators: one set describing an "A" performance, and the other describing a "B" performance. Learners compare their performance to these indicators through self-assessment, peer assessment, and various instructors' assessments. Frequent formative evaluation is provided to learners before the summative "grade" of A or B is assigned for each competency. (Learners who don't achieve a B level are given an "IP" rating: "In Progress.") Learners develop an action plan to address competencies they wish to develop further.

Here is an example:

Competency	"A" Level Indicators	"B" Level Indicators	Major Project Indicators
Apply current systems theory to problem solving. Competency Outcomes: Identify and describe current systems theories relevant to leadership and learning. Contribute to identifying the nature of problems and strategies for their solution. Apply current system theories to assist in solving problems.	All of B Level Performance, plus: Uses systems language and concepts to clarify and agree upon the nature of problems and the desired outcomes. Helps colleagues to evaluate alternatives, identify chosen action and determine criteria for success. Applies relevant theory suitable to the nature of the problem.	Demonstrates knowledge of a broad range of systems theories and of how diverse people work and relate to one another within possible organizational structures. Describes theories accurately and concisely. Draws valid and defensible conclusions.	Apply knowledge of changes in marketplace dynamics, the impact of emerging technologies on social infrastructures, the newly emerging nature of work, and cross-cultural issues to solving leadership problems in the major project. Employ strategies and approaches that creatively build on these trends, and that suggest positive directions for organizational growth and change. Demonstrate a deep and insightful analysis of systems issues and concerns, which is founded in the literature.

The source of evaluative criteria could sometimes be the learners themselves, who judge their own performance based on how closely it matches their future vision of themselves. Adult learners have their own purposes and motivation for learning. This is true even in situations where external stakeholders have input into the curriculum objectives and standards for evaluation. Consider *continuing professional education* (CPE). Content of CPE often responds to changes in legislation, new socio-economic pressures or technological developments. Employers encourage professionals to engage in CPE opportunities. But every adult educator who has facilitated a CPE program can testify that participants ultimately learn what they *want* to learn, depending on what problems they believe they must solve. Instructors of adult learners should remember that the criteria adults aspire to are not always the same as those set by the instructor.

The sources of criteria for evaluation serve as windows, creating frames through which the learner's actions will be viewed. The criteria for judging the learner's performance changes when the window changes. A learner who demonstrates a certain set of behaviours in a university classroom and the same set of behaviours in a workplace on-the-job training laboratory may be judged very differently in each instance.

Criteria evolve. Be open to change, and adapt criteria as you work with it and observe learners.

Indicators of Criteria

Indicators are specific learner behaviours for which an evaluator looks. Step one is to determine what the indicators should be prior to the learning experience. Step two is to look at what the learner actually says, does, and creates, selecting examples that are similar to the indicators established as the desired criteria.

Indicators can also be developed from the performances of the learners in a particular learning situation. When developing a new program, you may not know what sorts of behaviours to expect as learners struggle to develop new skills. You might get general benchmarks which you refine into indicator statements as you watch learners. Most importantly, indicators must be clear, specific descriptive statements of observable demonstrations: actions, speech, written expression, and products created by the learner. Any trained observer should be able to identify and apply the indicators when observing performance, and reach similar judgments.

Performance Indicators

Performance indicators are statements describing specific behaviours that evaluators will look for when observing and assessing, either after a learning program or on the job. Performance indicators may be relatively easy to establish for simple technical skills, but in the area of holistic behaviours that integrate values, attitudes, and multiple skills, reliable and observable assessment indicators are difficult to generate.

What are some characteristics of good performance indicators for complex skills and values? Here's a possible list.

- They help predict what will happen.
- They help determine how something is achieved.
- They depend on context.
- They value direction more than precision, and link process to product.
- They are simple.
- They use what people already know, rather than introducing complex new systems and processes.
- They influence and shape behaviour.
- They are comprehensive.
- They are based on actual observations of human activity situated in particular contexts, not on wish-lists of hypothetical expectations.

Think of a skill you've observed frequently or that you help people learn to develop. What specific indicators would you write that distinguish between a beginning level, a satisfactory competence, and excellence as it might appear to an observer?

Learner-Developed Criteria: Read-Around Groups

The following activity teaches learners one way of developing criteria. It also helps learners to see immediately how their own work compares to others, and to take responsibility for criteria used to judge their work.

Students in a college-level political science program are assigned a two-page composition within the first few weeks. They bring their compositions to class, leaving their names off the finished papers. Each student is assigned a number that is placed on the paper.

Students gather in small groups of five or six, and the papers are put in a pile. The instructor takes the pile from each group and gives it to another group. On a signal, members of each group take a paper from their new pile and read quickly and silently. After two minutes, papers are exchanged and each member quickly reads the new paper. The papers are exchanged again until all the papers in each group's pile have been read by each member.

The group now decides which papers are the "top three." They record the numbers of these three papers and one sentence summarizing what makes the paper a good one. The instructor then picks up the pile from each group and gives it to a new group. The process is repeated.

Afterwards, the instructor records the results on a flipchart.

Groups share their reasons for their top picks. These reasons become the criteria students used to judge a paper. The criteria are recorded, discussed, and turned into a grading rubric.

Moving Towards the Ideals of a Learning Organization

The following dimensions, described by Karen Watkins and Victoria Marsick (1993), characterize organizations committed to fostering a community of continuous learners.

- continuous innovation
- rewarding breakthroughs and initiative
- creative contention — where all processes and ideas are subjected to constructive debate and skepticism
- tolerating failure and mistakes and using them to improve
- reflecting on what worked and what didn't upon completion of projects and after decisions
- storing and retrieving this information for future use
- keeping and sharing "the recipe"—not just hoarding lessons learned in particular islands of the organization
- humility—learning from each other
- bench-marking—finding the best, studying them, and adapting the lessons
- collaborative advantage—listening and learning from each other inside and outside

If these are the desirable "standards" or criteria, what kinds of observable indicators can you think of that would provide evidence that an organization was moving towards these ideals?

Looking for Skill Indicators: Skiing

Janelle says she wants beginning skiers to learn to keep their weight forward, over their skis. From her experience of skiing and watching beginners, she knows two indicators of weight position. She knows that when the weight is forward the beginner can turn down a ski hill while holding a ski pole horizontally, always keeping the shoulders facing straight down the hill. When the weight is forward the beginner can also slow down or stop on cues from the instructor. Each beginning skier may demonstrate a hundred other behaviours, from bobbing up and down to turning wider rather than tighter. But concentrating on and working with these two indicators helps the instructor focus on the criteria—forward weight—under observation.

Thus learners focus on only a few simple things, which they are reminded of again and again as Janelle observes them and gives feedback. This helps avoid the overwhelming crush of information that can make learning a new skill difficult.

Involving Learners in Developing Indicators

Developing clear descriptors for indicators can be difficult. It is not enough to sit down and think about what, as a teacher, you want to or expect to see. The learner also has a stake in it. As always, it is important to consider the learner when determining the level of language and the audience for the language. The following example shows how to develop indicators.

If you use a Read-Around Group technique (see page 45), you might want to raise the following questions.

- Do all students agree with the criteria?
- What weight should be assigned to various criteria? (Which are more significant?)
- Can the criteria be broken down into levels?
- Should these criteria be applied to all written work done in the class? Why or why not?

Three good things emerge from this exercise. First, students see their peers' work at a glance, which is highly instructive for their own standard of writing and thinking. Second, students must think through issues of assessing quality in their own and others' writing. This helps them develop self-assessment skills. Third, the process involves students in developing the grading procedures that will be used on their own papers. This builds a sense of responsibility and participation and helps break down defensive attitudes that can erupt when students see the instructor as an adversary, who arbitrarily grades their work.

Developing Criteria

Markets establish the value of a product or service; however, the way people work within a company is not a commodity or service that can be sold, although it has an impact on sales and service. For example, Hewlett-Packard uses a technique it calls business process auditing to measure how efficiently it creates useful knowledge from information; that is, how efficiently the company learns. Specifically, it measures the changes in raw material as employees change that raw material into a product that can be sold to consumers.

When knowledge work has a well-defined output, like a purchase order, the change that happens after employees work with it can be measured in terms of information. When a new, streamlined telephone order-taking system is implemented, its results can be measured to show whether knowledge is being processed more efficiently. When a software package worth $1 million is modified by employee expertise to increase its value to $3 million, the employee knowledge has a value directly linked to the company's bottom line.

A Final Thought...

The purpose of this chapter is to look at the criteria you will use as you develop evaluation. If we could leave you with one thought, it would be to include learners more in the development of these criteria. Whether one's industry determines the criteria for learning or not, an instructor needs to help learners find relevance in understanding and mastering the criteria.

The goal of all learning should be intellectual and behavioural growth. We believe that the more learners talk and work together with their instructors, the more they will come to "own" their learning. Adult learners, especially, should have a voice in what they are doing and where they are going. Our experience is that constant, open, and honest dialogue creates a community of learning that can take on an extended life of its own.

5

Choosing a Strategy

Alternative Methods of Evaluation

As we have noted in prior chapters, assessment of learning is a complex and dynamic process, depending upon the interplay between context, purpose, learners, and criteria. It makes sense then that there would be multiple methods or strategies to measure learning. This chapter introduces a number of alternative types of evaluation. Most of these are more fully developed in the Toolbox section. Here we will present some considerations for choosing among the methods.

When learners and teachers hear the term evaluation, they often think only of tests: this is too bad. There are many other ways to discover information about learners' progress and inform them of it. These include checklists and anecdotal records, learner-teacher conferences, portfolios, journals, and class presentations.

We encourage instructors to evaluate learning at a variety of levels. It is important to both assess how well learners know and understand content and how well learners can apply, analyze, and evaluate concepts and create new ideas. Tests that use multiple-choice, true and false, matching, and fill-in-the-blank questions can sometimes effectively assess learner knowledge and comprehension. However, traditional paper-and-pencil tests are limited.

> The difficult we do immediately. The impossible takes a little longer.
> – George Santayana

Multiple Methods

The best way to meet the diversity of learner needs and preferences and to develop a rich, holistic understanding of what is really happening for learners is to use a variety of methods to collect information for your evaluative judgments. While any particular method may be limited in perspective or have practical drawbacks, it may also capture a particular dimension of the learning process that may be otherwise invisible through more standard evaluation tools. To help all learners experience success and enable them to show their strengths as well as their weaknesses, it is best to employ multiple methods. Use diagnostic processes as well as summative ones, encourage learners to formulate their own questions as well as answer the instructor's questions, and provide a variety of open-ended opportunities for them to show their critical and creative abilities as well as their abilities to memorize and apply concepts.

Good evaluation is a cooperative and ongoing endeavour that actively involves both learners and teachers. Evaluation procedures can be meaningful to both learners and teachers and an extension of learning for both. Evaluation methods can encourage learners to synthesize knowledge, rather than seeing it in isolated segments.

- Peer evaluation of learner performance or products.
- Review of learner performance on video by external expert or committee.
- Profiling—narrative, in-depth description of learner using appropriate categories.
- Portfolios or folders of work samples.
- Learning maps or personal scrapbooks.
- Journals or learning logs.
- Simulated cases or in-basket exercises for learner's problem solving.
- Role-plays of strategies for coping with situations.
- Debates, panel discussions, presentations or demonstrations.
- Learner teaches others, who are then tested.
- Informal conferences or formal interviews with learner.
- Focus-group discussions mediated by instructor.
- Checklists and rating scales.
- Standardized tests.
- Goal setting and review.
- Artifacts—circumstances, procedures, or relationships changed by learner's changed behaviour.
- Surveys (written questionnaire or telephone survey).
- Interviews (open-ended or structured questions).
- Observer's reports.
- Participant feedback and self-reports (satisfaction surveys, journals, etc.).
- Samples of program products (i.e., learner work samples).
- Tests of achievement.
- Records (program attendance, health records, financial data, etc).
- Institutional documents (curricula, history and background, policy documents, mission, etc).

Choosing Assessment Methods

An evaluation method simply provides a source of data to help you answer the questions that matter most about learners, within a particular context. When choosing a method, first examine the data source.

- What sources yield the best data to answer the most important evaluation questions?

- Do I have the time/resources/technical skills to obtain this data or process this data?

- Is the data source reliable and valid?

- Can the data be collected ethically?

- Will other users of the evaluation be confident in the data sources chosen?

Surveying the Learners

Before finalizing your choice of evaluation methods, find out from learners what sorts of assessment activities they are most comfortable with. If learners are unfamiliar with a particular assessment format or activity, their participation will not accurately reflect their learning. Too often instructors assume that learners have developed strategies for taking tests, or know how to write case studies, or are comfortable participating fully in role-plays. Simply ask the learners how they can best show what they know. Below is a sample survey to uncover learner evaluation preferences.

Questions to Consider Before Using an Evaluation Strategy

- Why am I using this particular type of evaluation?

- Why am I evaluating the learners at this time?

- What do I expect to learn about the learners as a result of this procedure?

- What do I want the learners to learn from this assessment activity?

- Does this method consider the learning objectives?

Techniques for Evaluating Individual Student Learning

Technique	Description	Advantages	Considerations
Paper-and-pencil test: objective (multiple choice, matching, true-false, fill in blanks)	Student selects most appropriate answer from several alternatives. Questions can be pulled from test bank.	Quick to score. Can be marked in class by students. Useful to survey or sample student learning. Can test student ability to analyze, apply, compare, and problem-solve. Avoids marking bias.	Higher-level questions are difficult and time-consuming to prepare. Limits student responses. May provide inaccurate responses due to misinterpretation of questions or reading ability. Provides no information about where or why student answered incorrectly. Time consuming to prepare questions. Easy for students to cheat or guess.
Paper-and-pencil test: essay style	Student can discuss, analyze, describe, prove, trace, explain, and so on. More open-ended and fewer questions. Offers opportunity for students to demonstrate their own insights and reflections beyond the instructor's perspectives.	Less preparation time than multiple choice. Student can demonstrate support and reasoning for their answer, personal interpretation, and creative thinking that the question doesn't anticipate.	Time-consuming to mark. Students' writing ability may limit their demonstration of thinking and knowledge. Criteria for assessment of each answer must be worked out carefully, and unexpected responses must be anticipated and considered.
Student demonstration of skill	Student performs a maneuver according to standard stated in course objectives.	Can be performed live or on videotape. Quick to assess using tools such as checklists. Corrective feedback can be immediate.	Objectives must be stated in specific detail. Students must know the expectations for skill mastery. Assessment criteria must be clear. Consider training peers to give constructive feedback in practice.
Informal student writing	One-page memos to instructors in class; journal writing; learning logs. Marked by viewing selected pages, skimming holistically, or having students periodically prepare short summaries.	Provides valuable information on how students are processing the learning, kinds of problems and questions that some are reticent to raise in class. Helps students track own learning process. Can act as a basis for formal writing assignments or projects.	Unfamiliar to some students—must use coaching and patience. Be well organized before reading (mark selectively and skim). Marking can be time consuming. Use results to modify instructional approaches.

Techniques for Evaluating Individual Student Learning

Technique	Description	Advantages	Considerations
Student-created product	Presentation; piece of writing; display; video; dramatization; product suited to course content (graphic, chart, artwork).	Good learning opportunity for students. Usually involves research. Most products (except writing) can be quickly scored with clear, specific criteria.	Students may need help developing projects. Ideas may be grandiose or impractical in terms of time. Fosters learning of multiple skills.
Informal student observation	Instructor observes students informally as they discuss in small groups; or assesses panel presentations in front of class.	Quick way to get instant information about the level of student understanding. Instructor must know clearly in advance what to listen for.	Focus on one group at a time. Consider using checklists. Some students get quiet or nervous when observed.
Student self-assessment (based on own goal setting) and interview with instructor	Student presents personal learning goals and self-assessment. Instructor helps student plan future learning goals based on progress, and can help identify appropriate resources.	Helps students take responsibility for own learning and evaluation. Mirrors workplace (goal-based performance appraisals). Reduces cheating. Often leads to powerful, meaningful learning, greater motivation and commitment to learning process because of self-directed nature.	Interviews take time. Consider meeting students throughout class periods when others are working on projects. Keep interviews focused. Some students need a great deal of assistance the first time they set goals. Refer to goals often throughout the course and demonstrate your commitment to your students.
Peer assessment	Using criteria provided by instructor or established together, students provide written or oral feedback to one another.	Students internalize criteria and can assess themselves more accurately. Provides wide range of feedback to each student without taxing the instructor. Develops better understanding of the expected standards and evaluation process.	Peers must be carefully trained in applying the assessment criteria effectively. Model and monitor. Train students in appropriate ways to give feedback.

- Have I adequately prepared my learners for this type of evaluation procedure? Have I reviewed enough?

- Have I accounted for the various ability levels, learning styles, and skills within this class?

- Have I planned time to do follow-up activities after the evaluation?

- Have I taken the test to make sure that it is as free from problems as I can make it?

- Is there anything about the format or layout of the test that makes it difficult for learners?

- Did I make the test easy to grade?

Questions to Consider After Using an Evaluation Strategy

- Did the learners understand what was asked on the evaluation?

- Do the results indicate that learners were prepared for this activity?

- Are the results consistent with results of other evaluation activities?

- If I use this procedure again, what changes will I make to it?

- What other methods of evaluation might be more appropriate?

- Were there questions learners missed that were my fault? If so, did I make up for it by giving them the benefit of the doubt?

- Did the test differentiate between the learners who prepared and those who did not?

- Is there evidence of cheating? If so, what can I do about it?

Involving the Learner in Assessment

Recently, views of evaluation and learner assessment have changed. Educators have begun to realize the importance of not only including the learner in the evaluation and reporting process, but also having the learner play an active or even directive role in assessment. Learners are increasingly encouraged to have learner-teacher conferences, to have input into the criteria used, and to set priorities about what is most

Determining Learner Evaluation Preferences

Put a check mark in the box that best describes how you feel about the items listed.

3 = very comfortable with this method

2 = reasonably comfortable with this method

1 = not comfortable with this method

3	2	1	
☐	☐	☐	1. Solving problems
☐	☐	☐	2. Writing letters and journals
☐	☐	☐	3. Delivering an individual oral presentation
☐	☐	☐	4. Having private conferences with the instructor
☐	☐	☐	5. Creating a display, art, or drawings
☐	☐	☐	6. Reporting the results of an Internet search
☐	☐	☐	7. Building products
☐	☐	☐	8. Performing on video
☐	☐	☐	9. Collecting samples of my work
☐	☐	☐	10. Writing opinion essays
☐	☐	☐	11. Writing tests or exams
☐	☐	☐	12. Creating my own evaluative tools
☐	☐	☐	13. Attending lectures and writing summaries
☐	☐	☐	14. Presenting orally in small groups
☐	☐	☐	15. Creating role-plays or drama
☐	☐	☐	16. Evaluating myself

important to evaluate. Given that most adults were not educated this way, what preparation of learners would be required in your context to help them enter the evaluation process responsibly and thoughtfully? What are some potential benefits and problems of this approach?

Questions to Consider Before Evaluating Learners' Progress

- Will this be graded? Should this evaluation be used to show a learner's accomplishment? Should it show something else?

- Is this evaluation relevant?

- Are my expectations too high? How much is effort worth?

- Should the learner who scribbles something quite good (but not up to her potential) get an 85 percent while the learner who sweats over his or her work gets a 55 percent?

- How can I encourage learners to do assignments that will not be graded?

- How can I be sure that I don't create more work for myself than I do for the learners?

- How much should I comment? Can I evaluate something without comments?

- What do I say to learners who want to discuss the specifics of their mark? How should I respond to learners who complain all the time?

- When should criteria be presented to the learners? How much should learners know?

- How can I be objective, especially in a written assignment? Is encouragement more important than objectivity?

- Do my evaluations reflect my original objectives?

- What is important enough to evaluate? Is it more important to leave some things alone?

- Do learners know what I think is important? If I am too specific, will I curtail their creativity?

- How do I reward learners for their efforts when their final product is not up to par?

- Are learners able to express what they think is important?

Management and Record-Keeping

The organizational aspects of evaluation are crucial and should be as carefully considered as the procedures for instruction and evaluation. Record-keeping should include more than quantitative representations of progress. Qualitative information can take the form of anecdotal descriptions, checklists or rating scales. Self-reports are useful for saving instructor time and providing an important perspective in records.

Record-keeping procedures should be manageable, efficient, and practical. It is wise to find and learn to use a computer grading program to collect and store grades generated by evaluation. These programs are cheap, easy to use and adapt, and can provide printouts of learners' grades.

Many online courses that use objective tests have automatic scoring and record-keeping systems built into the course design. See Toolbox 10: Assessment in Online Courses, for details.

A Final Thought...

Assessment should be consistent with how learners process and express their knowledge. Some learners can express what they know much better through poetry, storytelling, conversation, dance, or art than in formal writing. Different cultures, different types of knowledge or skill, different workplace environments, and different learner ages and stages, all influence the sorts of things learners can do best. It would be unfair to evaluate new knowledge using a medium or method that is foreign or limiting to that learner, unless part of the objective is helping the learner master new expression.

Also, different instructors prefer different methods of evaluation. As we evaluate more, regardless of whether we do it in qualitative or quantitative ways, we do at least two things: we find out more about the learners and the effect of our teaching and we help learners become more comfortable with evaluations. Like many other things, the more common something is, the less frightening it is.

6
Evaluating Technical Skills

"Factual" and "Procedural" Knowledge

Before we can think about how to evaluate a technical skill, we need to understand more clearly just what is involved in the process of learning that skill. This chapter considers various aspects of evaluating the technical skills of students and, just as important, how to create the right learning framework so they can develop these skills in the first place.

> "What do we live for if not to make the world less difficult for each other?"
>
> – George Eliot

The term *technical* comes from the word *technology*. Technical skills most often include the ability to use technology, usually the ability to perform specific procedures that involve action. Technical skills usually also involve decision making. In simple language, when performing a technical skill, making one choice could be considered correct; another choice could be considered incorrect.

An example of a technical skill is knowing how to operate a tool or machine that performs a necessary task in the workplace. Or a technical skill could involve knowing how to use a computerized machine. It could include a complex set of sub-skills, such as using the different functions of an elaborate word-processing package. Technical skills might be inter-connected with knowledge, attitude, and intuition, such as the skill of executing a difficult passage on a musical instrument.

Two Kinds of Knowledge in Technical Skills

Factual knowledge differs from **procedural knowledge** in the following way: Factual knowledge is what you "know" and procedural knowledge is what you "do."

To help evaluate technical skills, most educators separate knowledge into two forms. These are simply called *factual* knowledge and *procedural* knowledge. Factual knowledge is usually what we consider *content*. For example, operating an electric meat slicer might involve the factual knowledge of naming the parts of the machine, stating the pertinent safety precautions, or listing the procedures. Procedural knowledge is the knowledge of how to perform certain actions. Procedural knowledge for operating the meat slicer might be knowledge that allows the learner to operate the machine independently, safely, and correctly.

If you're like most teachers who are teaching technical skills, you probably already believe that procedural knowledge is the main emphasis of your instruction. Factual knowledge may be nice to have, but it is not crucial. In fact, some people who are quite expert at doing things—performing technical skills—can't name the parts or describe what they are doing. You probably also know that procedural knowledge is developed through action—usually repeated action, practice, and experience. Procedural knowledge gradually becomes internalized until it is so much a part of us that we are not aware of it. Most people learn new skills by practising them until they are comfortable doing them without coaching.

Operations Involved in Learning a New Skill

Operation 1: Knowing How to Do It

Knowing how to do things includes the techniques and judgments we can see when we watch someone perform a skill. Often, however, people who perform a skill well do it almost without thinking. They cannot say what it is they are doing or why they are doing it. The skill has been internalized. But most people do not start out knowing how to do things instinctively. Beginners behave differently from seasoned performers, usually proceeding slowly, double-checking all the steps of performing a new skill.

Knowing that beginners differ from seasoned performers has a number of implications. First, as an instructor, you cannot evaluate the whole process right off the bat. If performance is truly learned from experience, teaching a technical skill often takes time. Final evaluations, before learners are ready, can be devastating.

Second, a technical skill often consists of a series of smaller skills, so when teaching it is best to break down the process into smaller steps. For example, Jim remembers a quite wonderful teacher—in this case, one who taught him the technical skill of reading the musical score for Handel's *Messiah*—who broke down complex musical phrases into much simpler pieces. Those who were learning to read the music didn't have a clue as to which musical passage they were learning; but when the time came to look at the entire musical score, they were amazed at how easily the difficult technical passages seemed to flow. Jim believes that if he had had to face the complete score from the beginning, he would have been overwhelmed.

Operation 2: Knowing What to Do and When to Do It

Although technical skills can sometimes be taught in small incremental steps, in the real world they are neither performed one at a time nor in splendid isolation, and several skills must sometimes be performed simultaneously. Workers facing a problem must decide which action will best solve the problem. They can either draw upon a repertoire of skills they have developed, or they can improvise and learn their way out of a new skill problem facing them.

Using and relying on previously acquired skills has several implications for evaluation. To begin with, if individual experience differs, it would be silly to start all learners at the same place. A better idea is to pre-test learners prior to beginning the learning task. Assuming that everyone in a group has the same skill levels can lead to problems. First, you can lose people by assuming they know too much. No one likes to appear stupid. Second, you can bore students by starting at a too-simple level of instruction. Nothing is less motivating than boring instruction. Third, starting everyone at the same level can create a series of practical problems. One group can be bored, another lost. Those well versed in the material have a tendency to chat away, disturbing and sometimes embarrassing those whose lack of experience forces them to pay strict attention. An additional problem can occur if this second group comes to think they might be stupid because they don't know how to do things that, obviously, seem so easy to others.

To help students learn technical skills more efficiently, find ways to evaluate how well beginning learners perform skills in isolation. First, learners need a place to practise and concentrate on what they are doing. Be sure to set up situations that also evaluate the way learners perform these skills in real-life contexts. For example, a simple technical skill like foul-shooting in basketball can be enhanced by the learner's isolated practice. There is no one else to distract a foul-shooter in an empty gym where the sub-skills and routine can be practised until they are second nature. However, without practice in a game situation, the learner is not able to feel the pressure of competition, noise and distraction, and fast pace that a game brings.

Both isolated practice and real application are important. It is up to the instructor to find ways to assess how well learners choose and use skills in different situations. Only then can learners assess whether they can invent and improvise new skills when necessary to solve problems.

Operation 3: Knowing the Consequences of Actions

When we teach learners a new skill, we often tell them why they should use a particular method or set of steps by emphasizing the consequences of other actions. Recently, we went white-water rafting in Colorado. The teacher and guide was very explicit about the consequences of particular actions. For example, he told us, "If you people in the front of the raft don't duck low when we hit the 'hole,' the front end will ride high and

Dimensions of Mastery

A learner may demonstrate a skill after it is first learned in the classroom, but how do you assess real mastery? Here are some suggestions.

1. Check to see if the learner knows which skill to use in different situations.

2. Check to see if the learner can perform the skill correctly without hesitation or evident fear of error.

3. Check to see if the learner can improvise and modify the skill to accommodate different situations.

4. Check to see if the learner can perform the skill on cue, without immediate prior practice.

Evaluating psychomotor skills

When you write indicators to describe the levels between a novice and an expert performance of a skill, remember that skilled psychomotor performance usually involves:

1. Speed and accuracy

2. Accurate conception of the task to be performed

3. Coordinated movements

4. Efficient use of cues in the situation

5. Confident attack of the situation (reaching for correct tools without hesitation, and so on)

6. Adjustment as required to meet changes in the environment and situation

we might flip the raft." Needless to say, this information seemed important for us to know. This sort of approach is common in most effective workplace safety training programs. Participants are often shown graphic examples of accidents that happen if certain procedures are not followed.

Research suggests that a key difference between experts and novices in any practice is that experts develop a broad knowledge of consequences through experimenting, analyzing their results, and watching others experiment. This experience allows them to anticipate the consequences of alternative actions. The instructor's task is to help learners review unanticipated outcomes so they can learn from their mistakes. Some people try to forget mistakes, hide them, or rationalize an unwanted outcome as an anomaly. (Someone once said that if the definition of insanity is finding out what doesn't work and persisting in doing it, then most humans are insane.) Learners need to develop the ability to predict the consequences of their actions and make a habit of reflecting on their experiences to develop their knowledge of consequences. We also need to emphasize, in our teaching and evaluation, the importance of thoughtful trial-and-error risk taking as a way of continuous learning.

Situated cognition describes the idea that learning occurs as humans interact with the world. The learning that happens is shaped by the context or "situation" in which the learning occurred.

Context and Transfer in Skill Learning

Skill learning happens within a particular environment, using particular tools, surrounded by particular people. This context shapes the way the learner comes to develop the new skill. Research in **situated cognition** shows that understanding of a newly learned skill is actually rooted within the situation where a person first learned it. For instance, motivated learners will often imitate exactly, and usually unconsciously, the most subtle behaviours demonstrated by a role model. This is why people have such a hard time unlearning particular habits they may have developed during skill learning. Professionals often complain that the textbook methods they are taught in classrooms actually hamper their performance in the thick of practice.

In a particular workplace the learner's way of developing a new skill will also be shaped by the belief systems, the subtle rules and norms of behaviour, the shared understandings that define what are problems and what are not, and the range of possibilities for action.

One problem facing instructors is how to help learners transfer skills from the classroom to a workplace or other real-life situations. However, research is showing that learning is rooted in the actual situation (Lave and Chaiklin, 1993). People evolve ways of performing skills according to what works best and quickest on the kinds of messy situations in which they must perform, the tools available, and the particular methods the community around them endorses. Learning is never simply absorbed in a workshop and transferred to the workplace. People live and use their skills very differently in both places as they learn how to *participate meaningfully* in each community.

Coaching and Evaluating Skills

Cognitive apprenticeship is becoming a popular system for helping people learn a technical skill through ongoing coaching and evaluating in several systematic stages, listed below. If you want your instruction to be helpful, it is rarely enough to measure what students have learned at the end. Learning is complex, dynamic, individual, and incremental. Most teachers observe and assess on an ongoing basis as learners attempt a new skill. In the steps outlined below, the instructor is referred to as a "coach" to emphasize the activities of continual guidance and encouragement.

Demonstrate and Describe

The coach demonstrates the task, explaining his or her thinking about important steps, the choices being made, and their rationale. Some demonstrate the whole sequence of actions at normal speed, then break the skill into small chunks that are demonstrated slowly. The learner observes and questions.

Practice Plus Formative Evaluation

The learner attempts to model the task being learned, talking through the thinking process. Throughout this phase the coach watches the learners try the task. The coach may or may not give assistance. Formative evaluation is constant and includes listening to learners articulate the reasons for their choices of action as they move through the task. Good coaches emphasize positive feedback. They point out what the learner is doing that is desirable. Good coaches also limit feedback because, when learning something new, most people cannot deal with instant corrective feedback on every aspect of their performance. Most learners need many trials before they can implement changes.

Scaffold Plus Formative Evaluation

Good coaches do what is called **scaffolding** in cognitive apprenticeship jargon. During scaffolding, the learner continues to practise the learning task with feedback from the coach. Gradually, however, the learner moves to greater independence. During this time, formative evaluation continues, and a good coach assesses more than the learner's gradual mastery of the task. The coach also assesses when to hold back advice, offer encouragement, describe what's happening, pose questions to help learners notice what they're doing, further demonstrate a small aspect of the task, or correct an action directly.

> **Scaffolding** is the idea that one learning builds upon another. It is usually impossible for humans to make huge learning leaps; instead, most of us make incremental steps where our learning is based in part on what we already know.

Independent Trials Plus Summative Evaluation

Learners perform the task autonomously, with assistance and/or feedback from the coach only when requested. At this point, most evaluation is summative. The coach's tasks are to observe the learner performing the task and to score the performance, looking for consistency over several trials. Test developers suggest that mastery can be reasonably assumed when the learner performs the skill correctly without feedback on three consecutive occasions.

Continuous Evaluation

As an evaluator, it is probably wise to remember that anything can happen once—especially if it's something negative for the learner. Trust good evaluation, but remember that evaluation is subject to all sorts of actions and events—including miracles. For important tasks, it is therefore crucial to measure changes in a learner's skill performance over time and in different contexts in order to provide a true (valid and reasonable) assessment.

Self-Evaluation

Finally, the impetus and judge for assessment gradually shifts from the instructor to the learner. This shift does not often happen automatically! The chapter on self-assessment presents detailed suggestions for encouraging strong, effective, ongoing habits of self-assessment in learners.

A Final Thought...

Learning new skills and abilities requires trial and error and includes the willingness to take calculated risks, the willingness to make mistakes and the ability to learn from them, the ability to see cause-and-effect relationships of actions and consequences, and the ability to generalize from specific experiences to other situations. However, it is probably most important to remember that, of the many technical skills an evaluator may possess, it is the ability to build a comfortable, encouraging learning environment that is most crucial to helping students learn. Students learn best when they are stretched and encouraged to take risks. Our experience is that learners will respond and progress in an atmosphere that is critical, but supportive.

7

Evaluating Performance

Standard-Setting, Observation, and Interpretation

Performance objectives are controversial. Educators argue and debate over their value and the extent to which they should be used. Some believe that outlining, following, and evaluating performance objectives is the only way that learning can be seen. Others counter that performance objectives evaluate only a very narrow aspect of education. However, one thing is certain: if you are dealing in performance skills, your objectives should be clear, understandable, and easy to measure.

J im's introduction to performance objectives was as a young, frightened, novice teacher. Early in the morning on the first day of school, the administrators led the teachers into the concrete auditorium, darkened the lights, and flashed up a short movie. The movie was about behavioural objectives, and starred a little cartoon fish. The hero, or victim as he turned out to be, was looking to travel somewhere; but, sadly, he had not outlined a specific plan. As he swam around in circles, he frantically inquired of all the denizens of the deep, "Do you know where I'm going?" None knew. Finally, he met a shark and asked the same question, "Do you know where I'm going?" "Right this way," the shark invited, and pointed to his gaping mouth with his large fin. The little fish swam inside and was devoured.

The point of the story, for new teachers, was obvious. If they didn't write good behavioural objectives, they would surely die! At least, as the administration of the school pointed out, they would not know where they were going and would ruin the lives of all the students who had put their trust in them. (Better a shark should devour you.) Even for fresh, young teachers, the juxtaposition of a cartoon fish with apocalyptic warnings of imminent disaster was a bit laughable; however, there was a point.

Defining Objectives for Competency

Competencies are general descriptions of the abilities needed to perform a specific role in the organization.

Unlike interpersonal or problem-solving capabilities, technical skills are usually determined ahead of time. They should be taught according to objectives that are described in precise, specific detail. Ask the following four questions.

Who?

Are the learners complete beginners with no experience using this particular skill? What abilities and background do they have that may be helpful in learning this new skill? What characteristics do they have that may affect the way they perform the skill?

Will Do What?

This is the content of the task you want them to be able to perform at the time of evaluation.

Under What Circumstances?

This is the situation in which learners must perform the task. Who will they work with? What tools will they use? What time pressures and other task pressures create the context in which they must perform the skill?

To What Level of Performance?

What is the minimum level of performance needed? Is there a range that is acceptable? Is it important *how* they perform the skill? What are the most important qualities of performance they will demonstrate? How many correct trials must be performed?

Here are some examples of instructional objectives.

- **Example 1**

   Incomplete: Students will understand the dynamics of a vertical organizational chart and describe the lines of authority. *Revised:* Given a diagram of a vertical organizational chart (condition), the first-year management students (who) will identify in writing the five lines of authority (will do what) and list the three characteristics of each, stating what it is, its organizational function, and why it is important (level of performance).

- **Example 2**

   Incomplete: Students will understand the parts of a single-cycle internal combustion engine and the flow of power. *Revised:* In the final 15 minutes of today's three-hour class, given a drawing of a 24-volt DC starter motor (condition), each student (who) will correctly label and in a short sentence describe the function and relationship of 18 parts of the starter motor (what and level of performance).

Pre-Test/Post-Test Approaches to Determine Skill

An evaluation design that utilizes pre-tests and corresponding post-tests is the most common method of measuring skills learned during a particular course of instruction. Any test is a one-shot measure of something. In the case of using a pre-test/post-test design to measure technical skills, the instructor's first task is to find a way to test to what extent learners

Performance Observations

When observing and judging a learner's performance, ask yourself the following questions:

- Is the performance I'm seeing obstructed by anything (such as the learner's mood, physical condition, or anxiety at being watched)?

- Is the learner engaging in the performance with the willingness needed to demonstrate her best competence?

- Is the learner demonstrating something under artificial conditions that cannot be repeated in realistic, fast-paced conditions? Or is the learner demonstrating something now that will deteriorate over time in everyday conditions?

- What parts of this performance are truly significant in terms of the overall objectives?

- What am I possibly missing as I observe?

Assessment Cautions

When doing assessments, remember:

- Don't get trapped into rating what can be most easily seen and rated, losing sight of the core goal.

- Many raters use intuition. This is fine, but begin and end by describing the evidence that supports and sparks a particular judgment.

- Know what specifics to look for, but also know when to be open to new information. A clear focus helps you filter out the mass of information.

Occupational standards define the skills, knowledges, and understandings necessary to undertake a particular task or job to an understood level of competence, and are often established by the industry they pertain to, for example, architects, lawyers, doctors, teachers, or social workers.

can perform the desired skill. The next tasks are to design instruction and teach what learners need to know to achieve the objective. The final step is to re-test the students to see whether they can perform the task in a way that meets the instructor's or the program's standards.

Although working from pre-determined objectives can help you give clearer and more precise directions, there is also a drawback. When working solely from pre-determined objectives, you presume that you already know every skill and particular situations in which learners will use the skill. This precludes the possibility of learners finding new ways to do things that may not fit your expectations. We are not suggesting that you ignore pre-determined objectives or other evaluating activities. But use evaluative techniques with caution—always trying to measure the impact these evaluation activities have on the learners and how they learn.

The pre-test and post-test should be congruent with the objectives you have set as an instructor. A test can be oral, behavioural, or written. Tests that measure technical skills, however, are usually demonstrated, either in a simulated situation or in the actual workplace.

For example, an instructional objective might be that new trainees for the position of hotel service representatives enrolled voluntarily in your course will be able to follow the five steps stated in company procedures for welcoming and registering a guest, obtaining the necessary

Using Existing Measurement Tools

One way to save the work of constructing an evaluation instrument is to use a pre-existing tool. A fast way to find what you need is to post a question on the adult education network on the Internet. Unfortunately, the proliferation of assessment instruments has cluttered the market with inadequate tools; you'll need to choose carefully

Here are some considerations when selecting or designing an instrument for educational assessment, adapted from the psychometric standards used by the American Psychological Association. Obviously these apply only to certain kinds of measurement tools.

- **Validity**—What does the instrument measure? Will it be useful?
- **Reliability**—How stable are some of the scores from the measurement?
- **Objectivity**—Can the instrument be scored by

untrained judges, or is it objectively scored with grids, optical scans, and so on?

- **Availability**—Can the instrument be obtained easily? Are full instructions available?
- **Cost**—How expensive are the materials, booklets, and so on, and scoring methods?
- **Time**—How much time does the test itself require? Does it require one-on-one work with test-takers, or can it be delivered in groups? How long does scoring take?
- **Sophistication**—What background is required to use the instrument? What skills and knowledge must test-takers already have (i.e., reading level)?
- **Complexity**—What kind of feedback can be derived from the items? How complicated is the interpretation?
- **Supplementation**—Will the instrument yield data that adds to what participants already know?

Chart for Assessing Observable Outcomes

Note: An outcome is an observable result, usually taking the form, in learning situations, of a behavioural pattern, specific demonstration, or product created by the learner. If you can stand using a checklist-type recording format, here are two samples for your instructor's kit-bag.

Individual Learner Checklist

Assessment Outcomes

	Emergent	Basic	Proficient	Strong
Outcome 1				
Outcome 2				
Outcome 3				
	Little or no presence of the characteristic	Some (or beginning) presence of the characteristic	Detailed and consistent presence of the characteristic	Highly inventive and mature presence of the characteristic

Class Checklist

	Helen	Jim	Sue	Francois	Hank
Outcome 1	E	E	E	B	E
Outcome 2	S	E	S	E	E
Outcome 3	S	N/A	N/A	B	E

Instructor Self-Evaluation: Teaching Technical Skills

☐ Did the learners ask questions throughout? (Was I accessible?)

☐ Did several learners mirror a specific skill well? (Did I demonstrate clearly?)

☐ Did several learners mirror a specific skill poorly? (Do I need to improve my method, skill level, communication?)

☐ Was any review area misunderstood by most of my learners? (Do I need to change my teaching style?)

☐ Did the learners use resources (tools, texts) effectively? (Did I teach them to use their resources well?)

☐ Did the class repeatedly perform skills effectively? (Did I teach skills in proper sequence with clear progression?)

☐ Did I hear learners discussing concepts related to the skill I consider important? (Did I focus effectively on these concepts?)

Developing Indicators To Rate Levels of Technical Skill Performance

This example, from trainer Mark Davis of Atco Electric, shows the process and detail required to create effective assessment tools. Technical expert-instructors compiled specific descriptors of different performance levels based on their experience observing trainees. New trainees were consulted to determine which skill areas they felt were most important. The tools were then pilot-tested and refined further.

Note how the descriptors can be applied relatively easily by any trained observer to derive a numeric assessment for a learner's performance. Also, the descriptors make it very clear for learners what the desired standards are and where their performance can be improved.

Sample Objective

Upon completion of the Cable Preparation and Component section of the training course, each individual will be required to complete an elbow, a sleeve, and a termination that meets the manufacturer's specifications.

Several dimensions of this objective are assessed using a five-point rating scale. Here are two:

Tools

5—Uses all cable preparation tools correctly and to their full capacity. Demonstrates confidence and competence in selecting and using correct tools without hesitation. Able to assist instructors with other trainees' instruction.

4—Selects and uses all cable preparation tools correctly. Asks questions when not sure.

3—Selects appropriate cable preparation tools for use in specific tasks. Does not use tools to their full capabilities.

2—Requires continuous instruction and supervision when working with the cable preparation tools.

1—Uses wrong cable preparation tool in the practical application.

Safety

5—Good practice of all applicable safety rules.

4—One safety infraction.

3—Two safety infractions.

2—Safety infraction with "incident" (accident). Note safety rule with complete documentation.

1—Disregard for safety rules.

information, and responding to the guest's special requests. The company might want trainees to follow these same five steps every time they register a new guest, independently and without supervision. To test how well learners could do this before instruction you might ask them to list the five steps, set up an experimental guest registration situation and let them show what they would do, or have them read a case study description of a poor task performance and respond to it.

The pre-test/post-test format puts the control of evaluation into the hands of the tester. The decisions might be the instructor's or they might belong to an external agent the instructor represents, such as a college curriculum or occupational standards.

Advantages

There are a number of advantages to the pre-test/post-test format.

- It allows you to compare results and clearly show the changes in a learner's behaviour.

- Pre-test results help establish a baseline, against which growth can be compared. Both learners and teachers can see their progress, even in circumstances where the growth is small or does not achieve the standards specified in the objectives.

- With caution, results can be interpreted over time. The results help teachers examine the instructional methods or resources they are using. The post-test supposedly measures the growth of learning. The relative effectiveness of the learning program can then be assessed.

Disadvantages

A pre-test/post-test format does have some disadvantages:

- A learner's performance might be affected by fatigue, illness, or other factors of concentration or motivation. As a result, the difference in pre-test and post-test results may be an invalid measure of learner growth.

- An inadequate testing situation or test questions can yield performances that do not determine the learner's degree of skill mastery.

- Many things can affect the learning that takes place between the pre-test and the post-test. Learning is not always the result of instruction. Life experiences, such as learning from other courses, chance meetings

Skills as Intellectual Capital

Thomas Stewart (1997) reports that when the Canadian Imperial Bank of Commerce decided it needed to better manage and measure what it calls "intellectual capital," CIBC began by abolishing traditional training. Training costs, it decided, are unjustifiably high and don't contribute to a real employee change in skill that increases the company's value.

So CIBC developed a competency model, listing about four dozen skills employees should have. Employees are responsible for learning these skills on their own—using books and software at their branch's Learning Room, or shadowing colleagues.

CIBC charts the growth of what it calls intellectual capital along various indexes. The flow of knowledge is measured from people (new ideas generated) to structures (new products introduced) to customers (percentage of income from new revenue streams). For example, rising customer satisfaction scores and faster complaint resolution show growth in employee skills valued by CIBC.

with people, or a sudden surge of motivation can all have an impact. As a result, it is difficult to decide the effectiveness of instruction solely from pre-test/post-test.

Choosing Criteria for Evaluating Performance Objectives: Begin with the Learners

We have been stressing two things about choosing criteria: be absolutely clear about the basic outcomes that should be evident in learners' performance, and begin with the learners.

Focusing on the learners will help you to be more selective. It's easy to become idealistic and to expose learners to everything you know or think is important about a subject. Many university courses include impossibly titanic reading lists compiled by instructors with more enthusiasm than experience. Begin with manageable objectives. Some instructors plod through a course, top to bottom, year after year, without noticing where their learners are having difficulty. They haven't connected the objectives to the learners. Judith Newman (1991), former dean of education at the University of Manitoba, reminds teachers to ask themselves, "What are the two or three things you really want learners to know or to be able to do at the end of the course?"

One college teacher we know who gets consistently excellent results and warm reviews from students says, "I try not to think about covering the curriculum, but of uncovering what students can do and what they have to say."

Evaluating "Entry-Level Skills"

Thoughtful educators know that learning objectives emerge somewhere between what the educator values, what the learner wants to learn, and the curriculum that evolves during the teaching-learning process. However, the starting point is figuring out learners' current understandings and abilities. This is sometimes called "diagnostic evaluation," which implies that a learner is suffering a disabling condition that the educator will help cure. The term "needs assessment" is also problematic, casting the educator in the role of presuming to determine what "learning" another person needs. "Entry-level skills" is more neutral, implying that the learner does things a certain way before entering an instructional program.

Prior Learning Assessment (PLA)

Prior learning assessment (PLA) is a process being adopted by many post-secondary institutions and adult education programs through which learners seek academic course credit for their life experiences. Many adults have developed valuable knowledge and skills throughout their study, work, travel, volunteer, family, and leadership experiences in life outside a formal education program.

PLA tries to recognize this life experience so that learners can avoid repeating courses presenting knowledge they have already gained, and show they have met the entry requirements to enter courses at their own level of understanding and skill.

Most PLA processes use a variety of tools designed to help learners reflect on, articulate, and demonstrate their past learning. Here are some examples of common tools:

- **Portfolio:** learners assemble a file containing descriptions of their learning supported with documentation: samples of their work, letters from supervisors, demonstrations of accomplishments, etc.

- **Analysis:** learners critically assess their life and work experiences and describe the specific learning outcomes they have developed through these experiences.

- **Skill Development Profile:** learners complete a variety of questionnaires self-assessing their prior experiential learning, and areas for future skill development.

- **Challenge Tests:** learners challenge a particular course by completing various written and non-written assessment activities, including tests, simulations, interviews, etc.

- **Interview:** learners are interviewed to help them articulate their achievements and the learning outcomes of their past experience.

The institution then matches the learner's experiential learning as reflected in PLA to its own established academic standards, so that credit can be awarded by a credentialing body.

Many learners need help completing a PLA process, and institutions often provide workshops to assist in the process. PLA provides a rare opportunity to explore life experiences and accomplishments in depth, and so can really build a learner's confidence and pride. PLA also can be a helpful ongoing process of reflection and self-assessment for the learner. It focuses on competency and understandings rather than grades and is often billed as a useful career planner. It helps learners actually recognize what they know and can do.

The downside of PLA is the difficulty of articulating experiential learning. Not all learners have the means to express or demonstrate their understandings, especially when PLA often depends on writing ability. Secondly, institutions ask learners to organize their life experiences according to only those competencies and concepts that the institution has decided are valuable. This may narrow and exclude the rich experiences of many adult learners.

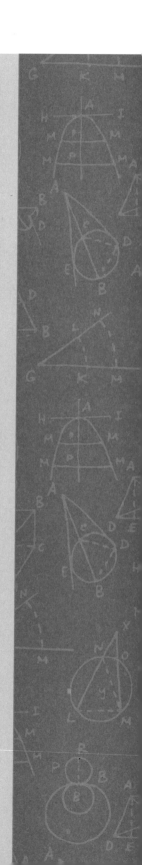

There are four main ways to evaluate the entry-level skills of adult learners: a special test, general observation in everyday activity, learner's self-assessment, and reports from those who can reliably observe the learner's performance. The most effective way is by using a combination of these methods. And, of course, this initial evaluation must be talked through with the learners to understand why they do things the way they do before instruction, how they view their own current skills, what they think they need to learn, and what they mean when they describe these things. Effective evaluation of entry-level skills usually occurs through back-and-forth dialogue, which can extend over a long period of time in cases where entire programs are being developed for a diverse group of learners.

Supervisor reports can provide helpful information about the learners from others who have watched them work. These reports must be read carefully. Reports are open to wide differences in interpretation, and need to be checked and double-checked against other sources of information.

Prior Learning Assessment (PLA) systems are gaining wide appeal as a more rich, holistic way to capture learners' entry skills than tests. Refer to the box on page 73 for more details.

A Final Thought...

In their place, performance objectives can be very helpful. If they are written well, they outline learning in a very precise way. They will spell out exactly what needs to be evaluated and, simultaneously, what should be taught. However, performance objectives are only suitable within a particular context—where the learner outcomes must be standard and there's little room for creativity. Used outside this specific area, performance objectives may be stifling.

8

Evaluating Growth in Conceptual Knowledge

How Do People Come to Understand Something?

We know that learning is not a process of simple consumption. However, many evaluation measures still work from this assumption. To design more effective measures to evaluate knowledge, we must understand how people develop concepts and thinking skills.

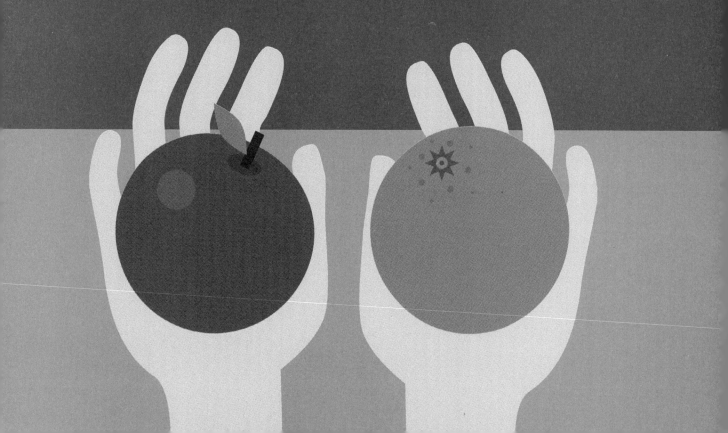

"Our culture is the sea in which we swim, as transparent to us as the ocean is to the fish that live in it."

– George Hein

When evaluating conceptual knowledge, we must be very careful not to make the mistake of assuming that each person uses the same images and words to make sense of the concepts taught in a course. Learners differ. And teachers have processed conceptual knowledge in a particular way, using their own experiences, words, and ideas. The tests they set reflect their own subjective ways of understanding the concepts, whether global, analytic, abstract, concrete, intuitive, logical, connected to internal experiences or external events.

So-called objective tests, such as multiple-choice or true-false item tests, purport to test a learner's knowledge of facts deemed important by the test designer. However, these items or concepts are represented in the test-designer's language. Learners are often frustrated by objective tests because the language may not match the unique way in which they've constructed a particular concept. They may know and understand the information being tested quite well, but the way the evaluation tool is formulated can confuse them enough to make them score poorly.

How do people come to know something? And how can we tell when they know it? Knowledge is a slippery concept that has been debated at length by philosophers and advertisers, engineers and theologians alike.

New Knowledge Is Actively Constructed, Not Passively Absorbed

The old "jug and mug" image of learning is rejected by most teachers, who realize that **conceptual knowledge** can't be poured into so-called "empty heads." People actively make meanings of their own from all experiences, including formal education. And all people construct knowledge differently. For instance, if you read a list of simple words to a group of adults—words such as car, fruit, holiday, winter—each person in the group will form a different mental image because each has a unique association with the same word. When presented with a new idea, we do the same thing. We compare it to the understandings and ideas we already have. We interpret the new idea by connecting it to personal experiences that illustrate it.

Conceptual knowledge refers to how people sort and then represent what they know in terms of main themes or ideas.

Conceptual Knowledge

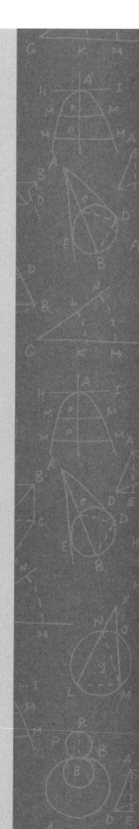

Sample Activities To Assess Learners' Growth

- Answer questions orally or in writing.
- Solve a problem, then analyze the problem-solving process.
- Create questions for other learners.
- Design assignments for products that would show a learner has attained each level of conceptual growth in Bloom's taxonomy.
- Narrate an example from their experience that illustrates the concept.
- Teach another learner the concept and answer questions.
- Make up stories showing application of a concept.
- Twist well-known stories, such as fairy tales, to show application of a concept.
- Role-play making a decision or solving an interpersonal conflict that shows the application of a concept.
- Choose a story from a newspaper or journal of interest to the learner that demonstrates the concept.
- Create an original process using the concept.
- Evaluate items applying criteria derived from the concept.
- Form a generalization for your personal action using the concept.
- Draw all the things you associate with the concept.
- Analyze a situation and suggest a solution, using the conceptual knowledge.
- Draw a symbol or image to represent the concept, then explain the choices.
- Choose five photographs to illustrate aspects of the concept.

We have used these activities ourselves with some success. For example, in an undergraduate course called "The History of Childhood," we wanted learners to understand and compare the ideas of various philosophers, such as Plato, Quintilian, Rousseau, and St. Augustine, concerning child-rearing and education.

Two groups of learners who enjoyed doing dramatic improvisations invented scenes showing a modern dilemma faced by the parents of a child (such as catching a child smoking cigarettes with her friends).

Other groups of learners pretended to be followers of a particular philosopher, for example, the neo-Platonists, the neo-Quintilians, and so on. Each group analyzed and evaluated the dramatic scenario from their own particular philosophic perspective, and made recommendations to the parents for the next action.

The activity revealed the level of understanding of each group and its flexibility in applying the concept to solve a problem. The activity was a good evaluation tool and, at the same time, furthered learning.

A limitation was that groups, not individuals, displayed the conceptual knowledge and thinking skills. This is why multiple assessment methods are helpful.

Everyone Creates a Personal Knowledge

Every new concept changes the way we think and act. Imagine your memory as a series of linked databases, like a personal Internet, into which you are trying to file a new bit of information. When we are constructing new ideas, we search our database to find corresponding information to help us understand the idea and to help us find a category in which to place it. We pull an appropriate file up on our mental screen, then add the new information to it. Our mental database works to shape and accommodate new information into our personal system. We might find that the new information does not quite fit existing files, which may force us to create new ones that then alter our existing database. When this happens, the new material has changed our mental structure. We have created knowledge.

Learners Construct New Knowledge in Different Ways

Socially constructed knowledge refers to the idea that knowledge is constructed by humans as they live within the world in response to what happens to them.

Research suggests that people perceive and process new knowledge according to their own individual learning styles. The Myers-Briggs Type Indicator and Kolb's Learning Style Inventory are popular, partly because adult learners often find that these psychometrics help them to recognize that they have a preferred way of learning that is different from others. Of course, such instruments have limitations because people are more complex than their learning styles; however, understanding that there are differences is helpful information.

For example, the Myers-Briggs and Kolb inventories suggest that some adults are "global" learners. They process information in large sweeps and prefer to look at the big picture. Other learners are "analytical." They process information in small chunks, preferring to go step-by-step and analyzing details. Adults also act differently. Some are eternal gatherers of information, who are afraid to stop searching and start doing. Others like to put new information to use right away, before learning anything further. Some talk and write about an idea in abstract form and others need to show their understanding through application or physical expression.

Listen carefully to what learners say, and imagine how they see things. When there is no allowance for differing perspectives, interpretations, or insights, some learners give up and passively wait to hear what the instructor wants. But knowledge and understanding grows when people ground concepts in their own language and experience.

Ongoing Self-Evaluation of Thinking Skill Development

Behaviour	Examples
I use errors as stepping stones for new ideas.	
I deliberately try to apply new ideas to my own work in different ways.	
I shift perspective with ease.	
I can empathize and respond to others' thinking.	
I weigh information carefully before creating opinions.	
I persevere in seeking ideas and solutions.	
I combine ideas in original ways.	
I produce many ideas with ease, such as in a brainstorming session.	
I seek information from several viewpoints.	
I generate, select, and apply criteria to evaluate what I see.	
I recognize when evidence is scanty or biased.	
I recognize assumptions, including my own.	
I can recognize and move beyond my own preferred beliefs and worldview, when there are good reasons to do so.	
I can tolerate uncertainty and ambiguity without forcing closure too early.	
I can hold two contrasting ideas in my mind at once and accept the paradox.	
In a conflict, I can recognize the insight available and remain open to learning.	

Some Assessment Measures Can Strangle Conceptual Growth

If you evaluate people's learning on what you've already decided they *should* learn, you may think you're making your expectations clear but you are clearly limiting their learning. This is exactly what you don't want when you are trying to develop thinking and creativity. Creative teaching demands that learners do not simply replicate current reality. Teaching adults means helping them take the initiative to push for breakthroughs, take risks, and make mistakes.

For example, the more specific you are in giving directions, the more circumscribed the learner's work will be. In some cases learners should follow directions exactly—as when learning a technical skill. But where conceptual thinking is involved, people need to work through a new idea for themselves. They play with it, change it to fit their own experience, challenge it, and add new dimensions to it. This is a necessary process for learners to take ownership of a concept.

Think of curriculum, not as fixed and final, but as a journey of possibilities. Listen carefully to what students say. Let yourself learn from

Changes in Evaluation Approaches

Conventional Evaluation Approaches:	Changing Evaluation Approaches:
Instead of...	Instructors now tend to...
■ reducing things to their separate parts to understand them	■ consider the whole, and its connections
■ deciding all the content that learners are to know	■ encourage learners to explore and discover
■ goal-oriented, linear planning	■ support a dynamic, non-linear change process
■ extrinsic motivation: punishment and rewards	■ build on people's intrinsic motivations
■ focusing on rational, logical learning	■ evoke intuitive and emotional knowledge
■ attempting to predict and control learner progress	■ understand that learning is messy, unpredictable
■ expecting certainty	■ tolerate ambiguity
■ measuring learners as if they were uniform specimens	■ realize learning unfolds differently for each student
■ assuming that objective, accurate measurement is possible	■ find dynamic ways to measure that grow with the learner

their fresh insights into the material you are teaching and their responses to your evaluation procedures. Ambiguity may be uncomfortable, but it opens a space where creative conceptual growth unfolds.

Putting It All Together

Thinking is complex. When humans change their thinking, they change their behaviour. For example, when we truly understand something new, like quantum mechanics, we solve problems differently. When we learn how to think in new ways about any subject, we behave differently. If we don't, we haven't really learned it. Whatever we learn, we use. We may be able to tell someone all about quantum mechanics, but still not understand it well enough to use it. What does this mean for evaluation?

Tests are often ineffective as indicators of conceptual growth

Often "objective" tests are used to provide mechanical measures of achievement. But objective tests, like multiple-choice and one-word answers, are never really objective. They represent someone's perspective on the knowledge being studied. They also cause a more serious problem: they tend to fragment concepts. Fragments are easy to test and measure, but reciting bits of information does not show learning or achievement. In fact, real learning loses its meaning when these fragments are separated from the whole that has been learned. In addition, these mechanical measures of learning tend to place boundaries on learners' thinking. Often, the thing that is being tested is the learners' ability to *guess* what the test-maker has selected as the most important knowledge. Someone who scores well on the test may actually be at a disadvantage: the very "skill" that allows a learner to be a good test-taker might, in fact, stand in the way of continual and dynamic growth.

Use of multiple methods is critical to serve learner diversity and avoid constricting innovative thinking

No single measure or test can be a reliable assessment of growth in thinking and conceptual knowledge. Each adult learner develops new understandings in different ways, and each has preferred ways of processing and demonstrating their learning. Some learners like to find theoretical patterns and make models. Others are impatient and bored unless they are actively using their new knowledge to make things or solve problems.

They learn by doing. Some learners like to talk through the relevance of the concept to their own past experiences. Others would rather write or teach what they've learned. Some want to pick apart every concept in detail until they internalize their knowledge deeply. Others go crazy with such a narrow focus. Some don't realize they have learned until they see themselves doing things they didn't know they could do. Some learners like to learn little bits about lots of things and are anxious to make connections and find the global picture.

Understand knowledge as fluid and constantly changing, not as a fixed commodity

These individual approaches to learning require different assessment methods. And understanding of a concept takes time. A learner might show theoretical knowledge and insightful applications of organizational change management after a week-long seminar. But after six months the same learner might remember very little of the concept; or this learner might have internalized a few key principles that he or she uses in developing company policy. After a year of experimenting with organizational change, that learner might be cynical about the usefulness of any of the concepts or might have personalized them into something new. He or she might not be able to state any of the concepts, but his or her attitudes toward change might be different than they were before the seminar.

A Final Thought...

Thinking about conceptual learning as a complex, long-term, and recursive process leaves us with some questions. At what point can we say that someone has learned the desired concepts? How do we assess the gradual growth of knowledge? What are some ways to assess knowledge without limiting learners? As you'll note in Sample Activities to Assess Learners Conceptual Growth (page 77) the best answer is this: Ask them.

As well, review Chapter 2's overview of different methods, Chapter 11's detailed description of dynamic assessment, and Toolboxes 1 and 2. Provide choices and invite learners to develop new ways of assessing their own growth. Learning continues to evolve, regardless of what the evaluation tells us. An assessment of learners' knowledge at the end of a course can only show their early progress. Sometimes a seed is planted during a course, but it may take years before new understandings become deeply rooted and fruitful.

9

Evaluating "Levels" of Conceptual Growth

Using Bloom's Taxonomy

Benjamin Bloom's taxonomy of how learners understand concepts is still widely used to develop learning objectives and evaluation tools and to create learning activities and questions for students that reach the "higher-order" thinking skills. Despite its limitations, Bloom's taxonomy can be useful in a variety of ways.

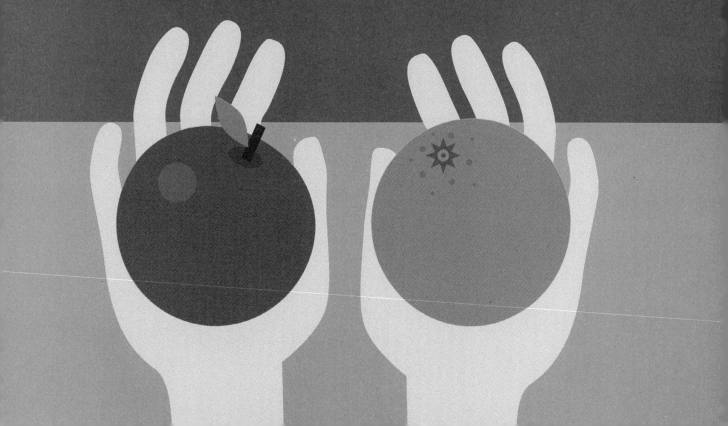

> "Life is short,
> the art long,
> opportunity
> fleeting,
> experiment
> treacherous,
> judgment
> difficult."
>
> – Hippocrates

In 1956, Benjamin Bloom first proposed his now-famous list to describe how learners develop their understanding of a concept. In creating this list, or taxonomy as it was called, Bloom was responding to a problem that troubled many educators.

At the time, learning was usually equated with rote memorization. To counter this belief, Bloom created a hierarchy of thinking skills. He hoped to remind teachers that a learner's ability to copy and regurgitate an explanation of a new concept did not equal knowledge of that concept. In fact, he noted that such simple-minded explanations were a long way from an ability to apply the concept to solve problems or create new ideas from it. Bloom especially wanted to draw attention to what he called "higher-order cognitive skills," and to avoid over-emphasis on memorization.

Although it is now common to be critical of his taxonomy, Bloom created a tool that can be used in a variety of ways—though its use should be confined to specific purposes, with careful provision for its shortcomings.

What Is Bloom's Taxonomy?

A **taxonomy** is a classification system; usually taxonomies move from simple to complex or from complex to simple.

Bloom's taxonomy categorizes conceptual development. According to Bloom, there is a logical order to cognitive ability. The "higher levels" (noted by higher numbers) are understood by Bloom to include each of the "lower levels." For example, a person who engages in the cognitive process of synthesis must also engage in the cognitive processes of comprehension and analysis.

Briefly explained and listed below are the categories of Bloom's taxonomy. Bloom's work has limitations, but we have found that it helps students become more thoughtful about evaluation.

Bloom's Taxonomy

Level 1—Knowledge: recalling information: identifying, matching, stating ideas.

Level 2—Comprehension: making sense of information: organizing and selecting ideas.

Level 3—Application: applying information: using facts, ideas, and principles in different contexts.

Level 4—Analysis: breaking down the information into its component parts.

Level 5—Synthesis and Creativity: restructuring the information to create new ideas and concepts.

Level 6—Evaluation: forming judgments, opinions, or decisions based on particular standards.

Using Bloom's Taxonomy

Bloom's taxonomy can help us vary the kinds of questions we ask learners, the types of tasks we use to evaluate their growth, and the sorts of assignments and activities they construct to demonstrate their conceptual growth. Use the verbs and sample questions listed below to create your own questions and tasks for learners, and also questions to ask yourself when you observe learner performances.

Level 1: Knowledge

Use verbs such as describe, label, identify, name, state, locate, list, define, outline. For example,

- Recall everything you associate with ... (the Kirkpatrick model of assessment).
- Who is ... (Malcolm Knowles)? What is an example of ... (a "soft skill")?
- Where ... (did the Chautauqua movement of adult education begin)?
- When did ... (William Deming present the world with the first Total Quality Management ideas)?

Level 2: Comprehension

Use verbs such as explain, give examples, summarize, rewrite, paraphrase, convert, distinguish, predict. For example,

- Explain ... (performance-based assessment in your own words).
- Summarize ... (the main advantages and disadvantages of pre-test, post-test assessment).
- Explain ... (the purposes of assessment).

Level 3: Application

Use verbs such as infer, change, discover, operate, predict, relate, show, solve, use, manipulate, modify, demonstrate, compute. For example,

- Demonstrate the use of ...
- Interview ... about ...
- How is ... an example of ... ?
- How is ... related to ... ?

Level 4: Analysis

Use verbs such as analyze, break down, differentiate, discriminate, illustrate, identify, outline, point out, select, separate, subdivide, categorize, classify, distinguish. For example,

- Find similarities (or differences) between ... and ...
- Classify ... according to ...
- Differentiate ... from ...
- What assumptions are necessary for ... to be true?
- What distinguishes ... from ... ?

Level 5: Synthesis and Creativity

Use verbs such as devise, compile, design, compose, explain, organize, rearrange, plan, combine, show relationships, synthesize. For example,

- Find a common theme among ...
- Use the technique of ... to do ...
- What would happen if you combined ... ?
- Devise a solution for ...
- Develop a plan for ...
- Develop a theory to account for ...
- If ... is true then ... might be true.
- Modify ... to ...
- Extend ideas on ...

Level 6: Evaluate

Use verbs such as judge, contrast, compare, evaluate, criticize, justify, draw conclusions. For example,

- How do you feel about ... as opposed to ...?
- ... is right because ...
- The evidence supports ...
- Do you agree with ... ? Why or why not?
- Prioritize according to ...
- What criteria would you use to assess ... ?
- I recommend ... because ...
- What is the most important ... ? Why?
- Is ... consistent with ... ? Why?
- Justify ...

Formats That Assess Levels of Understanding

Oral responses in whole-class discussion where the instructor or other learners pose questions

The primary advantage of oral discussions is that the whole class gets to hear different perspectives. However, there are disadvantages. One is that only a few learners are able to participate. Research confirms what we all know from experience: in plenary discussions, some voices are lost, particularly because some people do not feel comfortable speaking out in large groups. Some people feel marginalized by the group's power dynamics of career status, discrimination, ability, and selected values. It is also difficult for the instructor to facilitate the discussion and simultaneously make reliable judgments about learners' conceptual knowledge.

Group discussions can, however, work more fruitfully if they are planned well. Have some participants facilitate while the instructor observes, using a rating tool to record observation. Or teach learners how to observe and use the rating tool. Very simple rating tools are often as effective as complex ones. The tools can include a simple checklist to help the observer note who volunteers to speak and with what frequency, or what types of responses occur. For example, checklists can note how a participant states a concept (knowledge), explains a concept (comprehension), gives an example (application), raises a new question or applies the concept to a very different context (creativity), draws together different statements made in the discussion (synthesis), builds on another participant's idea, disagrees with another participant, or states an opinion giving reasons (evaluation).

Oral responses in small-group discussion where an instructor or other participants pose questions

One advantage of this format is that many learners can participate at the same time, but there are also disadvantages. Instructors often have difficulty relinquishing control of classroom activities. When many small groups are presenting all at once, the instructor simply cannot be present everywhere at the same time. Many very good teachers find this difficult.

For example, several years ago a terrible snowstorm made Jim more than an hour late to class. The students were presenting that day, and they simply took over the class. They did just fine. In fact, Jim realized that they didn't need him at all. Since then, he has typically included a day of class without him there. Students are not only quite capable of taking care of their own business, they also learn more about evaluation by actually engaging in it for real.

Oral responses to a partner

In this format, students work in pairs. A major advantage is that they are often more relaxed and personal in their presentations and responses. One of the disadvantages is that many other students' insights are not heard. You can counteract this by asking students to switch partners and present a number of times. This activity can turn a disadvantage into an advantage as students, with practice, become more comfortable presenting the material. The responses of the partner can also be used to shape and modify the presentation. This activity graphically demonstrates that presentations are dynamic and can be improved with formative evaluation.

Written response to a partner

Written responses have several advantages. First, feedback can be more thoughtful. Second, although it is not restricted to this format, with direction from an instructor, a partner can focus on and highlight a narrow aspect of the presentation. We have found that learners treat a written response more formally than an oral one. Sometimes we want our students to take special care. The instructor must rely on students having the ability and desire to work together, and the instructor must be able to give up the responsibility for all evaluation. Although it seems attractive, this is often difficult.

Written response to the instructor

One advantage of this format is that participants almost always believe that the instructor's feedback is worth more than that of their peers. Sadly, adult students seem more caught in this mythology than younger students. A second advantage is that the instructor can see the work of all the students. The biggest disadvantage is that the instructor actually sees all the work of the participants. Very late nights are common for instructors, especially those who insist on doing all the work.

Pick a test you currently use with adult learners, and try to classify its questions into Bloom's Taxonomy. Label each question as knowledge, comprehension, application, analysis, synthesis, or evaluation. Remember, there is no magic formula for categorizing questions; and, there is no right or wrong answer key. The purpose is to help you create evaluation activities that assess the levels of cognitive processes appropriate to your students' work. Our students typically find that their evaluation activities cluster at the low levels of Bloom's taxonomy. In fact, some have been shocked at the level of their evaluations and have been encouraged to change their work.

Also remember that some of Bloom's categories are not appropriate for all learning experiences or learner levels. The "perfect test" won't necessarily include a balance among all the categories. As you look at your own evaluations, simply ask if your test uses enough "higher-order" questions. Or do you find, as do many instructors, that most of your questions fit the "knowledge" and "comprehension" categories?

Limitations of Bloom's Taxonomy

Bloom's taxonomy can be a helpful starting point when teasing apart the elements and stages of a learner gradually understanding a new concept. It can also help create evaluation tools that go beyond rote responses and measure "higher-order" thinking skills. However, instructors need to be aware of the limitations of any list of categories like Bloom's. Below are some critical questions that are raised about Bloom's taxonomy.

- Does a learner need to progress through all the six levels described by Bloom when learning every new concept? For example, learning to name the parts of the human skeleton seldom involves creativity or evaluation. Learning to interpret sales charts may also be quite simple. There is no need to over-instruct or to use a cannon to kill a fly. While Bloom reminds us to consider higher levels of thinking, sometimes a low-level activity is appropriate.

- Does the learning of a new concept happen in sequential stages?

- Are the "higher-order" levels separate from the "lower-order" levels to the extent the taxonomy indicates they are? Comprehension, analysis, and creativity are often intertwined, and include all sorts of complex cognitive processes. Bloom's taxonomy should not be used to create a simplistic view of the world.

- Do all learners experience cognitive learning in the same way? Learners have different background experiences and understandings that affect how they will make sense of new concepts. Learners also have different learning styles and approaches to learning. Some need to experience learning through holistic, active experience. Some need time to think. Again, Bloom's taxonomy can simplify things that should not be simplified.

- Can levels of learning be described without attention to the context in which the learning took place? For example, a young Canadian woman who learns Italian during a year spent working as a nanny in Florence has likely had a different experience than a young Canadian woman who studied Italian at university.

- Can Bloom's taxonomy lead to teaching that causes knowledge to fragment? The vision of learning embodied in Bloom's taxonomy involves learning the language of a concept first, then breaking the concept into parts, then reassembling the parts into a whole.

Much of the theory about how adults learn is based upon the belief that adults learn concepts experientially. But this theoretical understanding does not correspond to Bloom's representation of the cognitive levels as application, then analysis, followed by synthesis and evaluation. For example, an employee experiences a conflict with a manager when she chooses to send an internal report to some of the department's clients. The shock of the manager's rage at this action causes her to re-evaluate what she thought was an appropriate action. She analyzes the conflict by assessing the various outcomes of her action and by imagining alternate solutions for the problems she's inadvertently created. In short, the real-life process is not nearly as cut and dried as Bloom's categories would make it seem.

A Final Thought...

Many of our friends who teach adults belittle Bloom's taxonomy. They find the taxonomy simplistic and limited for the complexities of adult education.

We agree that there are limitations. However, a knowledge of Bloom's taxonomy and the thinking behind its creation can help us judge and consciously design our own work. The focus on different thinking skills in Bloom's levels invites us to design and implement evaluation activities which are rich, challenging, and creative.

10
Evaluating "Relational" Skills

Caring About People

Have you ever known a person who just seems to enjoy people and whom people enjoy being around? These special people bring a vitality to whatever they do. What makes them so special? What skills do they have that others, who are just as intelligent and organized, seem to lack? And, more to the point of this chapter, can these skills be taught and evaluated?

Relational skills are those interpersonal behaviours that help people build productive relationships with others. Relational skills may have a concrete and observable dimension, but what really drives the important skills of relationship-building are a number of intangible attitudes. They include caring about people, seeing yourself more as a servant than a ruler, and having the ability to see another's point of view. Some writers call these relational skills "soft skills," but the term seems peculiarly vague and inappropriate for such complex learning.

> " Seek first to understand, then to be understood."
> – Stephen Covey

How to Talk About Relational Skills

Writing about relational skills can be difficult because the intertwining of skills, emotions, personality, and attitudes is complex. **Relational skills** include a willingness to listen, understand other perspectives, and reach out with empathy and compassion to build connections. They include communication skills: the ability to express ideas clearly, simply, and honestly, and to vary expression to meet the listener's needs. They also include personal skills: self-awareness, self-respect, patience, emotional balance, and ability to trust. In the workplace, relational skills include interpersonal skills like mediating a dialogue, handling complaints, giving constructive feedback, interviewing, coaching employees, delivering engaging presentations, and being able to work with a variety of people.

Relational skills include the ability to empathize, understand, motivate, and communicate with others. Those with good relational skills are able to see the world from another's point of view and recognize and understand problems and people as they operate in their contexts.

One problem in discussing relational skills is that none of them can be developed in a single period of instruction, whether it's a one-day workshop or a 12-week seminar. These skills are complex. Our best guess is that they are learned behaviours, developed over a lifetime of observing good models and practicing them in all the significant relationships of your life: seeing your grandfather shake hands with every member of the church every Sunday; being with a teacher who really cheered you on; having a close friend who listened to your problems over coffee; working through the thousands of conversations of a marriage; watching a gifted manager inspire and involve people in a community effort surpassing everyone's expectations.

Relational skills are more than just behaviours; they are entwined with values and culture, and underpinned by the particular ways we have come to think about other people. They are enmeshed with our sense of self, and they may border on spiritual dimensions. It takes time, experience, and many positive role models for most people to develop healthy personal and interpersonal ways of behaving. Changing one's behaviour involves unlearning old habits and opening to new habits, and can be a painful and lengthy process.

All healthy people develop relational skills, worked out in idiosyncratic ways. But what is right for one person in one situation may not be right for another. Deborah Tannen (1990) shows how some people use an "indirect" communication style, which seeks intimacy and connection. Others work from a "direct" style, which seeks efficiency and solution. The direct style can be misunderstood as blunt, insensitive, or even confrontational by the "indirect" communicator. Some communicators view themselves as essentially autonomous, separate from, and in competition with others. Others see themselves as essentially connected to others, and seek harmony and links to others' experiences. The most effective communicators allow for such differences, and try to bridge them to relate to others' meanings.

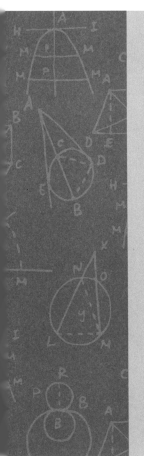

Emotional Intelligence

Relational skills are obviously closely woven with our emotions. Daniel Goleman, in his book *Working With Emotional Intelligence* (1998), argues for serious attention to be focused on feelings—our own, and the feelings of people we contact throughout our day. "Emotional intelligence" (EI) is the ability to understand and name how you and others feel, and to know what to do in response.

Five elements of EI are:

1. **Self-awareness**; the ability to understand one's feelings in the immediate moment, and how these influence one's thinking and behaviour.

2. **Emotional "literacy;"** the ability to name our feelings specifically and to talk about them openly.

3. **Empathy and compassion**; the ability to sense, understand, and be present for the emotions of others.

4. **Balance**; the ability to regulate one's own emotions, be comfortable with ambiguity and change, make choices and act through a healthy balance of mind, body, and emotions.

5. **Responsibility**; the ability to own, tolerate, and be accountable for one's emotions.

These elements imply certain relational skills which we can develop and possibly even observe and assess. A person with high emotional intelligence, according to Goleman, practices the following interpersonal skills:

- asks about and listens to other people's feelings, especially in decisions that affect them
- communicates his or her own feelings precisely to others
- validates these feelings by accepting and respecting them
- does not ignore, judge, ridicule, or trivialize others' feelings
- identifies the unmet emotional needs being expressed through others' negative feelings
- asks, what would help you and me to feel better?
- takes responsibility for generating options, choosing and acting to address negative feelings
- above all, demonstrates respect for others as unique and worthy of being taken seriously

The context in which people live and work also matters. Each person lives in a particular context that demands particular skills. Katherine runs Monday morning meetings in an authoritative, abrupt way. While some groups might openly rebel, her direct style perfectly suits the male aeronautical engineers she is briefing. They are too busy for "democratic discussion." In contrast, Mohammed's meetings with different group of engineers include time for socializing and inquiring after family and personal concerns before getting down to business. Katherine and Mohammed use what they know about their workers in planning their meetings.

Evaluating another person's relational skills is a highly political act, as is any assessment activity. Be clear about the particular values and cultural biases that inform the way you observe and judge someone else's relational skills. Attend carefully to the details of context, including the history of a situation, which affect the ways a learner approaches and responds to others. And always approach such evaluation by talking with the person to learn as much as you can about his or her understandings and choices.

Relational Wisdom

Having wisdom in relational skills depends on at least three kinds of knowledge: knowing how, knowing that, and knowing why. Daniel Goleman calls this "emotional intelligence" (see page 92). Knowing how involves the practical strategies people develop to solve problems. Knowing that is being able to predict the consequences of one's actions: if I do this, then that will happen. Knowing why is the understanding of values, motives, priorities that must be sorted out in making wise judgments.

The knowledge we have described above may be personal and may be displayed in different ways by different people, but it is practical knowledge. Peter Jarvis (1992) suggests that people construct practical knowledge in six different ways:

- through formal learning (observing, reading about, or hearing explanations)

- through trial and testing of this formal learning in practice

- through reflection on practice

- through forming personal rules of action

- through forgetting these rules as a new behaviour becomes integrated into one's everyday actions

- through continuous experiential self-directed learning which adjusts and refines the behaviour in new situations

There is a close relationship between the learner and the context in which practical knowledge develops. When developing practical knowledge, learners adapt to the demands of the environment as they participate in it, and continually invent new knowledge needed to cope with and solve problems that emerge within that environment. But as learners take action to solve problems, they also shape the environment. Francisco Varela (1989) calls this "laying down a path in walking."

What Can and Can't Be Measured

No one assessment tool can possibly measure relational learning. No instructor or curriculum, except in very specific circumstances where a course has been tailor-made for a particular individual in a particular context, can accurately determine what the expected, observable outcomes of relational learning will be before the learning experience happens. Even, for example, in a short course that teaches new receptionists skills for answering telephone calls effectively, each participant will be most effective when he or she develops a personal way of visualizing and creating early rapport with the caller, understanding and helping to resolve the particular concerns of each caller, and maintaining calm and prioritizing multiple demands in periods of stress. Some of these dimensions will remain hidden and impossible to observe within the course itself..

The question is how relational skills, which are so complex and contextual, can be evaluated. A variety of assessment tools can help. Performance observation, peer assessment, and video assessment are described in detail in the Toolbox section of this book.

However, the most important focus should be on developing learners' assessment of their own performances. Refer to Chapter 12 for specific suggestions. Toolboxes 1 and 2 on using journals and portfolios provide further specific suggestions for tracking growth.

Video and small-group feedback are also powerful ways to assess relational skill performance. If you are using video, remember that learners usually need time to adjust to the video camera before they can relax and perform the skill. Use several "takes." Small groups who observe performance can informally discuss their responses and evaluate the learner's performance. With this activity, it is always wise to let the learner respond to the review of her work. Often the discussions that follow can be particularly fruitful, allowing the thinking behind the action to come out. Finally, participants should be reminded that the advice they get from others is recommendation only, not direction. They can choose to use or discard feedback as they see fit.

These critical evaluative interactions can be insightful, but they can also be delicate. Remind participants how difficult it is to separate actions from people's feelings. Those being evaluated should try to listen with an open mind and exercise critical reasoning about whether or not to apply the evaluation. Even when a trusted friend evaluates your actions you may not follow the advice. What is good for one person is not always good for another.

A Final Thought...

We believe that being a good teacher and being a good person are not far removed from each other. In fact, some of the best teachers we know are also the easiest to get along with. In our work with learners, from Grade 2 to Ph.D. students, we have come to see that all humans respond to relationships, and good relationships are based on caring. If your students know that you really care for them and want the best for them, they will forgive you almost any mistake. If, on the other hand, they sense you are nasty and are "out to get them," they will forgive you almost nothing. Good relational skills are extremely important to teaching.

We encourage you to consider each instructional act you complete in its fullest impact—both as a technical skill and as a relational skill. If you do not consider the relational aspect, we believe you will miss the best part of the job.

11 Towards Dynamic Assessment

Capturing Learning in the Moment

Some educators calls conventional measurement "dip-sticking." Instructors think they can shove a dip-stick into their students' brain engines and check the level of learning, presumably to decide whether or not the student needs topping-up. To extend the metaphor, what does learning and teaching mean if you understand learning as "topping-up?" How can we capture the complexity of human understanding using a static instrument?

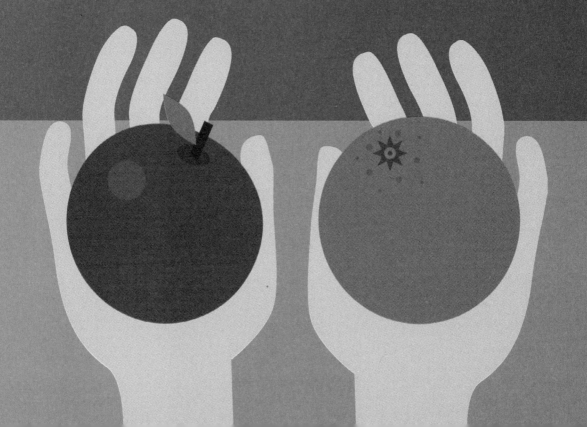

I magine photographing an apple blossom on a late April morning and trying to draw generalizations about the long-term growth achieved by the tree. You have probably noticed that the blossom appears and unfurls within a few days with a burst of life-energy that the casual passerby would easily miss. By the time we can see the apple tree's spring growth, many changes have already taken place deep inside. If it is impossible to capture in one static moment the various complex dynamics of growth going on in a plant at any given moment, how can we even begin to capture the dynamic complexities of human learning using a static instrument?

"Only those who risk going too far can possibly find out how far one can go."

– T. S. Eliot

The Problem with Conventional Assessment

To summarize points made in previous chapters, conventional assessment methods tend to be passive because the evaluator is in the position of "reading" the performance of the learner, who is viewed as a static object. Too often the evaluation and evaluator are assumed to be neutral, as though one human being can truly be objective in the process of perceiving, interpreting these perceptions, and making value judgments about another human being. The impact of the evaluation procedure itself on the learner's motivation and understanding is often not considered in conventional methods of mechanical measurement. Learners are not involved actively or even asked to assess themselves.

Conventional test construction often fails to consider socio-cultural milieu, socio-economic status, and linguistic and ability differences, which excludes some learners. Although these practices have shown themselves to be inaccurate and inconsistent, they continue to be used in prediction, decision-making, and inferences about everything from the leadership potential of employees to learner prospects for lifelong success.

Dynamic Assessment—An Empowering Alternative

Today's organizations are encouraging continuous learning in order to cope with rapid change. Conventional assessment approaches using predetermined standards to measure performance outcomes are incompatible with the continuous learning philosophy, which emphasizes risk taking, innovation, systems thinking, and reflective dialogue. Therefore,

Dynamic Assessment vs. Non-Dynamic Assessment

orientation	Dynamic assessment: process	Non-dynamic assessment: product
view of the learning process and knowledge	dynamic, unpredictable	predetermined, linear
assumptions about the learner	active—invents new knowledge	passive—acquires existing knowledge
assumptions about the evaluator	partial and limited—needs learner's perspective	neutral and objective—unchallenged authority
focus	whole learner situated in a particular context	isolated competencies
origin of standards	evolves with the knowledge invented in the process	externally determined and applied to learner
role of evaluation	ongoing, part of the learning process itself	end-point of learning
interpretation	what people learn, what they say they learn, and how they learn it	what learners can produce
purpose	recording, interpreting, and reinterpreting process	measure and judge according to existing norms

we need more dynamic means to measure performance and learning. *Dynamic* implies something alive and moving, rather than fixed and predictable. Dynamic assessment is grounded on four ideas:

1. Dynamic assessment understands that learning constantly unfolds, even—and perhaps especially—during the evaluation process. Learning does not stand still at the moment the evaluator tests the student. Dynamic assessment situates itself within the whole process of learning, acknowledging that learning is multi-layered. It avoids treating learning as an end product.

2. Dynamic assessment focuses not simply on what the learner knows or can do, but also on how the learner is developing knowledge and skill. The primary purpose of evaluation is to actively help learners move towards success. Dynamic assessment helps by assessing the process of learning, and by integrating assessment procedures into the learning process. Evaluation of many dimensions of the learners' meanings and practices, and the process through which they created these meanings, is followed by assistance and further instruction, which is informed by further evaluation. Dynamic assessment *involves* learners as active participants in the evaluation process, never treating them as passive objects to be weighed and measured.

3. Dynamic assessment recognizes that learners are individuals and that context affects learning. Dynamic assessment examines external conditions and internal impulses that affect the learning process: the culture and power relations embedded in the learning experience, the worldviews of the learner, and, most importantly, what is valued as knowledge and who decides this. Dynamic assessment acknowledges diversity among learners, which means that cultural and social-political differences, gender and language differences, and learning style and ability differences are taken into account.

4. Dynamic assessment looks carefully at the community dynamics in which the learning unfolds. Learning cannot be evaluated simply by focusing on the performance of one learner in isolation, because learning is inter-connected with the shared meanings and relationship dynamics of a particular knowledge community. This is systems thinking. It considers how the parts influence and are influenced by the whole, and examines the purpose and connections of the whole. The observers themselves influence and even determine what is being observed in the learner. Dynamic assessment includes and interprets the community dynamics.

Jim Rough (1994), a consultant who teaches organizations how to shift their approaches to assessing learning, writes, "Our efforts to objectively measure the results of training are part of the old Newtonian way of thinking. When we seek to develop excellence, we are engaging in a transformation process and we should be using a new paradigm to guide us." He suggests that dynamic assessment approaches treat learning and teaching as artistry. Rather than measuring skills, such approaches facilitate transformation by supporting a dynamic process of change in people.

Approaches to Using Dynamic Assessment

1. Establish a general direction—a vision—for the learning. Then let it evolve as people begin to try out the new skills or familiarize themselves with the new concepts, reinventing the knowledge into something personal. For example, we might present a general ideal vision for effec-

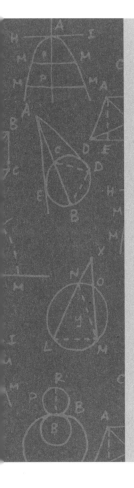

Case Study

Transforming Performance Measurement into Dynamic Assessment

Employees in a government department that provides consulting services in economic development for private business and industry must now produce monthly records describing their performance outcomes for a 30-day period. Senior directors were trying to train staff in the reporting and accountability procedures, but some staff were resisting. One of the first things the consultants did was to facilitate a half-day session of "naming where we're at." In small groups, staff generated words and phrases to describe their perceptions, feelings, and assessment of the current situation. These were then sorted into large-theme categories and posted on flip-charts around the room. The statements were anonymous—generated in groups, then distributed among many categories—but brutally honest and insightful.

Naturally there was some healthy venting. But after the anger and resentment had been cleared, the focus changed for all staff and managers. Rather than resenting and resisting the top-down push for "accountability" through monthly assessment, the department clearly needed to find ways to describe actions-in-process and gradual change. Rather than worrying about generating enough products to report each month, they needed to invent concrete phrases and terms to show upper management how the process parts of their work were significant in light of the organization's overall mission and objectives.

Their focus needed to shift to observing and assessing their own work, and finding a way to represent their growth and accomplishments in results-oriented language. As one manager put it, they needed to start thinking in terms of their time as if it were "billable hours." What did I just accomplish in that conversation? What did I learn? Is it worthwhile to me? Is it worthwhile to the organization's goals?

This is dynamic assessment. It focuses learners on their own efforts and progress. They ask questions such as: What am I choosing to read? To listen to? What tasks am I filling my time with? What are the most significant things I accomplished or learned this week? How do I know? There is a wealth of resources available now to help people evaluate their daily activity, to "put first things first" and assess their own continuous learning and growth.

tive interpersonal conflict management to a group of employees, teaching them models of conflict resolution and making suggestions for redirecting destructive behaviour. But the minute they begin to actually experiment with these models, comparing them to the messy value issues and political agendas in their company, they will begin to create a new vision of how relations in their office could be. They will adapt and personalize the models, and the gradual changes in their environment will in turn shape their vision.

2. List some expectations and indicators before you get going. What do you as facilitator expect to happen? What do participants expect? How will you know when it's happened? State all initial expectations, both instructor's and learners', clearly. These are flexible, of course; but once they're set out, they can then be examined, changed, and taken apart to challenge their underlying assumptions.

Have individuals list observable indicators of their vision — things they expect to observe around them, things they expect to see happening in themselves and in their behaviours. This gets people writing down what is important to them, what they'd like to see in their own behaviour and that of people around them. Later they can compare their pre-learning assumptions with the reality that unfolds in the learning process.

3. Track what happens over the course of learning. Tracking requires discipline. Establish a regular routine of noting observable indicators of change. Focus on observing carefully and finding ways to express what you see happen. Most people have difficulty perceiving things they do not expect to see. When people are learning and changing, they may create new solutions and ideas that are invisible according to pre-determined criteria. Focus not only on what can be seen, but also on intuitive insights. Watch for little indicators, not just sweeping changes that are impressive to report.

Draw from various data sources when tracking. Look at records such as absenteeism or customer satisfaction forms. Have individuals track their own thoughts, feelings, and behaviour changes throughout the learning process. Enlist various external observers to track growth from different perspectives: supervisors at worksites, instructors off-site, peers observing each other.

4. Interpret what is observed. Take care with interpretation: what may at first appear to be a moldy error may turn out to be the next cure for penicillin. Compare what you see to the original expectations of learners, instructors, and other stakeholders. Be alert to patterns that emerge, and unexpected but valuable results. Above all, be prepared to change the criteria for evaluating the learning according to what emerges in the process.

5. Talk about the learning process. Have co-learners or co-workers meet and discuss what they believe is happening in their own growth. Each person will bring a different perspective, but all viewpoints are necessary to form a rich, meaningful picture.

Small informal focus groups can meet to listen to one other and ask, "What is going on here?" Instructors can model how they understand their own growth and how they use personal experiences and language to make sense of the world they know. In highly sensitive situations, where anxiety levels are high and trust is guarded, try one-on-one interviews with people first.

6. Find a way to define the growth. Defining personal growth is much more difficult than reporting how people compare to pre-determined objectives and standards. In dynamic assessment we are asked to define things that are ambiguous and often too personal. Sometimes people ignore certain important parts of a learning or change process because these parts are perceived to be undiscussable; too "personal," or too threatening to harmonious relations. Sometimes it is hard to see yourself clearly or critically. Sometimes it is only possible to see growth after it has happened, when you are surprised by it. And, sometimes making personal claims about how we have grown is risky—we may have to take responsibility for those times we slip back into old ways. Often learners and even facilitators have difficulty expressing things that don't fit into neat measurement categories. Sometimes learners or facilitators neglect to mention important incidents or steps because they seem trivial, "soft," and unscientific, or far removed from the original expectations. Encourage open sharing of all and any insights.

Perhaps the most important and difficult part of dynamic assessment is finding a way to name what is actually happening; sometimes change is so complex or new that there is no easy or pre-existing language for expressing what people are doing and feeling. This gets at the heart of the difference from conventional assessment, which tries to make learners conform to pre-existing or idealized standards and mechanical measurements. Dynamic assessment plunges into the real muck of the learning process and tries to describes what is really happening, not what learners or instructors think should be happening. In dynamic assessment, people are asked to state, in their own words, "where they're really at" instead of where some indicator suggests they should be; such honesty opens up opportunities for more meaningful learning and evaluation.

How to Incorporate Dynamic Assessment in Classrooms

Dynamic assessment uses holistic measures, grows with the learner's growth, assesses the meanings the learner creates rather than measuring against some abstract ideal, and places high value on the prior knowledge, attitudes, and self-perception of learners.

Strategy 1: Using Learner Narratives and "Talk-Throughs" to Articulate Growth

- Story-telling has a rich tradition in learning processes. You can encourage people to tell the stories that matter most to them and reveal the greatest insights by modelling. When the facilitator takes the time to develop the personal aspects of an experience in all its contradictions and messiness, others will feel they also have been given permission to be honest and patient in sharing stories that reveal the process of growth.

- Writing is another common method that learners can use to describe how they think ideas through. However, some learners find it difficult to free-write without direction or structure. Try providing "starters" to stimulate writing, or suggest questions such as: What changed for you this week? What questions are you wondering about? What incident, person, or place this week contributed to your learning —and how? Questions can be used in various ways.

- The instructor asks the learner questions to gently probe aspects of the learning process. This simple evaluation activity provides direct information to the instructor and is helpful when learners are not willing or able to coach one another. This activity is only useful where one-on-one interviews are practical, such as in small classes where instructors can arrange a few minutes to talk with each learner while the others are working on something else.

- Have learners, in pairs, ask questions or write to one another about their learning process. This activity may be the most preferred. It allows each learner to hear a partner talk through a thinking process and to think about, and perhaps adapt, the questions to really probe the partner's understandings. This activity is also suitable for use in distance learning (see Chapter 16).

- Have students keep a learning log, writing down at regular periods what they are aware of learning. They might spend ten minutes at the end of each class session **free-writing**, without direction or structure, or using suggested questions. According to the comfort level of the learners, writing can be shared in pairs, with each partner "writing back" comments, responses, or questions.

A **narrative** is a story that describes a sequence of fictional or non-fictional events. It comes from the Latin verb *narrare*, which means "to recount."

Free-writing describes a process of non-stop writing for a set period of time, where writers do not edit but continue to write whatever comes to their minds. There is no judging or censoring what is written.

■ Ask students to draw their learning process as a river, tree, or map of their journey. They should illustrate obstacles and peaks, surprises, influences, and other aspects of a particular learning process that were significant for them. Have them share and discuss these drawings.

Strategy 2: Analyzing the Learner's Process to Evaluate Knowledge Growth

Journals have a long and strong tradition in many college and workplace settings. If journals are an established part of the learning program, both the learner and the instructor can examine them for knowledge growth. Many instructors appreciate the flexibility and tolerance for ambiguity that journals provide. The use of journals is enhanced by learners periodically reading their work to find and analyze recurring themes. How, for example, has the learner's thinking changed or grown in these areas? How well does the learner follow through on a particular question or theme to develop it? What appears to be the learner's approach to growth and learning?

Strategy 3: Analyzing Critical Thinking Processes

Stephen Brookfield (1987) identifies four dimensions of the process of critical thinking. We believe these dimensions could form a starting point for ways to *evaluate* critical thinking and generate descriptors specific to particular subject areas. However, we offer you a cautionary note. Critical thinking is a holistic process. Brookfield formulated these four dimensions to serve as indicators that critical thinking is occurring. These indicators should never be interpreted as a hierarchical model of "competency" in critical thinking.

1. Identifying and challenging assumptions: questioning the ideas, values, and other assumptions that underlie what things are said, thought, and done. One indicator that learners are growing is that they question the practices and beliefs that other people take for granted, and search for more accurate ways to represent their own experiences in the world. For example, Thomas Moore (1992) asks why cholesterol is necessarily bad for us. He questions the assumption that the heart is no more than a pump, that we eat to maintain the pump, and that cholesterol is an evil to be battled in our struggle against mortality. He discusses the role of the heart in life from a poetic, mythic perspective to challenge the predominant scientific paradigm of assumptions.

The term **critical thinking** or **critical reflection** defines processes that involve discerning, analyzing, and evaluating one's thoughts, activities or choices. Usually one thinks critically—such as listing pros and cons—about a specific issue in order to judge whether a decision makes good sense.

2. Challenging the importance of context: demonstrating awareness of the layers of interpersonal, social, political, cultural, and historical dimensions that affect any incident or way of interpreting an incident. One indicator to look for is whether or not a learner is considering and balancing other people's perspectives with one's own opinion. Another is to consider origins of practices and beliefs, and to weigh consequences of change in terms of the affect on aspects of context.

3. Exploring and imagining alternatives: realizing that taken-for-granted practices and beliefs can be changed, and that one's norms can be replaced. One indicator of learning is asking what lies beyond, and what options are available. Another is the ability and willingness to think beyond apparent obstacles and to create visions.

4. Reflecting with skepticism: refusing to accept any ideology or assertion at face value. One indicator of critical thinking is scrutinizing proposals, policies, and media messages carefully, noting incongruencies or inaccuracies. Another is observable confidence in challenging others' ideas and judgments where these do not match one's personal experience.

Brookfield also suggests regular self-examination to evaluate progress in developing the capacity to reflect critically. When taking stock, people look back over their actions and choices and their critical analysis of these actions to make judgments about their effectiveness in changing some aspect of their lives. People can also assess their past ability in order to recognize their patterns of behaviour, their habitual responses, and their own insights into their assumptions and motivations. Most of all, Brookfield stresses how important it is to evaluate critical thinking processes to help people realize the value of time spent in critical reflection, especially in a world that is focused on observable actions and measurable productivity.

Strategy 4: Encouraging Individuals and Groups to Engage in Self-Assessment of Growth

Self-evaluation is a habit of reflectively reviewing and analyzing one's own actions, choices, and patterns of behaviour. Dynamic assessment relies a great deal on learners' ability and willingness to assess their own growth. Some need help to distance themselves from their own everyday practice. Others need help to appreciate, rather than castigate, themselves. Many need reassurance that time spent in thoughtful self-observation and self-evaluation is worthwhile. Invite learners to try the following activities.

Dynamic Assessment Incorporating Critical Reflection

Here are some specific activities for dynamic assessment incorporating critical reflection. All have been adapted from a popular resource of reflective activities: *The Fifth Discipline Fieldbook: Strategies and Tools for Building a Learning Organization* by Senge, Kleine, Roberts, Ross, and Smith (Doubleday, 1994).

Assessing Ability to Discern an Issue: The Five "Why's"

Each group of students chooses a specific problem to examine in the issue they are studying, or a specific problem they perceive as related to how they are functioning as a group.

The students write a sentence stating the problem. Then they explore answers through a succession of "why" questions. The following example was produced by a group of students that almost split apart due to interpersonal misunderstandings.

Problem statement: "We don't respect each other in this group."

- **First Why:** Write a question about this statement: "*Why* don't we have respect in this group?" And answer the question: "*Because* we don't listen to each other."

- **Second Why**: Write a question about this answer: "*Why* don't we listen to each other?" And answer it: "*Because* we don't take the time."

- **Third Why:** "*Why* don't we take the time?" "Because we give this discussion low priority— we rush to go on to other things we think are more interesting."

- **Fourth Why:** "*Why* don't we find this discussion as interesting as other things?" "Because we don't feel personally committed to this project."

- **Fifth Why:** "*Why* don't we feel personally committed to this project?" "Because we don't believe our plan of action is going to accomplish anything meaningful or contribute anything interesting."

At this point the group is beginning to get at the real problem behind the surface symptoms of trouble. The next step is to probe this problem and discuss possible solutions. (One solution might be to completely redesign the project!)

The following activities are excellent ways for groups to reflect evaluatively on their learning processes.

Assessing Ability to Appreciate Multiple Perspectives

This helps a small group of eight people explore a problem from multiple perspectives. Make a large cardboard disk about 18 inches in diameter. Write the problem in the centre of the wheel. Draw lines to divide the wheel into eight equal pie-shaped slices. In each space, write the name of a person or group who might have a particular perspective on this problem. Around the outside of the wheel, place the eight name tags representing each participant in the group.

Spin the wheel. Each participant now takes on the perspective in the wheel pie that comes to rest beside their name tag. Going around the group, each participant presents their understanding on this perspective, saying "From my perspective as..., the critical elements in this situation are..." Participants can consider the following elements in imagining what the perspective might be.

- **Time:** When did this become a problem for me, and when will it no longer be an issue?

- **Expectation:** What do I expect to happen? What are others' expectations of me?

- **Understanding:** What do I see that nobody else can see in regard to this problem?

Vision-Building: Assessing Assumptions

A group of students chooses a specific problem identified in the issue being studied, and work through steps to develop an action towards a solution to that problem.

The students create an ideal vision of the future, imagining the most desirable scenario possible in five years time. Using flip-charts, they brainstorm for answers to the following questions.

- What are we doing in this vision?

- Who else is involved in our activity, and what are they doing?

- What have we achieved?

- How do other people see us?
- How do we affect on other people and groups around us?
- What are our goals?

The students now examine the current reality of this situation through their perspective as this group of people. They ask themselves the following questions.

- What are our biggest problems?
- What are we doing now to perpetuate the problems?
- Who else is involved in our activity, and what are they doing?
- How do other people see us?
- How do we influence on other people and groups around us?

After each question, students should consider how they would assess their progress.

Recalling the Past

This activity invites learners to recall positive past experience of working in a team or doing a project, and to develop lessons from these for the project at hand.

Have the group of students work through the following questions, posting answers on flip-charts.

- Recall a time when you were part of a group you thought was "really great." What made it "great"?
- What can this group do differently to create the same kinds of feelings?
- What action can this group commit itself to?
- What indicators will we look for in the future to measure our growth?

- **Watch yourself.** Pick a specific period of time from the previous week, and visualize yourself in action. Fill in as many details of the people, place, and situation as you can remember, but focus on watching yourself like an observer. Note things to applaud, then suggest things to improve.

- **Tell about a critical incident.** Pick a "peak" incident in your learning or practice, and write it down or tell it to someone. Focus on who–what–why–where–when. The listener then helps the teller probe the incident with questions such as: Why did you make these choices? What were your intentions? What did you feel? What do you regret? Did you obtain the results you wanted? Why/why not? What assumptions were you making? What would you do differently knowing what you know now? How could you have changed the outcome?

- **Create a metaphor to represent yourself in practice before and after a particular learning experience.** Share and compare this metaphor in small groups. What is revealed by the changes in the metaphor?

Moving Towards Dynamic Assessment

Instead of ...	Try ...
1. Giving learners a test and marking it ...	■ having each learner construct a test for another student and mark it. ■ having learners work together to solve problems on a test, then determine what more they need to learn. ■ having learners try the test, rate their own performance against the answer key, then set new learning goals for themselves.
2. Having learners write an essay that no one but you will read ...	■ having learners write an article and prepare it for publishing in a local newspaper or professional periodical. ■ producing a class anthology of writings that are targeted for the needs of a specific audience.
3. Having learners complete all evaluation tasks individually and competitively ...	■ having learners create products in small groups and together evaluate the process and dynamics they experience, as well as the quality of the product.
4. Having learners deliver oral presentations for grading by the instructor ...	■ having learners teach the class a concept, or hold a public forum, presentation, or panel discussion for the benefit of the community.
5. Having learners create a "dummy project" for the classroom ...	■ developing a project that will contribute something concrete to the community.
6. Observing learners performing a single skill in an isolated way, on cue and in the protective environment of the classroom ...	■ placing learners in a real-world situation to observe their ability to perform the skill as part of the multiple demands of other tasks.
7. Having learners discuss case studies in the artificial classroom atmosphere ...	■ having learners observe and work with people in real cases to design solutions and try to implement them.
8. You setting all the evaluation tasks ...	■ having learners design tasks that can demonstrate what they believe they have learned.

Constructing Tasks for Dynamic Assessment in Classroom Situations

In contrast to standardized tests and other traditional forms of assessment, dynamic assessment is based on authentic tasks and matches learning in a particular situation with the evaluation procedures. There are three dimensions to the tasks used in dynamic assessment.

1. Tasks used for the purpose of rating performance are meaningful not artificial or meaningless outside the learning situation. They are derived from real-world contexts, not from school-world contexts.

2. Tasks are relevant to the content and context of the course as you delivered it, not imposed from outside the relationship between the instructor, the learners, and the curriculum.

3. Tasks integrate evaluation with ongoing learning. In authentic assessment, the task itself is valuable as a learning experience.

The list of suggestions on page 108 shows how to modify evaluation practice in classrooms to move towards dynamic assessment. A useful resource for further exploration is *Dynamic Assessment for Instruction: From Theory to Practice* (1996) edited by Michael Luther, Esther Cole, and Peter Gamlin.

A Final Thought...

We believe evaluation should be dynamic and flexible. The conventional methods of assessment, such as tests, one-shot observations, and end-of-course assignments prepared for grading purposes, have two problems. They are static, and their orientation is passive. They create a two-dimensional still photograph of something that is really multi-dimensional. The process of learning is always moving and shifting. It can never be contained in a snapshot.

So, why do we continue to use only conventional methods of evaluation? Perhaps because we are so used to these familiar methods that we haven't seriously considered alternatives, or our institutions or communities sanction standardized measurement based on observable, pre-determined performance outcomes. If evaluation is to change, to become more dynamic, more process-oriented, more flexible, and more learner-centred, we must change it. We must engage in dynamic assessment of and critical reflection about how and why we evaluate, then adapt to any new knowledge gained. Let us walk our talk.

12 Helping Learners Evaluate Themselves

A Critical Goal of Learning

Adult learners have been well socialized by our North American system of schooling. They expect their learning assessments to come from an external authority, such as a supervisor or instructor. This chapter outlines how to determine whether self-assessment is appropriate and how to help students develop skills in this area.

elf-assessment refers to "the involvement of students in identifying standards and/or criteria to apply to their work, and making judgments about the extent to which they have met these criteria and standards" (Boud, 1991).

The purpose of this chapter is to outline ways of determining the appropriateness of self-assessment for your particular context, ways of introducing self-assessment, and ways of helping learners develop skill in self-assessment. But first we want to point out that self-assessment is not appropriate for all situations, all learners, or all instructional contexts.

The methods of getting learners involved in **self-assessment** that are covered in this chapter include reflective writing, such as journals and learning logs (containing summaries of learning, narration and analyses of critical incidents, and daily notes about ongoing progress), reflective dialogue with others, portfolios of work samples, and interviews between learner and instructor or supervisor.

> "An intellectual is someone whose mind watches itself."
> – Albert Camus

Why Is Self-Assessment a Critical Goal?

Many learners are uncomfortable when asked to assess their own learning. They don't know how to begin. They don't know how to set assessment criteria or choose which aspects of their own performance and understandings to assess. Instructors of adults should therefore be prepared to help them develop the skills and tools they need for self-assessment, and to work with them until they develop a comfortable level of expertise.

Some adults need help moving past initial resistance; they believe that teachers who encourage students towards self-assessing abdicate the instructor's responsibility to evaluate learners. Sometimes adults are wary of sharing their most honest self-assessments with supervisors or instructors who, they may believe with some justification, may use self-assessment information "against them."

Does self-assessment sound like too much work? If so, consider why the investment of time and energy in self-assessment is not only worthwhile, but critical in a world of fast-paced change.

Self-assessment is the act of identifying standards or criteria and applying them to one's own work, and then making a judgment as to whether—or how well—you have met them.

- **Self-assessment increases people's openness to learning.** People in the habit of assessing their own learning are more aware of their moment-to-moment thinking processes, more apt to learn from their mistakes, and tend to seek feedback.

- **Self-assessment develops and sharpens work-related skills.** The practice of self-assessment improves the ability to focus (setting and following goals), communicate (listening, interacting, seeking and giving feedback), and think critically (reflecting critically on experience, finding and solving problems, and questioning).

- **Self-assessment fosters responsibility.** People who assess themselves take ownership for their quality of work and tend to continuously monitor their progress. They think in terms of meeting their own standards and tend to be highly motivated.

- **Self-assessment fosters greater reliance on internal criteria.** People become more confident as they set personal standards and compare themselves to organizational and professional standards. They recognize the values in their own criteria, such as honesty, quality, making a difference, and integrity.

- **Self-assessment increases self-awareness.** People build self-esteem as they monitor their own competence, and take responsibility for changes in their own beliefs and concepts.

- **Self-assessment enhances a sense of direction.** People who continually assess their own learning have a sense of where they've come in their journey. They can set a course for themselves, confirm their direction, and establish new directions.

Using Self-Assessment

Before beginning self-assessment, instructors should think carefully about the context, learners, and other stakeholders. The introduction of self-assessment in any culture where learners are used to being dependent on external appraisal, such as in a workplace controlled through hierarchies or in a formal institution of higher learning, will not automatically change adults into capable assessors of their own activity and learning. Furthermore, it is unfair to set up a system of self-assessment and then stand by as someone judges learner performance and holds them accountable to external criteria.

It is also unfair to expect learners to enter into the spirit of self-assessment in an environment characterized by a controlling hierarchy, a competitive reward system based on externally defined outcomes, and accountability imposed top-down. Self-assessment does not easily co-exist in a system where rigid specifications govern learning.

Introducing any practice of self-assessment will affect other courses and programs, learners, and instructors or supervisors within the same system. Power dynamics exist within courses and between staff and students. Catherine Marienau (1994) points out that students may question the link between course outcomes and their assessment. They may be disappointed by the lack of external feedback, and they may question other assessment practices when they become comfortable with self-assessment.

Beginning Self-Assessment

Plan Carefully and Explore Consequences

Examine constraints in resources, policies, general practice and culture, staff philosophy, disposition, and expectations of learners in your institutional context. In planning self-assessment, involve other colleagues who are affected by the learning program. Before choosing a method for self-assessment, explore alternative methods of self-assessment and their potential consequences, including both the probable and the desired outcomes. Methods can rarely be used without having to adapt them to your own situation and the needs of your learners. Plan self-assessment within the entire program. Self-assessment should be balanced with feedback from an external source to provide different perspectives. For example, qualitative peer feedback could be successfully used with staff, supervisor, or instructor feedback.

Involve Learners in Planning.

Learners can and should be invited to influence the procedures and criteria of self-assessment. If, after a suitable trial period, the self-assessment method requires modification, changes can be worked out with learners. Be very clear before the instruction begins as to how self-assessment will intersect with other sources of feedback. If summative assessment will be produced, be explicit about how it will be derived. Learners may need to "learn" more about how and why to self-assess. Provide some examples and illustrate the benefits of self-assessment.

Don't Worry If Initial Responses Are Less Than Enthusiastic

Participants may be cautious about self-assessment until they are sure that no one will trick them by administering an external examination or by telling them their criteria are wrong. Some may miss the concrete nature of external assessment. Some may be worried about self-disclosure in their written journals or frank discussions with someone else about their own learning progress and dilemmas. Some may simply find self-assessment a waste of time, especially if they are insecure or do not trust their own standards as a reliable measure of their own performance. Self-assessment is not as easy as it may seem. Be patient, and do not take these natural reactions personally. Instead, expect them and be ready to address these fears and resistances.

Give Clear Guidelines and Models

To help learners become more comfortable with self-assessment, provide clear procedural guidelines. Whether or not they are developed with learners, the guidelines should be explicit, written forms that suggest a procedure and a rationale for self-assessment. Provide models of what excellent work looks like. In some cases, it is appropriate to show models of clear descriptors and indicators to help learners internalize standards for their own performance.

Be Helpful and Understanding

Support learners by giving feedback to help them develop criteria for their own learning and performance. Allow students time to talk through the development of self-assessment skills, and to share their frustrations and other feelings. Give them time to work through the process before "rescuing" them or, worse yet, dumping the idea of self-assessment because of problems encountered at early stages. Reinforcement may help at the beginning, either through peer discussion groups or talks with instructors about what they're doing and discovering. But be careful. Supportive reinforcement can become the external approval many learners seek. One student asked us to read over his learning journal each week, because he wanted to make sure he was writing what he thought we wanted.

Help Learners Develop Self-Assessment That Works for Them

Like any new learning, self-assessment needs to be incorporated into daily routine in a deliberate and conscious way. Some find self-assessment tough at first, because there is no immediate pay-off for their effort. Some feel guilt about taking the time for the reflective activity of self-assessment, or they simply can't find the time in their helter-skelter work lives. Help them identify times or strategies that work for them.

Help Learners Determine What to Monitor and How to Make Sense of What They See

Have learners begin by describing a skill they can now perform successfully. Then ask them to develop criteria to measure their performance in a way that helps them determine their level of learning and areas where they need improvement.

The following pages present several tools, strategies, and exercises to try. Help your learners find one or two that work for them.

Effective Course Closure Through Self-Assessment

Gary Wagenheim stresses that instructors need to place just as much emphasis on course or assignment closure as on openings. Students need time to reflect on what they've done in order to fully integrate and synthesize their learning.

Wagenheim describes in the *Journal of Management Studies* (1994) an exercise he uses to close course activities. He asks learners to respond to these leading statements:

I'm left feeling …

Something I learned about myself …

Something I learned about others …

Something I learned about groups …

Participants write responses to complete these stems using different coloured markers, sometimes drawing pictures or symbols. The instructor joins them in this activity. In small groups or pairs they talk about their responses, then post them around the room. Sensitivity to people's comfort levels is required to facilitate this exercise.

Ronda Beaman of Northern Arizona University writes: "What most of us do not do is bring closure for ourselves or our students. Like the good book you had to put down unfinished, we leave our courses with unchecked emotions, unanswered questions, unrealized relationships" (How to End Courses, 1995).

"Ladder of Inference" Left-Hand Column Exercise

The following activity was proposed by Chris Argyris (1990) to help people uncover the leaps of interpretation they make in conversations, jumping to conclusions using their personal "Ladder of Inference."

Have students write a brief paragraph describing a problem they have encountered.

What do you want to happen, and what do you believe is blocking you? Can you recall a frustrating conversation related to this problem?

Then have students divide a page lengthwise into two columns. In the right-hand column, write down "What Was Said." Write everything you can recall that was actually stated in that dialogue. In the left-hand column, write down "What I Was Thinking." Include all the thoughts and feelings you had but didn't say. Focus especially on the meanings and interpretations you drew from the other person's words.

Students can do two things with these columns:

1. have the other person involved in the conversation do the exercise, then compare the columns and talk out the unsaid things and the inferences each person was making. Or,

2. students can analyze their own columns.

For example, students can ask themselves questions to help focus the activity: What led me to think and feel this way? What was my intent? Why didn't I say what I was thinking? What assumptions did I make about the other person? How did I contribute to the problem?

For excellent descriptions of the "ladder of inference" and in-depth instructions for using the left-hand column exercise, refer to Senge et al., 1994, *The Fifth Discipline Fieldbook*, pp. 242-252.

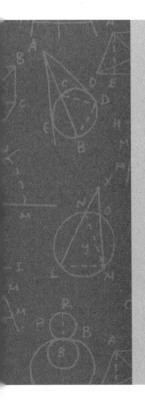

"PAPA": Participant Action Plan and Analysis

Another method that has become popular in some organizations is the "PAPA" approach to self-evaluation: Participant Action Plan and Analysis.

- The evaluator determines, by interviewing participants, the breadth of training that will be taken in light of the needs of the organization.

- An action plan is created with learners. This plan is continually revised as learners progress through course activities. Learning objectives shift as the learners become immersed in the process of learning and discover new threads they could not have envisioned at the beginning of the process.

- Follow-up activities are planned by learners, specifying the kinds of action they will take when they are back at their jobs.

- Further follow-up happens several months after the training, through interviews or questionnaires with learners. The follow-up determines the changes that learners are making in their ways of working and thinking over time. It also examines the effects of the learner changes on work environments.

- Learners determine, with input from the evaluator, their next action steps.

- An analysis of the entire process is reported in written form by the evaluator and communicated to both learners and the organization.

- This approach relies on the instructor/evaluator to provide direction. It would be most appropriate where learners are uncertain or unfamiliar with the course content or the process of self-evaluation. PAPA may need modification with more able or autonomous learners who wish to take more personal control of self-assessment.

Methods That Prompt Ongoing Informal Self-Assessment

The following list of practical ideas and activities is designed to help learners develop their skill in self-assessment. This skill involves valuing reflection and self-assessment, self-awareness, attention to the moment, willingness to recall and analyze one's own thinking process, the ability to articulate and write about one's thinking, and the discipline to be precise.

- Invite learners to examine how much they currently need external validation for their efforts. Start with discussing what a grade means to them. Suggest that they think about past experiences that were graded, why they sometimes desire a high grade, and the usefulness of a grade in their continuing development. Help them to imagine the effect on their motivation, commitment, accountability, or learning in any classroom or work activity if no evaluation were given, if everyone were given the same grade, or if only two responses (satisfactory or unsatisfactory) were given.

- Help learners focus on the moment. Donald Schön at Stanford University is often credited with introducing the notion of reflection in action. He prompts professionals to learn from their own experiments and problem solving. Judith Newman has borrowed Schön's ideas and made this kind of critical reflection a keystone of her practice, described in her book *Interwoven Conversations* (1991). When teaching teachers, Judith interrupts her instruction or learning activity to ask, "What is going on here?" In other words, "What are you, as a learner, attending to? What are you thinking? What questions do you have? What have you learned in the past five minutes?" This helps students develop the habit of monitoring their thinking processes—the first step in self-assessment. The second step is getting learners accustomed to jotting down these reflections-in-action, so that they can track their learning process.

- Try an exercise, called Moments of Awareness, or MA, which comes from a group of educators devoted to promoting critical reflection and continuous learning (see page 118).

- Have learners write "quick-memos" during an instructional session, a business meeting, or a work activity. The quick-memo can be addressed to themselves or to someone else, such as a peer or supervisor (see page 114).

Getting on the Same Track

Have learners stop in the middle of a large group conversation periodically and do five things.

- Ask yourself what you are thinking and feeling.
- Ask youself what reasons are behind your opinions.
- Tell others the reasons behind your thinking.
- Ask others to explain their feelings.
- Ask others to explain the reasons behind their thinking.

Or, a facilitator might lead the group through questions at various points in a discussion to clarify what's being said.

- What data lie behind this statement? Are these data observable?
- Does everyone agree with the ideas being discussed?
- Can you explain your reasoning?
- How did we move from our data to our assumptions and conclusions?

Moments of Awareness (MA) Exercise

Organizational developers Chris Argyris (1990) and Donald Schön (1983) began teaching people to think about their "Ladders of Inference" in the late 1970s. Today this idea is used by groups to develop awareness of members' interpretations and perceptions. Each person interprets a conversation differently, but we believe that what we hear is what everyone heard and that our interpretations are truths everyone would agree with. We then draw conclusions based on this truth, and take actions based on the conclusions. This is "climbing the ladder of inference" (see page 116).

But others have climbed their own ladders and have different opinions about what happened, which might collide with ours. The result can be frustration or bewilderment. We might argue, give up, withdraw, or privately make negative judgments about others.

Have learners explore their own learning biographies, in one of two ways.

- Invite learners to recall incidents that are especially noteworthy as learning moments in their past. These are called "critical incidents." Ask them to describe the incident, recalling details about the time, place, activity, attitudes, and others involved. Then analyze the incident, examining possible underlying assumptions, motivations, learning style, and so on.

- Ask learners to trace the acquisition of a particular skill, understanding, belief, or attitude. Have them write about the activities, materials, personal motivations, emotions, involvement of other people, turning points, and disappointments or frustrations that unfolded in their learning. Then have them analyze this process and draw conclusions about their own learning patterns, preferences, and processes.

These activities are good starters for anyone beginning to keep a learning journal. Once they've tried to recall and explore their past learning, learners often develop a greater awareness of their current learning, which they can then track through their journal.

Balance learner reflection on past incidents and current moments with reflection about their future learning.

Reflection Notes for a Workshop

Two things I already know that were re-confirmed during this workshop as being important are:

1. _____

2. _____

Two new things I learned in this workshop are:

1. _____

2. _____

Two questions I still have are:

1. _____

2. _____

Three actions I will take to apply what I've learned today to my work are:

1. _____

2. _____

3. _____

Methods for Formal Self-Assessment

The Toolbox section of this book contains detailed explanations of many self-assessment methods. These include portfolios, journals, videotapes, interviews, and contracts. You may want to experiment with one or two methods, and balance their use with other means of assessment. Remember to plan and prepare learners carefully before introducing any new method. Even when using formal methods of self-assessment, learners may need help discerning what to notice in their own performance.

Learner self-assessment should be a significant part of any evaluation program. Even when you are working with standardized criteria or evaluating technical skills that must meet pre-determined standards, involve the learner in the process of assessment. Even when you think there is

Self-Assessment: Work Experience

One incident that happened in the past week where I believe I was performing very well, or where I felt good about what I was doing, is ...

- ◆ The skills and expertise I demonstrated in this incident are ...

_____

_____

- ◆ Other people were contributing to my positive performance by ...

_____

_____

- ◆ Other conditions (time/place, other situations, my attitudes, and so on) that contributed to a positive experience were ...

_____

_____

_____

One incident that happened in the past week that really bothered me, during which I did not feel good about what I was doing, is ...

- ◆ Conditions (time/place, other situations, my attitudes, and so on) that contributed to the problem were ...

_____

_____

- ◆ Other people were contributing to the problem by ...

_____

_____

- ◆ The skills or expertise I may have been lacking are ...

_____

_____

_____

Lessons from the past week that I'd like to remember in the future are ...

_____

_____

_____

_____

_____

_____

no time to do so, involve the learner. Why? Here's a quick summary of reasons for using at least some learner self-assessment during instruction.

- The learner's perspective is illuminating and can show difficulties in the learning process that the instructor may not understand.

- Because learning often occurs so gradually, we don't notice it; self-assessment is a powerful way for learners to see how far they've come in the learning process.

- Self-assessment compels learners to make precise judgments about their own performance. Learners become less dependent on external approval and begin to assume responsibility for their own progress.

- The practice of self-assessment teaches learners how to stop and think about how they are thinking and doing things now. It encourages reflection about how things were done in the past. It highlights thinking patterns—both their genius and their limitations.

An excellent resource for further exploration is David Boud's book *Enhancing Learning through Self-Assessment* (1995).

The next chapter offers many activities and tools to promote ongoing evaluation and self-assessment as an integral part of the learning process.

A Final Thought...

There are risks involved in moving entirely to a system of evaluation based on self-assessment. However, in this chapter we argue that self-assessment should be a primary objective in adult education. Self-assessment returns the ownership of knowledge, and the accountability for working and learning, back to the learner where it belongs. This does not mean that others are not important in our educational lives. However, there is a huge difference in learning from others and *depending* on others to teach you. Mature learners know, and act out, the difference.

Self-assessment is a continuous process that moves us to deeper, more compassionate, more resilient self-knowledge. Although self-evaluation may take more time and resources to teach and apply, ultimately self knowledge is our best resources for making informed choices in an unpredictable universe.

13

Integrating Ongoing Evaluation into the Learning Process

Continuous Assessment of Self, Peers, and Instruction

Too often, teachers and learners equate evaluation with something done at the end of a program of study, as useful to get a grade. However, to be effective, evaluation must be ongoing, continuous, and completely integrated into the learning process. Evaluation can come from a peer, an instructor, the consequences of the task itself, or oneself—through comparing one's performance with a model or set of standards or through sudden insight.

Instruction that is truly learner-centred and committed to helping people grow and improve relies on formative evaluation during instruction, not just summative assessment at the end of instruction. Formative evaluation provides feedback at the moment of practice, creating an opportunity to use the feedback to make corrections. It alerts learners to the experience and to what they are learning. Most important, it transfers the responsibility for monitoring learning from the educator or the educational institution onto the learners.

Many short workshops or courses that do not award grades or formally test learners can incorporate meaningful opportunities for evaluation during instruction. Even a half-day session can build in evaluative methods that are efficient, economical, and more useful than the "smile sheets" that tend to show only whether participants were entertained.

One of the most comprehensive examples we've seen of a workshop program that integrated multiple evaluation methods into every part of the learning process is described in Case Study: Ongoing Evaluation of Coaching Skills (page 125). But you can choose from a variety of activities that are not time-consuming or difficult to implement, listed throughout this chapter.

> "It is not the answer that enlightens, but the question."
>
> – Eugene Ionesco

Focusing the Learners on Assessment

We encourage you to spend some moments discussing your methods of assessment and your rationale for emphasizing it throughout the course. Here are some statements about evaluation that you may want to discuss with participants.

- All new learning comes from evaluating past experience: remembering it, analyzing it, making sense of it, speculating about its whys and its possibilities.

- Self-awareness is the goal of most learning, and self-awareness develops only through self-evaluation.

- Without the perspective and feedback of others, we are locked into our own self-reinforcing loops of behaving and thinking.

- What gets evaluated is what gets learned.

Begin a workshop by involving participants in an evaluation activity. This reminds them to monitor their experiences throughout the workshop, and become more aware of what is happening moment to moment.

You might try having them start by reviewing the recent past, asking themselves what they have learned in the past week or in the past 24 hours. Have participants explore why these questions are so difficult to answer.

Opening Evaluation Activities

Opening evaluation activities can help participants become conscious of their past behaviour and experience, their current skill levels, or their attitudes. A good opener focuses participants' attention on the topic, hooks their curiosity, and may serve as a preview of the learning objectives.

Evaluative openers can include personal inventories related to the course content, checklists of skills, non-threatening quizzes that test participants' understanding of the topic (true-false or multiple choice completed individually or in pairs), a case study or other problem for which they brainstorm for solutions either individually or in small groups, or a reflective exercise. There are some sample personal inventories included in this chapter.

Ask participants to mentally review their recent past actions in performing a skill or working with others, then evaluate mentally what they see when they watch themselves in action. What is working? What isn't? What could be fixed? On which strengths could they build?

Patricia Wagner of the Metropolitan State College of Denver sets up "evaluation awareness" of students right from the beginning of the course so that students develop understandings of the benchmarks they are striving for at each stage of the learning. She ends each class with the question, "What changed for you today?"

Opening evaluation activities can help participants become conscious of their past behaviour and experience, their current skill levels, or their attitudes. These activities also focus participants' attention on the topic, hooks their curiosity, and may preview the learning objectives.

Case Study

Ongoing Evaluation of Coaching Skills

When Collins Kavanagh Consulting of Toronto created what became a highly successful "Coaching Skills" program, they decided to make ongoing evaluation a key component. The program was designed to teach supervisors located in various branches of a national Canadian bank how to coach their subordinates in continuous learning. The program was delivered in two workshops spaced a month apart. At the end of the first workshop, participants were given coloured paper, glue and tape, crayons, magazines, beads, glitter, and other odds and ends and invited to create a map showing their "learning journey" since the beginning of the course. Before leaving the workshop, participants listed indicators in their own behaviours that would reveal their integration of these skills into their ongoing practice, and built an action plan for themselves. Some of the coaching indicators include:

- I state the constructive purpose of my feedback.
- I describe my observations specifically.
- I share my specific reactions to what I observe.
- I offer suggestions.
- I close with an offer of support.

In the action plan, they outlined specific tasks they would remind themselves to do daily to practise coaching skills in their supervisory behaviour. Finally, participants were shown how to create a reflective journal, log, or scrapbook to record quickly and efficiently their daily progress, as well as questions and issues that arose.

A short while after the first workshop, Collins Kavanagh Consulting mailed a package to each participant. The package contained a reminder of the concepts and skills presented in the workshop and a list of self-assessment questions to guide participants' review and summary of their journal findings. Participants were also invited to a second workshop to share their experiences putting their coaching skills into practice.

At the second workshop, participants shared stories from their practice one at a time. In small-group dialogue they helped each other make sense of what happened, returning to the evidence and viewing the story from different perspectives and examining their own underlying assumptions and interpretations of specific incidents. Participants then examined one another's progress in implementing the coaching skills. They identified the techniques that didn't work in their own context, shared solutions, uncovered underlying problems in their implementation of coaching, and identified areas for further work.

Then participants developed indicators to ascertain whether the coaching techniques were in fact improving the bank's results. Participants listed observable successes of coaching in their branch (such as customer satisfaction reports, bank staff visibly helping each other and sharing information more frequently, effective and efficient implementation of new initiatives such as the telephone banking system, fewer line-ups in the bank).

Six months after the second workshop, Collins Kavanagh Consulting facilitated small focus groups of the participants to explore the following questions.

- To what extent are you using the coaching skills in your regular practice? How do you know?
- What evidence of positive outcomes have you noted in the branch that can be attributed to coaching skills?
- How can the outcomes of the coaching techniques be assessed continually in the future?

An ongoing evaluation mechanism based on observable indicators and regular discussion became integrated into each bank's regular procedures.

Listening Skills Inventory: Coaching Skills for Supervisors Workshop

Rate yourself from 1 to 5 for the following skills. (1 = never; 5 = always)

____1. I always attempt to give every person I talk with equal time to talk.

____ 2. I really enjoy hearing what other people have to say.

____ 3. I never have difficulty waiting until someone else is finished talking so that I can have my say.

____4. I listen even when I do not particularly like the person talking.

____5. I The sex and age of a person makes no difference to how well I listen.

____6. I assume every person has something to say and I listen to each person equally.

____7. I put away what I am doing when I am listening.

____8. I always look directly at the person who is talking, and give them full attention.

____9. I encourage others to talk by giving them verbal feedback and asking questions.

____10. I encourage other people to talk through non-verbal feedback, using gestures, eye contact, and facial expression.

____11. I ask for clarification of words and ideas I do not understand.

____12. I am sensitive to the meanings conveyed by the speaker's tone and gesture.

____13. I try not to interrupt a person who is talking.

____14. I withhold judgments and opinions until I have heard all that a person has to say.

____15. I make mental outlines of the points a person is trying to make.

____16. I consciously develop my listening skills in all communication situations.

____17. I try to visualize what another person is describing.

____18. I am patient even with inarticulate speakers, and try to understand their point.

____19. I try to understand another person's meaning, motivation, and feelings when they are speaking.

____20. I respect every person's right to their opinion, even when I disagree with them.

80-100 points: a good sensitive listener; **70-80 points:** makes an effort to listen well but could improve focus and concentration; **below 70:** listening skills need work. What are the key areas that could be improved?

Mid-Process Evaluation Activities to Be Used During Instruction

In the middle of a session, ask learners to stop and check the pulse of their learning. What connections are they making? What concepts aren't making sense? What questions for further inquiry are beginning to form? What areas need further practice?

The easiest way to involve learners in a mid-process checkpoint evaluation is to ask them how things are going, what they are feeling, what they are learning, and what difficulties they are experiencing. Allow them time to reflect, and be ready to listen patiently. Reminding learners regularly to examine their own learning process helps them to establish a reflective habit. Here are some activities for class situations.

- In the midst of a lecture or discussion, stop and ask learners: What ideas are bubbling in your head right now? How are they useful? Sometimes a question alone is enough to jog class participants from the complacency of passive listening.

- At the mid-point or the conclusion of a discussion (small group or large group), ask people to summarize the most significant ideas they've heard, then organize these ideas into themes or categories (main ideas and sub-topics, or according to different perspectives, or some other classification scheme). If learners are able to, have them synthesize their jottings into a two- to three-sentence statement and share this in a small group.

- At the end of an explanation, ask learners to paraphrase what they have heard and understood.

- After a practice session, but before giving feedback, ask learners to tell or write about aspects of their performance that seem to be strong. Ask them to tell or write about the aspects they would change.

- After learners have worked their way through solving a problem or developing a new procedure, have them write down the process they used, then analyze the effectiveness of this process. Ask if there are better alternatives. Or have learners describe their procedure to one or two others, and compare the process they found themselves following with the steps others followed.

Mid-process evaluation is a term used for formally or informally "checking in" with students on any number of criteria in order to develop critical thinking and self evaluation skills.

Personal Inventory: Powerful Presentations Workshop

Inventory Objectives 1 = poor, 3 = good, and 5 = excellent	YOUR SKILL LEVEL				
	1	2	3	4	5
VERBAL					
1. Allows sufficient preparation time					
2. Uses preparation time efficiently					
3. High familiarity with content					
4. Uses several resources					
5. Plans creative content and presentation ideas					
6. Organizes material systematically					
7. Develops a clear purpose					
8. Edits speech carefully to eliminate redundancy, etc.					
9. Uses humour or stories to illustrate material					
10. Handles questions effectively					
11. Handles mistakes and interruptions effectively					
12. Is able to speak improvisationally					
VOCAL					
1. Clear speech—good articulation					
2. Full resonant tone					
3. Good volume; well projected					
4. Enthusiastic and dynamic					
5. Well-controlled pace					
6. Appropriate pitch and vocal emphasis					
7. No distracting "tics" or vocal fillers					
VISUAL					
1. Assured, sincere approach					
2. Relaxed, personal, natural style					
3. Assertive posture					
4. Direct eye contact with audience members					
5. Open, free gestures and movement					
6. Warm audience rapport					
7. No distracting behavioural habits					
8. Effective use of visual aides to illustrate key points					

Note: Rating sheets, such as this, contain strong assumptions about what is "good" and what is "right." They also leave wide gaps for interpretation. We suggest you use such scales—whether self-scored by learners, peer-scored, or instructor-scored—only in the context of critical dialogue with learners. Which items here make sense or seem useful? Which should be modified or thrown out altogether?

- Stop the class and have people share, in pairs or trios, a story from their own experience that illustrates one idea they've learned so far that is particularly meaningful or useful for them. Debrief in a whole-group discussion.

- If learners use journals, create a regular habit of stopping the class and having members write in their journals for five to ten minutes. You might offer one of the following suggestions to get them started.

  - Describe a new thing you've learned so far today that is especially interesting or meaningful to you, and show how it connects to something you already know.

  - Explain one thing you've learned today that is relevant to your work. Show how you might apply it outside this class.

  - Think of two different examples from your own life experience that show this concept working in action.

  - Write a metaphor to explain this concept. Make sure you show what you've learned so far.

  - Write about something you've heard with which you totally disagree.

  - If you had to stand up and respond to someone's ideas (instructor, peer, or writer) you've encountered so far today, what would you say?

  - Write about a difficulty you're having in understanding or applying what you've learned today.

  - Jot down individual words and phrases to summarize the main ideas you've learned today on the left side of your page. On the right side, jot down questions, feelings, personal connections, and off-shoot ideas.

- Remind learners to compare what they find themselves thinking and doing at this point to where they were at the beginning of the instructional process. Invite them to step back from the moment-to-moment activity and locate their performance.

- When teaching a technical skill, have learners repeatedly attempt the skill as soon as possible after the demonstration. Key areas they don't completely understand will become immediately apparent. Effective instruction involves a continuous loop of corrective feedback and further practice.

> " I cannot teach anybody anything, I can only make them think."
>
> – Socrates

Personal Inventory: Change-Management Workshop

1. On a scale of 1 to 10, how would you rate the amount of change you have had to cope with in the past few months of your life at home or at work?

   1 = no change
   5 = significant change—I can feel it
   10 = overwhelming change—I fear I can't cope

2. Describe the one change that has been most difficult for you to deal with in the recent past?

3. How are you responding to this change (in your feelings, interpersonal behaviour, work habits, attitudes, decision making)?

4. Describe a change with which you coped previously.

5. If you were to explain the process you went through in this change as a series of stages, how would you label each stage? List the stages and write a phrase explaining what happened in each.

6. How did this experience of change affect you (in your behaviour, your interpersonal relationships, your feelings and attitudes, your work habits, and so on)?

7. What did you find most helpful in supporting you through this change (family, supervisor, support groups, religious person, spiritual faith, education, and so on)?

8. What lessons about yourself and about ways to cope with change from your past experience can you apply to the present?

Action Plan

What is one thing in your behaviour that you want to change using some of what you've learned today?

_____

_____

_____

_____

_____

How will you know when this behaviour has changed? (List three indicators that an observer might notice.)

_____

_____

_____

_____

_____

Write down three dates on which you will review your behaviour and note any changes, the presence of any of the indicators from the list above, the absence of some of the indicators, and suggest reasons for any unexpected behaviours you notice.

Checkpoint 1:   Date _____ Changes I've observed: _____

_____

_____

_____

Checkpoint 2:   Date _____ Changes I've observed:_____

_____

_____

Checkpoint 3:   Date _____ Changes I've observed:_____

_____

_____

_____

Case Study

Checklists for Monthly Self-Assessment on the Job: Tracking Leadership Skills During Organizational Change

Highland/Corod Inc. is a western Canadian oil company that has recently undergone a series of changes involving restructuring, a new mission and values statement, refinement of Total Quality Management initiatives, and implementing coaching and emphasizing results-oriented performance outcomes. Training has been conducted through short intensive workshops. To ensure implementation, Michele Ho Leung has introduced ongoing assessment techniques to all field supervisors, regional and service centre managers. One of these measures is a self-assessment form in leadership skills, which supervisors and managers complete monthly. The form lists 14 objectives, of which five are shown below:

Individual Self-Assessment of Leadership Skills

Name _____

Using the following scale, assess your current performance.

1—Needs development—I don't practise it right now.
2—Working on this—It needs some attention.
3—Well developed—I use it regularly in my leadership role.

Rating	Assessment Area	Action To Be Taken
	I understand and can state what the mission of the company means to me in my job, and I have shared this with my people.	
	I communicate my goals to my people and help them in setting theirs.	
	I have identified the predominant working styles of the people I deal with (using the model presented) and have applied my new knowledge to improve relationships.	
	I have defined areas of responsibility for my area, I understand what constitutes poor/great performance, and I have established "what's in it for me," for both my people and me.	
	I set performance expectations with my people, manage the performance cycle, and keep records of examples of poor/great performance for my people and me.	

■ When teaching interpersonal skills such as interviewing or listening, have learners practise the skill through role-play immediately after instruction. Learners can work in pairs while the instructor circulates among the students to get a feel for what further instruction is needed. Instead of giving direct feedback to individuals, try stopping the group and giving two or three specific pointers for everyone to think about. Then allow further opportunities for practice.

For mid-process evaluation, you might ask two pairs to work together. For instance, when teaching teachers how to manage interviews with parents, we had one pair observe another pair and provide feedback to the "teacher" of the role-playing pair

For more specific ideas, refer to "Peer Assessment" in the Toolbox section. For some excellent suggestions about giving and receiving feedback during instruction, consult *The Art of Teaching Adults* by Peter Renner (1993).

■ Throughout the instructional period, have learners keep ongoing records that document their progress. One example is Ongoing Self-Evaluation of Thinking Skill Development in Chapter 8 (see page 79).

■ One instructor hands out four cards to each learner with one letter printed on them: A, B, C, and D. Periodically in the class he reads aloud a multiple-choice question about the content he is explaining and asks students to hold up a card representing the correct answer. At a glance he can see the level of understanding in the class.

Follow-Up Activities for Ongoing Evaluation

One of the most effective ways to ensure the ongoing monitoring and growth of learning is to provide learners with ways to continue evaluating themselves after instruction is complete. Below are some methods to consider.

■ **Action plans.** When you reach the conclusion of the learning experience or instructional event, have learners choose a task or activity they engage in frequently that they can improve by implementing what they have learned. (Note that the focus is on what they *will* change, not just what they want to change. Willing is commitment.) Ask learners to write down their plan. A sample Action Plan (see page 131) and Monthly Self-Assessment on the Job worksheet (see page 132) are included in this chapter. One consulting firm that offers leadership development has learners write down three action goals for the next six months. The firm keeps these sheets, then mails them to learners at the end of the six months.

- **Follow-up groups.** Encourage learners to meet periodically in small groups after the instruction period is completed, with or without a facilitator, to share ideas and problems with implementing the new learning. Email offers a forum for such follow-up meetings. Tele-conferences or video-conferences are other possibilities. Some groups meet at regular, informal breakfast meetings. Group discussion in any medium is an excellent way to talk through the issues and difficulties of trying to adapt new ideas to one's own situation. Fellow learners can offer empathy and comfort, provide guidance and suggestions, show gaps or blind spots using a critical perspective, share resources, or remind one another of objectives and criteria.

- **Journals.** Runners training for marathons often keep diaries to track their progress. They systematically and briefly note specific indicators of changes in their body and their overall progress. The tracking helps them become more attuned to their body's unique process and responses to different conditions and types of training. Over time, the information helps them adjust their training schedule and other variables (sleep, work, nutrition) to achieve peak performance. Can this concept be applied to your own and others' learning in non-sport areas?

A Final Thought...

Obviously, we believe evaluation is important. But, if we could pick only a small number of things we'd like you to remember, one of those things would certainly be to think of evaluation as a natural and thorough part of all teaching and learning.

Only by thinking of evaluation as more than grades can learning and teaching become positive and enriching experiences. The central point of this discussion is about power and control. If evaluation comes only at the end, the teacher is the authority and has all the power and control, and learners become passive. If, however, the evaluation of both the teacher and learner is ongoing, continuous, and integrated, learning and teaching become shared activities of teamwork and community.

14

Evaluating for Grades

What's in a Number?

We hope this chapter will help you to use grades more efficiently, more creatively, and more ethically. However, before discussing how to use grades constructively, we believe it is important to look at them critically. The more you know about grading, both good and bad, the more you will be able to use grades properly.

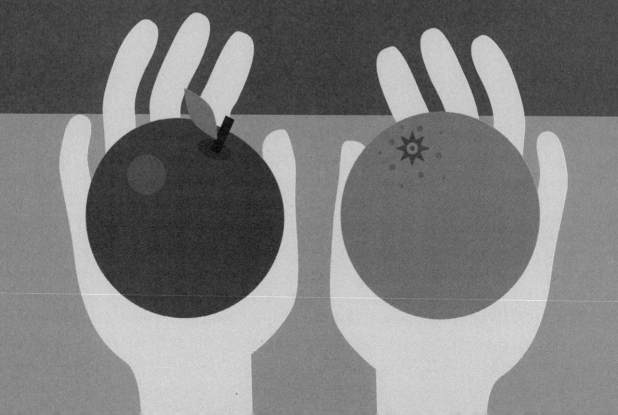

> "If I ran a school, I'd give the average grade to the ones who gave me all the right answers, for being good parrots. I'd give the top grades to those who made a lot of mistakes and told me about them, and then told me what they learned from them."
>
> – R. Buckminster Fuller

Number grades, as the term implies, use numbers instead of letters. Often, a learner's work within a course is thought of as adding up to 100 percent with the smaller evaluative activities of that course split into parts that add up to 100 percent. The different numerical weights are based upon different worth or values.

Grading by numbers is based on the premise that a number is a useful and reliable tool for differentiating human achievement and progress. A number grade is a normative assessment that uses criteria applied universally, is based on the laws of averages, assumes that human learning within a limited time period can be validly and reliably assessed by a third party and that assessment can be represented by a numeral.

But these assumptions about grading are questionable. Agriculturists evaluating soil examine 16 different dimensions of soil, each of which can be rated using 50 different criteria. The dimensions of soil are so wide ranging and the variables affecting assessment so complex that any single number obscures important characteristics that truly differentiate soils. Further, soil specialists claim that subsuming all these assessments under a single numeric "grade" would be inaccurate, even absurd. If soils differ so radically, how dare we assign a numeric grade to the living magic and complexity of individual human growth and learning?

The Meaning of a Grade

A number grade is an arbitrary symbol. Although it seems concrete, a grade is imbued with many taken-for-granted cultural meanings. This can be good. For example, asking adult learners what grades mean to them can lead to fruitful discussions about how we attach self-worth to a number, about personal expectations often derived from parental emphasis on report cards and high grades, about the limitations of a number grade, and about feelings of dependency and defensiveness.

Many students believe that a grade is like a reward; they talk in terms of the grade they deserve. Many students and instructors believe that a grade represents competence and hard work. Because their life experience has taught them that they are generally competent and hardworking, most adult learners naturally believe they deserve high grades. The problem for instructors is that a grade becomes a commodity in an exchange relationship—proper payment due for effort or for adherence to all course demands. Not only is hard work difficult to assess and quantify, but the nature of its relation to learning is debatable.

Our students often tell us, "I want to see where I stand in relation to everybody else." We appreciate their honesty, but why do they want to know? What use is such knowledge to their own growth? Perhaps their many years in a competitive school system has taught learners that people should be ranked from poor to weak, from good to excellent. Maybe we have all learned that comparing our own performance, knowledge, effort, and creativity to others is the best way to gauge our value. What an endless treadmill this thinking condemns us to.

No one approaches a new concept or task with the same unique talents, history, sense of self, style, purpose, obstacles, ways of viewing the world, and ways of acting in the world as any other person. Instead of ranking people by comparing them to each other, encourage learners to compare their present performance to their past performances (self-referencing) or to standards of quality they personally want to achieve (criterion-referencing). Grading activities should celebrate learners' uniqueness, not emphasize their deviation from some artificial "norm."

Self-referencing asks learners to compare their present performance to their past performances..

Criterion-referencing involves determining a learner's grade by comparing his or her achievements with clearly stated criteria for learning outcomes or clearly stated standards for performance. There is no pre-determined grade distribution with criterion referencing.

In **norm-referencing**, learners are awarded grades on the basis of their ranking within a group of other learners. Usually grades are "curved" using a pre-determined grade distribution.

What Does a Grade Mean to You, the Instructor?

When thinking about grading, ask yourself the following questions. Does a grade represent the quality of the products prepared and submitted by the learner over a period of time? Or does it represent only the quality the learner is finally able to produce by the end of the course? Does the grade represent the amount of knowledge the learner is able to remember and verbalize at the end of a course of study? Or does the grade represent the amount of progress made by a particular learner since the beginning of the course? Does a grade show what percentage of the course skills the learner can be counted upon to use when necessary? Does a grade show exactly what a learner has learned?

It's important for adults to analyze and examine the meanings they give to a grade as well as the limits of the grade itself and what purposes it serves. If numerical grades exist chiefly to serve institutional purposes, not the learner's need for feedback, then everyone must understand that constraint.

What Grading Means in an Educational Institution

In some institutions, learner performances, understanding, and products are rated in individual marks, which are then weighted according to importance and subsumed into a single grade percentage ranging from 1–100. Sometimes these grades are translated into symbols, as illustrated in the letter–grade systems. Usually, the grade percentage range is established by a particular instructor or department or institution.

Giving Learners a Choice in Evaluations

Assignment List: History Course

The following assignment list was distributed to students enrolled in a course called the "History of Childhood" at Concordia University College in Edmonton, Alberta.

1. Choose any two of the following, selecting from the list below of educational philosophers:

- an argumentative essay of five pages, analyzing the perspective of a particular philosopher on childhood;
- a series of journal entries from the perspective of an educator or philosopher writing about children;
- a written dialogue between two educators or philosophers on the subject of children;
- a descriptive account of a contemporary parenting dilemma, with analyses from the perspective of a historical philosopher; or,
- a response from an historical philosopher's viewpoint to a contemporary article about childhood.

Philosophers:
- Rousseau
- Dr. Spock
- Plato
- Quintillian
- St. Augustine
- Comenius
- Locke
- Luther
- Neill

2. Choose any two of the following formats to present to a small group in the class:

- a children's book you create yourself;
- a dramatized script or puppet scenario of the discipline of children from different periods of Western history;
- a dramatized scenario from a playground garnered through observation, plus your analysis of this scenario;
- a dramatized interview between a contemporary writer and a historical writer on a contemporary issue of childhood;
- a photo-essay of your own childhood;
- a photo-essay or video documentary of children focusing on a contemporary issue;
- a children's song, a poem for children, or a short puppet drama for children that you write and perform;
- an analysis of video clips of advertising or television shows for children; or,
- a report that shows what you saw when you followed children through a toy store.

Some instructors use a point system rather than percentage grades. Each assignment or performance task in the course is allotted a number of points, which are added and translated into a symbol grade. The total number of points possible can range as low or as high as the instructor wishes; they do not need to conform to the arbitrary number of 100.

Grade Curves

Sometimes grades are ranged over a curve, such as a normal probability curve. When graphed, the height of the curve at a given point indicates the proportion of cases at that point. The majority of learner grades centralize around the mean, and the least number of grades occur in equal proportion at both top and bottom of the range of grades. An instructor who grades students "on a curve" matches the class list of grades against the proportions indicated by the normal curve. If the top mark is 76 percent, this grade is awarded an A+ or a 4.0. If the class average dictated by the institution must be no more than 3.2, this number (3.2) becomes the mean for the normal curve and the student grades are ranged according to the proportions dictated by the normal curve.

A number of different research studies have found that the bell curve used in educational assessment is inaccurate and invalid in class sizes fewer than about 60 people. However, many post-secondary institutions continue to derive student grades through "normalizing" practices.

> **Grade curves** refer to the ranging of grades over a curve, such as a normal probability curve. When graphed, the height of the curve at a given point indicates the proportion of cases at that point.

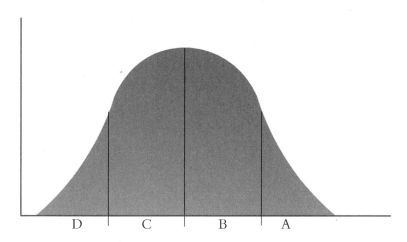

A typical **grade curve** is shaped like a bell, with the largest number of learner grades falling in the middle range. For example, on this curve, the majority of grades would be B's and C's, with a limited and equal number of A's and D's.

The Politics of Grades

Grading is philosophically, socially, and politically driven. In the university credit courses we teach, we try to clarify the artificial demands of the institution and the effect these demands have on the grading process. Some departments in our institution assume that rigorous instructional standards are demonstrated by low class averages. Our class averages must meet or fall below grade point averages set by the university. There are few exceptions allowed—even in small or specialized classes, or classes characterized by unusually gifted learners with much experience and background knowledge, or classes led by instructors who motivate learners to achieve high levels.

The reason careful consideration must be given to the system of grading is that, for many adult learners in an increasingly competitive and credential-focused society, the stakes are high. Sometimes government funding for adult learners is tied to scholastic performance. Upgrading adults often must work hard to achieve the grades they need to meet increasingly high entrance requirements for post-secondary training programs. In certain occupations, grades are examined carefully by employers and certificate-granting agencies. In some institutions, teacher evaluation, program evaluation, and even institutional accountability is linked to learners' achievement as demonstrated through grade point averages.

This practice continues despite research evidence supporting arguments that grade point averages are of limited use as indicators of student learning and overall progress. Some argue that inconsistency among instructors' teaching styles and evaluative procedures makes valid comparison of student scores difficult. Some argue that the common practice of comparing student entry scores and student exit scores to determine the "value-added" worth of an educational program ignores the many factors other than the program that have influenced student progress.

When the institutional philosophy and approaches to grading are not congruent with the instructor's approach, instructors can and often do choose actions such as the following:

- **Fight the system.** Some propose and win the right to use alternative grading practices. Some post-secondary instructors award "credit" or "non-credit" for successful course completion, along with written evaluative comments. Judith Newman (1991) claimed to have awarded every student a "9," the top possible mark, at the beginning of her classes. This practice, of course, was integrated with a thoughtful philosophy and emergent curriculum valuing trust and commitment, all of which were communicated clearly to students throughout the course. Incidentally, this instructor reported that not once did a student fail to meet her expectations of achieving a standard of work worthy of a 9 grade.

- **Subvert the system.** Because a number grade is a slippery thing, which can change according to the weighting of a particular assignment, an instructor can sometimes manipulate the numbers to produce the final grade outcome that seems fairest. Some instructors deliberately build in a percentage of marks to be awarded for "class participation," "daily course work," or "discussion" to help redistribute marks when calculating final student grades. Not only is the calculation of grades hidden, but the instructor can make judgments that are not reported or accountable to any standard or criteria beyond his or her own feelings or intuition.

- **Teach learners to ignore the system.** This approach says, "Yes, I know it's unfair; but, it's the system and you all chose to enroll in this particular institution knowing that it rewards academic performance, uses bell curves, and favours conventional learning methods." The instructor may offer alternative evaluation: "We'll do the mid-term test, one essay, and a final exam for your stanine mark, but don't expect these marks to reflect what you think you've learned. Instead, we'll build in opportunities for peer assessment and ongoing formative feedback to meet your needs."

- **De-emphasize grading.** When the instructor focuses on learner improvement and growth, and stresses that not everything students do will be graded and that they will be asked to do work that will really help develop their learning, adults sometimes catch the spark and quit worrying so much about the number.

- **Work with learners and other instructors to change the system.** Change happens slowly, but when both learners and instructors disagree with particular assessment practices, they are more likely to be amenable to new ideas. Many alternate means of assessing learners—such as portfolios, journals, self-assessment, and peer assessment—are described in this book. You might try teaming up with even one other instructor, and propose a pilot project to introduce one or more of these to develop grades for learners.

Dimensions of Student Evaluation

Balance of focus is important in deriving a grade. As much as possible, instructors should strive to allow students to "stretch and show" in activities that balance focus on talk and writing, solo and group, formal and informal, and process and product. One course should create a grade from a blending of learner assessments.

- some skill performance and some discussion/explanation *about* the skill;

- some written products created over time and some written products created on the spot;

- some on-the-spot performance of skill and some rehearsed performance of skill;

- some oral communication in various contexts, some written communication, and some visual communication of learning (through art, role-play, graphics, charts, and so on);

- some individual activities, some small-group activities, and some large-group activities;

- some activities that show comprehension of a new concept, some that show interpretation, some that show its application, some that show synthesis, some that show creative new ways of using it, some that show evaluative judgment of the concept (different levels of Bloom's taxonomy);

- some formal, serious activities for assessment and some playful, fun activities for assessment;

- some final product assessment, and some assessment of process.

Deriving the Grade: Issues to Consider

Even if you do not like grades, you will probably be forced into the problem of trying to represent very different factors with one overall grade. When producing a learner's final grade, think very carefully about the components of that grade. Below are some suggestions for constructing a more meaningful final grade.

Choose meaningful assignments that allow students to demonstrate what they know in real-life situations

Remember the principles of authentic assessment. Try to design assignments that allow relevant real-life applications of the newly learned concepts or skills, or assign projects integrated with issues learners are actually grappling with in their work or family life. Avoid assignments that have no useful function outside the purpose of the grade. Where possible, build in learner choice. Don't leave choice too wide open or learners may flounder, spending days just deciding what to do. One creative example of assignments inviting learner choice presents a selection of topics and formats. The learners pick and choose to design their own assessment activities. (See Giving Learners a Choice in Evaluations, page 138.)

Balance different types of activity for assessment

A common complaint among adult learners is the preponderance of print-based activities for assessment. Written essays, reports, and papers are the sole evaluative data in many post-secondary courses. Yet the work-world increasingly functions in oral or electronic communication media. An introductory business course in a local college, "Organizational Communication," assessed learners using two written examinations, one individual research project, and two short essay papers. One instructor finally pointed out the absurdity of the fact that, in a course devoted to understanding human communication, not a single assignment for assessment compelled learners to work together and demonstrate team skills, to use skills in small-group dialogue, to show their ability to listen critically, to speak extemporaneously in an informal situation, or to speak formally to a large group.

Another area of concern is test writing for the purpose of grading the learning of skills. Would you rather emphasize a person's ability to talk about the components of good listening habits, or a person's ability to be willing and able to listen deeply to others? Would you rather have learners of first-aid pass a written test on the procedure to stop profuse bleeding, or demonstrate their ability to think fast in an emergency situation and do what needs to be done?

Balance each of these dimensions when planning a series of assessment activities for producing a grade.

Make sure the majority of the work evaluated reflects the most important skills/knowledge of the program

Different weights given to a series of assessment activities can change learner grades dramatically. When items are given proportionately large weighting, such as a project worth 40 percent of the course grade, the sub-items they contain, such as the components within that project, need to be weighted carefully.

Examinations traditionally are given a disproportionate amount of weight in a course. It is assumed that learners demonstrate their level of knowledge at the conclusion of a program. But for learners who do not articulate knowledge well, or who aren't naturally good writers, or who don't perform well under the pressure of an exam, a final examination worth 30 to 50 percent of an overall course grade can be disastrous and will not reflect what they actually know. Learners should be informed of the value given to different assignments, and helped to plan their investment of effort accordingly.

Alternative Methods of Deriving Grades

Alternative 1: Non-Graded Courses

Some instructors either award "credit" or "satisfactory" to learners who have completed the whole program or simply record it as "complete" or "incomplete." The advantage of a credit/non-credit course is that learners are more receptive to feedback. Because they are not worried about losing marks and figure that if they work hard they'll get credit, they often relax and focus on improvement. Instructors are released from the burden of playing "the heavy" at the conclusion of the course after taking on a nurturing role throughout the program. The disadvantages are that some learners are motivated by grades and some institutions view credit/non-credit courses as lacking rigor. Credit/non-credit courses also may affect students' applications for scholarships.

Questions to Ask

- Which concepts and skills are the most significant?

- Which assignments or activities will consume the most learner time and effort?

- Which types of assignments or activities are more difficult or easier for learners?

- Which units of the course should receive equivalent weight?

- Which aspects of learner performance (individual and small group) are more significant?

- Should learner progress and effort throughout the course or learner competence at the conclusion of the course receive more priority?

Alternative 2: Self-Assessment Approaches

One way to include a learner's self-assessment in the final calculation of a grade is to allot a percentage of the course grade to a score learners give their own work, using criteria they have developed and applied to their own performances. These criteria can be developed as a class, in small groups, or by individuals. Documentation of the criteria and the way they were applied should be filed along with the grade.

The grade might include any combination of the following: the learner's assessment of his or her overall growth since the beginning of the course, progress in particular areas, effort committed to course work, contribution to others' progress, the learning process undertaken by the student, or confidence in mastering particular course requirements.

Alternative 3: A Performance Approach

A performance approach is a quick, simple system that records whether the learner completes assigned tasks. The instructor establishes an acceptable standard of performance, then notes which learners have done the work. In operating a piece of heavy equipment, a list of steps that must be followed are checked off as the learner proceeds through them satisfactorily. In a writing course, the instructor may specify a minimum of five journal pages to be completed each week, or two business letters handed in each week. Credit is given only if the work is completed. The advantage of the performance approach is efficiency. The disadvantage is that good or poor work is not differentiated. Quality might slip unless instructors have clearly established standards for what constitutes completion. There is no provision for interpretation or judgment: the performance approach is best suited to concrete, demonstrable learner performance, such as technical skills.

Maximize Your Minimal Time

Assessing learner work is time-consuming and you can quickly become bogged down in mind-numbing stacks of papers. Or you can create a marking plan that allows you to enjoy and even look forward to sessions of reading student work. Here are some alternative possibilities and time-saving suggestions.

Give Less Written Feedback

Feedback should be plentiful, but written feedback on final papers is time-consuming and, judging by the number of learners who simply glance at the final grade and comments, may be the least effective way to communicate suggestions. Instead, focus on providing feedback when learners are in the early stages of designing their assignment, then in various stages of the drafting/revision process (refer to Toolbox 3: Assessing Written Assignments). Try to circulate regularly among learners and find moments throughout instructional time to give quick verbal feedback regularly to everyone.

Decide how valuable your written feedback will be on a particular assignment. Most instructors do not thoroughly read or comment extensively on every assignment. It is pointless to engage in the time-consuming activity of correcting spelling and grammar on a paper unless it will be revised for publication. A general comment at the end of the paper suggesting that the learner try to proofread more carefully, or see you for help with comma splices, or find a friend to help edit may be more helpful. Sometimes a quick personal comment responding to something specific in the work is sufficient.

Use Holistic Grading

Rather than two or three major assignments that you must read and respond to in detail, consider having students submit several shorter assignments that you skim, then grade quickly and holistically (refer to Toolbox 6: Rating Scales, page 231, for holistic scales). Make one or two specific comments on each assignment. Learners can practise the skills of doing the assignments and being accountable for them, without placing a huge burden of marking on the instructor.

Holistic Grading attempts to consider an evaluation of the entire as a whole rather than breaking it into discrete pieces and grading those pieces.

Use Non-Written Products for a Portion of the Assessment

Alternatives to taking home a briefcase bulging with written assignments include asking students to present research results orally, to present an argument on a particular issue in a debate, or to present findings of a small-group project in a display or role-play. All can be scored during a class presentation and are equally as valid as paper-and-pencil tests or written essays!

Expand Use of Peer Feedback

Some adults are suspicious of peer feedback. Some may still believe that the instructor is the only authority in the room worth listening to; they have paid for the "expert" feedback of that instructor, not the untutored opinions of their peers. Some have had less-than-useful experiences with peer feedback.

Difficulty with peer feedback comes when you throw learners into pairs and expect them to automatically have the personal courage, the intellectual ability to observe another's work critically, and the right way of phrasing responses. However, showing learners what to look for in each other's work, giving them protocols to guide their feedback, and providing opportunities to respond in meaningful ways allows students to share rich evaluative feedback with one another and learn the valuable skills of providing feedback. (For more on the benefits of peer feedback, see Toolbox 11, page 254.)

Grade Less, but Don't Reduce the Amount of Valuable Activity You Assign for Learning Purposes

Portfolios of products, journals, or writing folders promote intermittent grading (out of a large volume of learner writing or other products, only a small portion is selected for formal grading). Most adults understand that not everything they do requires formal feedback, nor do they need the incentive of a grade to motivate them to do a particular assignment. Other incentives work just as well, such as trading their work with another learner, each reading and responding in a written format to the other's work; orally and informally presenting their work to a small group; or displaying their work for others to review.

Reporting Grades to Learners

Task 1: Communicate clear criteria and prepare learners for summative evaluation

Ideally, learners should be given a written list of all assessment activities and assignments, along with a statement of the criteria that will be used to judge their performance, and the percentage weight each assignment will carry in calculating the final grade. Encourage learners to keep track of their own grade throughout the course, using the percentage weights to calculate where they stand. This practice keeps the grade in the hands of the learner, reduces surprise when final grades are given, and promotes early attention to slipping grades.

Task 2: Give sensitive and helpful formative and summative feedback

Number grades should be accompanied by comments. Even small assignments that are quickly skimmed and given a holistic grade should be accompanied by written or verbal feedback, however brief. If you're pressed for time and working with a large group, develop a checklist that can be prepared quickly for each learner, accompanied by a short written comment. Prepare students for final grades, posted as a list of numbers beside students' ID numbers, in class by providing them with a description of what each number grade or range of grades represents.

Some instructors hold brief one-on-one conferences to discuss the learner's work in the course. These can take place during a program or at its conclusion. The conference can take many forms: describe learner and instructor perspectives of the learner's progress and possible areas for further growth; explain evaluative criteria, how they were applied, and the learner's performance viewed through these criteria; establish goals for future improvement; together develop an action plan for learner improvement.

Task 3: Deal with learner concerns about a grade

If a learner approaches you with concerns about a grade, make an appointment. If the student is very upset, give yourself thinking and planning time and the learner, cooling-down time. At the appointment, try to discern why the learner is upset. Was there an unclear understanding of the purpose or criteria for evaluating the assignment? Did the learner feel unjustly rewarded for much effort? Is the student projecting personal disappointment into anger at you? Does the learner have a history of aggressive action when expectations are not fulfilled? Is the learner fearful of failing?

When it is your turn to talk, help the learner understand the criteria being applied in the evaluation. Rather than defending your decision, ask the learner to defend a change in grade. Then focus on helping him or her find concrete ways to improve or grow. Work towards a win–win

> "To suggest is to create; to describe is to destroy."
>
> – Robert Doisneau

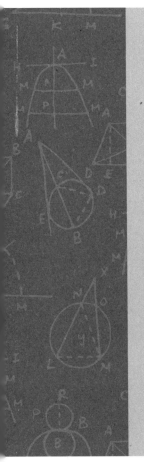

> "Curiosity is one of the most permanent and certain characteristics of a vigorous mind."
> – Samuel Johnson

solution. Perhaps the learner could revise an assignment for re-scoring, write a make-up test, or create a new assignment to make up some grades.

If your talk does not resolve the issue, be open and helpful. Suggest that the learner formally appeal the grade. Most institutions of formal learning have clear policies in place for students to appeal a particular assignment or course grade. Such policies may involve a different instructor re-scoring the assignment, then a decision made by a committee based on evidence submitted by the student.

Trouble-Shooting

What do you say when they ask, "Where did I lose marks?"

Our standard response is, "You're not losing marks, you're gaining them." The learner starts at zero at the beginning of a graded course and accu-

Four Small-Group Grading Approaches

Peer Grading

Every member gives other members of the group a grade plus their criteria for that grade. A variation occurred in a college business administration course emphasizing teamwork. The instructor scored the team's final presentation and written report. Each member of the team gave every other member on the team a percentage grade, based on a perception of each member's relative contribution to the total project. The instructor then calculated an individual mark for each team member, based on the average percentage awarded by the other members of their team, and the total team mark awarded by the instructor. The person who worked the hardest, according to the team, received the highest mark—often higher than the group grade. The person who worked least, according to the group, received the lowest mark. This system depends on a high degree of learner maturity, critical thinking, and honesty.

Shared Grading

Every group member gets the same grade. Make it clear at the beginning of the project that all will share the grade. Suggest strategies that divide the workload fairly. Group members can submit a self-assessment describing their own involvement in the project. Group work can fall apart if the group includes a difficult, uncommitted, or uncooperative member. In some projects, let groups choose their own members, giving time for the class to get to know each other before choosing. Sometimes a "difficult" person is simply a poor fit in a particular group.

Individual Grading

Every member of the group receives an individual grade for a product, such as a report. The small group works together to research or create the material, but the final score reflects the product of each individual. The disadvantage of this method is that group process and interpersonal team skills are not acknowledged. The message to learners is that, once again, product counts more than process.

Self-Grading

All members grade themselves. Learners provide a written description explaining the assessment and how it was derived. The instructor may use this grade as part or all of the assessment. The remainder of the grade may be the group's score, given equally to every member, an individual grade based on the individual's own product, or a combination of these.

mulates marks through effort, progress, and achievement. However, some learners believe they've started at 100 percent; their grade indicates places where the instructor has taken away marks for errors. Try to help these learners develop a new perspective: 72 percent indicates they are already 72 percent of the way towards a goal. It helps first to show the learners what they are doing well, what areas of their performances are strong, and for what they have already been awarded marks. Then, moving away from the issue of grades and marks, help them see specific areas they can improve, and suggest concrete steps towards improvement.

How can you award grades for class participation?

"Class participation" is a grading category commonly used to award marks for a variety of miscellaneous elements: attendance in class, active contribution to class discussion or small-group activity, and compliance with small ungraded assignments that are assigned, such as having everyone bring an article related to course material to share with a partner.

Be careful not to award class participation marks based on who talks most! Learners participate differently. Some listen deeply and carefully; some never fight for "air time" in a large-group discussion; some enliven small-group work with imaginative play and humour; some encourage others' ideas but don't spotlight themselves; some prefer small, intimate, lengthy conversations but are silent in fast-paced, public discussion; and some would rather write responses than respond orally. These learners are often ignored by evaluators who think effective class participation means talking.

How do you award marks for individuals in a group when effort and quality of work is inconsistent among the members?

Scoring projects completed in small groups or teams can be an adventure. Sometimes groups work exquisitely well; other times you may be called on to mediate the group process. To avoid having to referee for learners as they struggle into new territory, spend time in plenary sessions up front, discussing strategies for effective teamwork, identifying the group's particular strengths and team-building skills, and exploring the stages in the process they will likely follow. Some instructors allow a group to ask a non-cooperative member to leave. This person then completes an independent project. This action may help the group, but it does not help an individual develop interpersonal or cooperative small-group skills.

Assessment of Class Participation

Three Grading Alternatives

1. Instead of daily attendance, which creates problems when the instructor is constantly placed in positions of deciding what constitutes legitimate absence, create a checklist of tasks that are simply scored periodically throughout the course with a 3-2-1 scale or checkmark. The checklist could include small-group activities conducted during class that end in informal presentations, or small in-class assignments (write a response, explain a procedure, read another's work and respond to it, create a poster, present an idea).

2. Devise periodic in-class surprise tasks and quizzes. Give credit for completion to all those who participate.

3. Have learners describe their own approaches to class participation. In small groups of learners, generate ways to assess class participation that can be applied fairly and consistently to every member of the group. Periodically, have small groups review and assess their group process and dynamics (refer to Toolbox 11, page 254, for rating scales for small groups).

If you stay in touch with groups throughout their project, you will become aware of interpersonal or task problems that arise and can help facilitate group strategies for dealing with problems. These strategies include open talk, helping each hear the others' perspectives on the issue, clarifying and objectifying the problem, peeling back the layers of the problem to find the underlying source, allowing all members to state their feelings about the process orally or in writing, and brainstorming alternate solutions.

How can you award grades fairly for portfolios or journals?

When grading portfolios or journals, develop specific grading criteria. Even if you want to award grades holistically, develop indicators to help you clearly and consistently identify what you're looking for. Clarify grading procedures for learners at the beginning of the journalling process and provide them with a written description of criteria; examples are also helpful. For additional specific help and sample rating scales, refer to Toolboxes on journals and portfolios.

How can learner effort be assessed for grading purposes?

Grading *effort* can be difficult, but worthwhile. First, ask yourself why you want to award marks for effort. How will this help a learner? What information will it provide to others responsible for the learner's further performance and growth? How is effort relevant to the overall goals of the program? In the case of teacher education, some university instructors award marks for hard work because they believe this is a quality required of new teachers, perhaps far more than specific content knowledge.

Second, determine the concrete, observable *indicators* of effort in the context of the program. Some considerations might be attention to detail in presentation, work hours reported by the learner or observed by the instructor, difficulty of the task, breadth of resources, initiative in finding resources, ease of access to resources, and thoroughness of treatment.

But remember, what gets measured is what becomes valued. Is sheer effort a dimension you want learners to value? How important is effort relative to thinking and interpersonal skills, attitudes, behaviours, and beliefs? Some adults believe that long hours spent in independent study or practice are a virtue, however inefficiently or misguidedly such hours may be employed. So be thoughtful when devising a way to grade effort. Plain dogged hard work, if it is thoughtless, does not guarantee success in learning, career growth, or skill improvement.

How should tasks be weighted to construct the final grade?

Instructors usually divide a course into parts or categories and find a way to evaluate each part. Parts may be divided according to any organizing principle that enhances the overall purpose of the course. In each part of the course, an individual's learning is formatively assessed through feedback and through a grade for process or development, then summatively assessed through an assignment, task, or test at the conclusion of that part. A final project, task, or test is sometimes used to assess the individual's overall learning at the end of the course. Each part of the course should be weighted according to its significance to overall learning goals. The amount of class time spent and the learner's commitment of energy and time should also reflect the significance of the overall purpose. Here are some examples of course organization schemes.

- A small number of general themes around which the literature of the course is organized. A university course called "Introduction to Adult Education" contains five units, each assessed through a concluding assignment: Providers and Participants in Adult Education (10 percent); Overview of Historical Canadian Programs (15 percent); Philosophical Frameworks (30 percent); Principles of Program Planning (30 percent); Contemporary Issues of Practice (15 percent).

- A number of different skill areas. A course preparing adult trainers could include writing, speaking, preparing lesson and unit plans, consideration of alternative ideas, and setting competencies for evaluation.

- A sequence of teaching units or modules, each occupying a period of time. A course in international sociology is broken into six, two-week units, each examining the work of a different theorist, each weighted equally through equal numbers of questions on the final examination.

- A list of different tasks the learner must perform at the conclusion of the course. A course for dental hygienists may be organized according to clusters of learning objectives, each stating a skill the learner must perform correctly. Each skill or task is weighted differently according to its importance.

- A series of projects students complete or experiences they move through. A management course for public administrators is conducted

> "I am always doing that which I can not do, in order that I may learn how to do it."
>
> – Pablo Picasso

entirely through a simulation involving different in-basket exercises each participant must successfully complete at the class meeting each week. Each week emphasizes a different aspect of administrative performance: interpersonal skills, conflict mediation, finance and budgeting, problem solving, visioning, and crisis management. The participant is given a general score each week from the ratings earned (1-2-3 scale) for performance on each administrative in-basket task. Each part of the course is rated equally to make up 80 percent of the grade. At the conclusion of the course the participants write a reflective paper, worth 20 percent, about their administrative style and areas for growth.

What do you do when high-performing learners produce a class average that is higher than the institution will allow?

Enjoy the class and try to work out something with your immediate supervisor. Obviously, you can't make this claim all the time; but, if you have a track record, your supervisor should allow some flexibility for "the class from heaven."

What do you do when the class averages for a particular task are either too low or too high?

With a small group of learners, grades for particular assessments often do not show a balanced spread. If the marks are high, which often happens in oral presentations or group projects, the cause may be any of the following:

- They are all motivated learners, who worked hard to perform well.

- It is a topic learners are generally familiar with or found easy to master.

- The instruction was successful, helping and encouraging everyone to succeed.

- It was an assignment or performance task in which all learners were able to excel.

- The criteria do not distinguish effectively between stronger and weaker performance.

- The evaluator is reluctant to award lower scores.

If the marks are low, as in the case of an examination, the reasons may be any of the following:

- Certain test items require information that the learners don't have.

- The test focuses on minutiae when the course breadth is considerable.

- Test questions are ambiguously worded or can be answered effectively in different ways.

- Your teaching has emphasized one set of concepts and the test has focused on another.

- The test is too long or test-taking conditions hindered successful learner performance.

- Learners lack the knowledge to complete the assignment, such as strategies for taking tests or writing essays.

- The evaluator's expectations for learners are unreasonably high given their current stage of development.

- Learners are unmotivated, or unprepared (perhaps they didn't understand the rigour of assessment).

- Learners are experiencing unusually high degrees of stress.

After reviewing the situation, you may decide to make some changes. For example, marks can be scaled up or down. If the assessment tool is at fault, you may choose to deliver further instruction and redo the assessment. You can allow learners to redo the assignment or test. You may decide not to include the grades in the final assessment; however, if some learners have done well on the assignment, it would probably be wise to offer compensation. Perhaps you could give everyone equal credit for completing the task. Finally, you can approach learners with the issue, present options, and invite them to discuss and choose an action. If they, too, are teachers, the lesson they learn can be important.

How should overall learner growth be considered in the final grade?

Pre-test and post-test are the most common ways of determining learner progress. A good pre-course assessment can determine a learner's entry-level knowledge and skills. Some pre-test methods include paper-and-pencil test, formal skill demonstration, conference with the learner, self-assessment or written description of prior learning and experience completed by the learner, informal observation of the learner's behaviour in situ, or a combination of these methods. Prior Learning Assessment is also gaining serious attention in many adult education programs and post-secondary institutions. (See box on page 73.)

The post-course assessment is compared to the skills assessed in the pre-test; both should test the same learner understandings and ability to solve problems. If the pre-test was qualitative and interpretive, such as a conference or written description inviting the learner to reflect on life experience or discuss relevant understandings and perceptions, the post-test should use similar criteria. A letter or number can be chosen to represent a person's level at the program's conclusion from a holistic scale presenting clear descriptors for each level. This level is compared with the pre-course level, and the amount of variation is calculated and included as part of the course mark.

It's important to remember when determining pre-course and post-course skills that not all learning registers itself in levels. Nor can learner growth or lack of growth be attributed to a particular program. Many factors influence learning: family issues, domestic arrangements, life crises, access to other resources, or direct help and indirect support from family, workplace, and community. The issue of measuring learner growth should be approached cautiously and humbly. It should never be reported simply as a quantity, without some qualitative commentary.

Calculating and including learner growth as a percentage of the learner's grade acknowledges that each adult enters a learning program from a different point. Each brings unique knowledge and experience to a new learning situation. For some, the growth is the most important part of this process, not the rating of their final achievement. Including learner growth in a grade recognizes and celebrates learner effort and gain, even when the final achievement may be less than triumphant when viewed against external criteria.

Including learner growth as part of a final grade has two disadvantages. First, it penalizes learners who enter the program with a high degree of understanding, skill, and familiarity with course content. Their growth will not be as dramatic as those completely unfamiliar with the content. Second, some learners may have learned a great deal at deep levels that cannot yet be expressed. During a course, people can experience transformations that begin percolating at pre-verbal levels. Few post-course measures can detect such growth, especially when one considers just how brief most courses are.

How do you balance the difficulty of the task with the quality and control evident in the final product?

A task with clear boundaries and a narrowly limited scope is easier to manage than one with a more challenging range and depth that stretches the learner. This is why the quality of the final product, whether measured according to organization, control of format, elimination of errors, or style, should be balanced with a consideration of the degree of difficulty involved.

Dimensions of difficulty will vary with the nature of the task, but might include the following:

- The breadth of items that are being considered.

- The depth of understanding of items (increasing from comprehension to interpretation, application, analysis, synthesis).

- The complexity of embedded meanings in items under consideration.

- The complexity of relationships among items.

- The originality of perspective on items being considered.

A Final Thought...

Grades—we seek them, but we hate them. Grades can motivate; and grades can defeat. Like death and taxes, few instructors can avoid grading. Our formal systems of education demand them.

We encourage you to remember how important grades are to learners. Grades do motivate, and they do reward. But make sure your work as an instructor emphasizes more than grades. The most mature learners consider grades important, but they do not value their work simply by the grade someone else gives it. Encouraging students to grow past a reliance on grades is a step in the right direction. Instructors who emphasize grades first are placing giant roadblocks in the path of students as they head toward intellectual maturity.

15

Assessment *for* Learning:

Creating Ongoing Conversations with Learners

It used to be that learners felt powerless in the face of the judging teacher. Fortunately, this is no longer true. This chapter outlines the positive growth in learning that can occur when learners and teachers work together to negotiate learning. Assessment for learning suggests that teamwork between learners and teachers can help produce successful learning.

Adults, even those who are quite successful, never seem to forget how embarrassing it is to fail—especially in front of others. Most of them have grown up in schools where teachers believed the way to "achieve" learning was to create anxiety so that students would "pull up their boots" or that the "tough would get going." As a result, for many adult, assessment has been intimidating. However, adults want to be "lifelong learners." They also know that others—often their teachers—can help them learn. How can we create assessment that is more supportive, ongoing, and less intimidating?

The highest degree one can achieve from an institution is a doctor of philosophy (Ph.D.). Many are fortunate enough to have achieved one. To gain that credential, years of hard work and study are required. One must take courses, propose and complete a major research project, then write and defend the project before a group of peers. All this work is supervised by a more experienced professor—a mentor who works with the graduate student, or candidate, over a long period of time.

The supervisor of the Ph.D. candidate spends much time meeting with the student, discussing the student's work, the student's progress towards goals, the student's research and publication plans, and in all probability the student's future academic work. This relationship often works well and can become the cornerstone for a lifetime friendship or working relationship. The relationship is conversational and goal-oriented. It is also, at heart, the foundation of what is called *assessment* for *learning*.

What is assessment *for* learning, and how does it differ from other forms of assessment? **Assessment *for* learning** is an idea originating in K–12 pedagogy, but as demonstrated by the relationship between graduate students and their supervisors, it clearly has the potential to work exceedingly well with adults. Basically, the power of assessment *for* learning is that it occurs *during* the teaching and learning process rather than after teaching and learning has been completed. It is not directed toward measuring how much a learner has learned after a unit of study, rather, it is primarily focused on how learners might improve the quality of their work during their study.

If you think this sounds like formative assessment, you are correct; however, it is formative assessment with a twist. That twist is the creation of a dynamic and ongoing conversation between the teacher and learner—the goal of which is that the learner comes to better understand

> "Perhaps self-reference is the best tool of all for leaving behind the clock-like world of Newton. We need to be able to trust that something as simple as a clear core of values and vision, kept in motion through continuing dialogue, can lead to order."
> – Margaret Wheatley

Assessment *for* learning stems from the belief that assessment should represent more than a summative evaluation of what has been learned, but should be used by the learner and teacher to track and plan future learnings and is, thus, an important part of the learning itself.

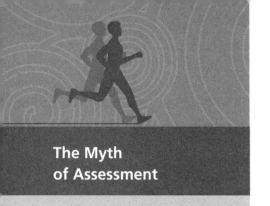

Although Stiggins (2002) does not explicitly make the connection in his article, hero mythology is strong in American lore and culture. Joseph Campbell described this well in his book *The Hero with a Thousand Faces* (1949). This heroic myth—Campbell calls it the monomyth—is often referred to as a "hero's journey" and describes a basic pattern found in many narratives from around the world; but, it is especially illustrative of a North American approach to overcoming challenges.

The mythology of the "hero's journey" implores us to believe that "when the going gets tough, the tough get going"; or, when faced with difficulties, one just needs to redouble the effort. This cultural paradigm translates into assessment practices, such as setting high academic standards and raising the bar in an effort to "drive" learners to achieve. The problem is that although this might have worked to spur industrialization and North America's material growth, it works less well when applied to the deeper and more autonomous learning requirements of learners today; yet, it remains deeply rooted in our North American psyche.

and consequently own the process for her or his own learning. The goal of assessment *for* learning is to facilitate learning independence.

The Problem with Traditional Assessment

In a 2002 article in the eminent North American educational magazine *Phi Delta Kappan*, Richard J. Stiggins lambastes traditional standardized "American-style" assessment, calling it a crisis and suggesting that few school officials know how to address this crisis. Specifically, he notes that the questions we typically ask about assessment put us within a "rewards–punishment" metaphor, which includes the mistaken belief that punishment for substandard work will motivate learning. Although Stiggins is speaking about K–12 education, his argument echoes into adult learning. Furthermore, although Stiggins speaks critically about the "American system," it is difficult not to see North American education as a whole—and the Canadian system specifically—mirrored in his critique.

Although Stiggins (2002) argues for K-12 learners, most adult educators and trainers understand that all learning takes place when learners experience success, not failure. Assessment based upon punishment for "substandard" work assumes that learners are "reluctant," – that is, they don't really want to learn and must be forced, against their wills. If Stiggins is correct, what a horrid place any learning setting is when a learner underperforms and assessment becomes punitive. Also, Stiggins notes that the assessment community has made a huge error—it has acted as if the task were to discover more sophisticated and efficient ways to create valid and reliable *test scores*. By doing so, he believes we have equated learning with frequent and intensive testing and have mistaken accountability for learning. Instead of seeking to become better at measuring outcomes, we should be seeking ways to help our assessment practices maximize the most positive impact on learners and their learning processes—which assessment for learning research suggests would lead to more positive outcomes.

Stiggins is correct when he notes that assessment practices throughout North America have centred upon two purposes: to inform decisions and to motivate learning. Both these purposes, he notes, are problematic. He comments on the fundamental grounding of such assessment practices, suggesting that educational policy makers have built education success upon a worldview of an individual learner's heroic action in the face of struggle (see "The Myth of Assessment").

Instead of perpetuating the "win or lose" philosophy of traditional assessment, Stiggins, promoting a different vision, asks two critical questions: (1) How can we use assessment to help learners *want* to learn? and (2) How can we help learners feel *able* to learn? He suggests that, contrary to the mythology that fostered the "pull up your socks" mentality, a huge segment of learners simply do not redouble their efforts when challenged. Indeed, they respond by giving up because they feel the task is hopeless. He reminds us that many political and educational leaders have never really experienced the painful, embarrassing, or discouraging trauma of chronic and public failure. Instead, Stiggins points out that summative assessment (especially standardized testing) has the dichotomous impact of enhancing one person's progress (those who are successful) while discouraging another person's progress (those who don't experience success).

What is Assessment *for* Learning?

Assessment *for* learning is a simple concept. Instead of using assessment to *measure* a learner's achievement, assessment for learning involves using educational assessment to *raise* a learner's achievement. This approach is based on the belief that learners will improve if and when they understand the goal of their learning, when they accept and can relate to this goal, and when they engage this goal dynamically. When these three principles are brought into focus, learners will come to play an active part in their own achievement. They also learn *how* to learn.

Stiggins offers an even more powerful vision. He suggests that rather than have assessment provide *proof of* learning it should provide *information for* learning. In other words, Stiggins believes that shifting towards assessment for learning can help teachers use assessment to establish a more positive relationship with the learner, as well as a continuous flow of information about the co-articulated goals for achievement back to the learner, so that the learner can better see how she or he can advance toward those learning goals. Thus, instead of being a static *check on* learning, assessment can become an interactive *guide to* learning.

By now you may be seeing one of the key differences between standard assessments and assessments *for* learning: Standard assessment is more static and creates products of measuring learning; whereas assessment *for* learning is dynamic and supports process of measuring learning

Evaluation as Myth

Are Your Curriculum and Evaluation Practices Based on Myth?

Joseph Campbell's study of literature, *The Hero with a Thousand Faces* (1949), noted that many myths were universal and survived for thousands of years. These myths, he noted, shared a fundamental structure that could be organized into a number of discrete stages that included:

1. A call to adventure, which the hero has to accept or decline;

2. A road of trials, where the tested hero succeeds or fails;

3. Achieving the goal or "boon," which typically results in the hero's gaining of important self-knowledge;

4. A return to the ordinary world, again where the hero can succeed or fail;

5. Applying the boon, where the hero's new insights can be used to improve the world.

It is not difficult to imagine these stages within the context of the North American education system, with, for example, a university degree as the goal or "boon," which allows the hero to "make something of himself."

When teachers assess for learning, they work to:

1. Understand and articulate learning goals for their learners, in advance.

2. Inform learners about those learning goals in ways learners comprehend.

3. Learn to better translate learning goals into appropriate assessment practices that reflect how learners are actually doing.

4. Use assessment to help learners build confidence and strategies that eventually help them become responsible for their own learning.

5. Give learners specific, frequent, and descriptive—but not judgmental—feedback that offers insight about how to progress toward learning goals.

6. Adjust pedagogy based upon the results of frequent feedback to learners.

7. Help learners engage in regular self-assessment that honestly reflects learning progress.

8. Involve learners in communicating with teachers and peers (where appropriate) about their achievement and learning growth.

Stiggins also argues that learners become more confident as they watch themselves progress and succeed. Success is cyclical: when learners experience success, they work harder and smarter to achieve more success. There is usually a correlation between hard work and achievement, so this work pays off in even greater success. As a result, learners gain a sense of control over their own learning, make better decisions about their learning, and assess their own progress towards learning.

Ideas for Using Assessment *for* Learning

Basically, assessment for learning involves helping learners become effective partners in their own ongoing assessment practices. In other words, while the curriculum or the learning goals might not change, assessment pedagogy shifts so that teachers and learners work more closely together to build, monitor, and plan learning and assessment. Thus, learners engage in their own empowerment when they become better able to use assessment information to set their own goals, to understand what quality work looks like, to self-assess and make learning decisions related to their own improvement, and to learn how to communicate their progress toward—or success in achieving—established learning goals.

Teachers and learners might work on many tasks to make assessment practices more understandable and more supportive of learner independence in self-assessment. However, all such tasks share one characteristic: they involve teachers and learners working together collaboratively—as a class or one-on-one. These tasks are dynamic and are unique to each learner and context.

- Working together to analyze samples of good work and discussing what makes these samples good;

- discussing the need for scoring guides or rubrics as they pertain to learners' work, and engaging in activities that help learners evaluate their own and others' work against these rubrics;

- co-creating assessment rubrics and standards that work for individual learners within the context of their own needs, goals, and standards for what is being learned;

- revising their own and others' work based on appropriate standards;

- communicating with other learners about their growth and monitoring their own progress.

Key to all these activities is the building of a deep and rich conversational space where, through dynamic responsibility, learners come to own their own learning.

At the heart of these learning conversations is the ability to engage in effective feedback and insights about learning. Effective feedback is honest, considerate, descriptive, specific, and timely. It is built on an accepted relationship that is learner-focused. Although the teacher remains the teacher, effective feedback does not create status or distance between a teacher and a learner, but describes how a student's plan or work could be improved in specific terms learners understand. Furthermore, effective feedback is reasonable—there is a rationale for it that is honestly shared. By contrast, ineffective feedback is often based upon the teacher's approval or disapproval of a learner's performance, which suggests that a teacher is right and the student is wrong or that the teacher has the higher status in the relationship. In either case, it suggests that the teacher knows something that the student does not know. If this is the case, should we not be asking: "How do we ensure that the student knows all that he or she must know in order to achieve?"

Questions...

Learners Must Ask Themselves

Where am I trying to go?

Where am I now?

How do I close the gap?

How can I modify my learning to get there?

How will I know if I have been?

Teachers Must Ask Themselves

Where is the learner trying to go?

Where is the learner now?

How can the learner close the gap?

How can I modify my teaching to help the learner get there?

How will we know if we have been successful?

Principles of Assessment *for* Learning*

1. Assessment **for** *learning should be part of effective planning of teaching and learning*

A teacher's planning should provide opportunities that help learners obtain and use information about their progress towards learning goals. The philosophy of assessment for learning is based upon a caring and considered relationship between teacher and learner and upon a dynamic interplay and continuing conversation between them. Such conversations require flexible time allotments that allow responses to initial learning (we must start someplace) and emerging knowledge and skills (we must be open to new ideas about moving forward).

Planning must consider formative assessments; that is, as teacher and learners converse, they always work together to ensure that learners understand the goals they are pursuing and the criteria that will be applied in

---

* Principles of Assessment *for* Learning *(pages 161–168) is based on "The 10 Principles: Assessment for Learning," Qualifications and Curriculum Authority (Great Britain).*

assessing their work. Although there is a sense that assessment for learning is more collegial, that is not to say that all learning is based upon learner desires. Assessment for learning does not reshape traditional or accepted curriculum; it does, however, reshape the teacher–learner relationship, and may require a reconsideration of pedagogical approaches, which may take more time and teacher energy. For this reason, planning is essential.

Once the learner and teacher discover how a learner learns, assessment activities are planned, conducted, and interpreted by the teacher or the teacher and the learner so that the learner's activities might be more fruitfully charted. This process, directed by the teacher, becomes part of planned instructional activity. Learners, using this ongoing and iterative process, become better aware of how they are learning. And, for learning to be successful, the "how" becomes as important as the "what."

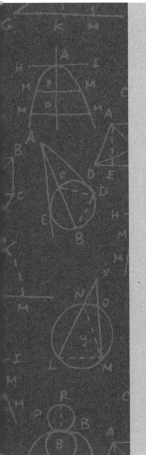

Inside the Black Box

In 1998, Black and Wiliam called the classroom a "black box," in which inputs (learners, teachers, resources, management rules, and expectations) are followed by outputs (knowledgeable learners, teacher job satisfaction, high test results,). Because the relationships that exist within the black box are less than positive, they argued for formative assessment by asking and answering three key questions:

1. Is there evidence that improving formative assessment raises standards?

2. Is there evidence that there is room for improvement?

3. Is there evidence about how to improve formative assessment?

Their extensive review of research that allowed them to say yes to all three questions. Their synthesis pulled together the findings of studies across a range of ages, subjects, and countries that correlated formative assessment with substantial learning gains, especially with learners often thought to have learning difficulties. They noted a number of successful activities found to work with all age levels—and that promise to work with adult learners. These included such things as enhanced feedback, learner involvement, and using results to alter teaching and learning strategies. They also discussed the impact of self-esteem on motivation, and the crucial importance of self-assessment.

Black and Wiliam demonstrated that providing ongoing feedback had unprecedented positive effects on learner achievement. Their work suggests that the fundamentals of assessment *for* learning can help low-achieving learners (especially those at low socio-economic levels) close the achievement gap.

Black and Wiliam note that self-assessment, "far from being a luxury, is in fact an essential component of formative assessment. When anyone is trying to learn, feedback about the effort has three elements: redefinition of the desired goal, evidence about present position, and some understanding of a way to close the gap between the two. All three must be understood to some degree by anyone before he or she can take action to improve learning" (p. 143).

2. *Assessment* for *learning should focus on how learners learn*

As noted, a key process that underpins assessment for learning is the "conversation" between learner and teacher that has, at its end, the goal of helping a learner to understand how she or he learns and to plan further success in learning.

Therefore, one key to using assessment for learning is ensuring clarity or transparency of movement toward curriculum goals, which requires learners to be actively involved as part of the conversational process. Such back and forth activity differs from a teacher telling and a learner listening. In using assessment for learning, teachers are able to gain greater input from learners about how they are proceeding at any given time. It is then up to the teacher to use the information provided to create appropriate feedback that inspires a conversation about how to move a learner forward. Discussions between teachers and learners centre on how learners and teachers can together set a direction that allows the learner to make fruitful progress. While it might seem that a teacher "loses authority" in using assessment for learning, the opposite is true.

It might be more accurate to suggest that assessment for learning *supports* traditional top-down curriculum, based upon greater empowerment of the teacher (away from relying on external evaluations) to chart a learner's progress towards traditional curriculum goals and objectives. As noted before, it is not so much the *what* of learning that changes, but the *how* one goes about learning. Eventually, the instructional goal is that learners become independently able to shape their own learning processes, no matter what the curriculum or content.

3. *Assessment* for *learning is central to classroom practice*

Teachers already constantly engage in assessment activities. Good lesson plans are well-considered lesson plans; that is, the activities, tasks, questions, and assignments a teacher chooses are based on that teacher's best sense of what helps learners understand the knowledge or skills that make up the content to be learned. Learners, in a typical learning activity, are asked to demonstrate the knowledge and skills to be learned. The teacher's task is to judge these demonstrations as a representation of how well learners understand a given concept or topic. In other words, teachers "listen" or "watch" what learners do (assessment in its most simple form), then interpret and judge whether learning has actually taken place and how learning can be improved. Such assessments are essential to every-

Actions that Support Assessment *for* Learning

1. Pre-test learners prior to a unit of study to discover what they already know. Shape instruction accordingly. Don't assume learners come empty.

2. Analyze specific learner needs for further knowledge, skills, or practice.

3. Regularly revise instruction based on assessment results and learners' progress.

4. Consider the effectiveness of your "standard" teaching practices. For every learner, ask whether these practices support that individual learner's goals. Although the "tried and true" remain so, some strategies might not fit current learners' needs. One key to assessment for learning is differentiating instruction for each student.

5. Talk with learners about their strengths and about their needs for improvement in particular areas. Continue these conversations formally and informally; these conversations are both social and instructional.

6. Create an open learning environment; do all five steps above *in collaboration with* your learners.

> "Learning is much affected by emotions from three sources: those we bring to the learning process, those that are generated during the learning process, and those which we feel when we receive feedback about whether we have succeeded or failed."
>
> – D. MacKeracher

day teaching practice. However, assessment for learning centres upon an *explicit* involvement of teachers and learners in reflection, conversation, and decision-making, which becomes the foundation of the assessment.

In an ideal world, teachers do not keep all their reasons or criteria for judgment in their head and simply assign a mark; they walk through, expressing out loud, how they arrived at their assessment or mark. This gives learners insight and guidance as to how to improve (as well as how to assess).

4. Assessment **for** *learning is an important professional teaching skill*

If assessment for learning is to have its desired effect, teachers must gain the professional knowledge and skills necessary to plan for assessment, observe learning, analyze and interpret evidence, provide important feedback to learners, and support learners toward self-assessment. These skills are more than analytical. Teachers need to consider learner needs—and these needs go beyond simply identifying and meeting content or skill-centred learning goals. Because assessment has an emotional impact, direct conversations with any learner must be sensitive and constructive—for example, one must consider how a student best takes in information. Even if very strong relationships are built between teachers and learners, these relationships remain power-laden. Conversations, as ongoing and edifying as they might be, never can ignore the fact that the teacher is the teacher, and the learner is not.

Thus, teachers need always to be consciously and cautiously aware of the impact that their comments, their feedback, and the grades they give can have on learners' confidence and enthusiasm for learning. Do these comments and actions encourage or erode a learner's sense of progress? Teachers should be honest, but constructive in the feedback they give. At any level, comments that focus on the content of *work* rather than the value of a *person* are more constructive. Appropriate feedback can aid learning and increase motivation. These are skills that teachers may need to learn more about to implement them effectively.

5. Assessment **for** *learning should consider the importance of individual learner motivations*

At the heart of high-stakes standardized testing, or even central to tests that evaluate an entire class using a single instrument, is the implicit belief that learners should be compared and evaluated *against* one another. For adults, however, most learning is individual. Adult learners tend to care about their own needs, interests, and—appropriate to this—success. They hope to succeed. They desire that their learning is personally relevant. They certainly care about their colleagues, but they "get it" that their colleagues—while sharing a learning experience—are really other people who likely have different skills and different needs than their own.

Thus, for most adult learners, evaluation and assessment is personal and not comparative or even competitive. And, learning happens best when sought by an empowered actor who assumes personal responsibility for her or his own education. A teacher can create a space for learning, but a learner ultimately learns alone. Learning is personal.

Assessment for learning outlines how teachers can encourage learning by creating conditions that foster individual learner motivation and success outside the context of comparison and competition. The most effective way to create conditions that empower individual learners is to emphasize achievement or even progress, rather than failure. Assessment that utilizes comparison with others—a sort of "look what happens if you don't drink your milk" approach, comparing a learner to others who have been more successful—is more likely to produce jealousy or shame and less likely to motivate learners. However, when compared to those who have done worse, comparisons might produce a prideful and haughty personality, and lead one to be less inclined to work on one's own achievement. Comparisons seldom produce true winners. In either case, comparison is less appropriate for learning than for buying a car.

Personal failure, as noted earlier, can lead learners to withdraw from learning experiences where they feel they are "less than good" learners. Optimum learning requires optimum motivation; and, rather than being a detriment, assessment methods can indeed enhance motivations when these methods create powerful insights a learner might use to negotiate a personal plan toward learning. Assessment should help protect learner autonomy, provide sensible choices, offer constructive feedback, and create further opportunities for self-directed and self-motivated learning.

6. Assessment **for** *learning should build a commitment to learning goals and an understanding of the criteria used to assess these goals*

If effective learning is to take place, learners need to understand what they are trying to achieve—and they must learn *why* they might "want" to achieve it. Understanding and commitment follows when learners help decide their own goals and identify the criteria for assessing progress toward and ultimately achievement of these goals. Teachers who regularly communicate reasons for assessment as well as assessment criteria help learners make better choices about how to reach their learning goals.

Note the term *regularly*. Often both teachers and students have lived in educational environments where there has been little, if any, formative assessment—the students do the work and the teachers evaluate that work once it is handed in, seldom giving substantive reasons or even comments for their grades. Students complain, but seldom confront or even ask questions of teachers. Assessment for learning differs from this because of the ongoing conversational relationships built both between teachers and learners (so that there should be no surprises in final evaluations), and between learners and their own goals (so there should be no ambiguity about what a learner is striving to achieve and why).

Perhaps these relationships are the most positive aspect of assessment for learning as a pedagogical idea. The process is almost *counselling* towards success, and involves regular discussions between learners and teachers—with discussions providing opportunities for encouragement and advice. Communication should focus upon ends that learners understand, provide examples of how learning goals can be met, offer opportunities for practice, engage learners in their own self-assessment, and finally establish and build productive relationships between learners and their teachers.

7. *Learners should receive constructive guidance about how to improve*

Contrary to some opinions, assessment for learning is not completely learner-centred. In fact, there is little revolution in curricula knowledge, skills, or even values. What has changed is the process by which a learner moves toward the "traditional" goals of the curriculum. A teacher becomes a dynamic partner helping learners move toward these goals by providing information and guidance. Learners use this needed information and guidance to construct suitable plans that move them toward their own learning goals.

Simply telling learners that they are not measuring up or are "missing the mark" does not help them make adjustments to their learning; learners need constructive help planning and implementing their learning. Teachers can help learners in three ways. First, they can help learners understand their own strengths and provide advice about how to develop these strengths. Second, they can provide clear and constructive insights about learner weaknesses or skills gaps and how these weaknesses or gaps might be overcome. Third, they can provide opportunities for learners to improve their work by providing feedback and encouragement throughout the learning process in ways that help the learners become self-aware and self-directed in their learning.

8. Assessment for learning helps learners self-assess their own work

Self-assessment is a "big picture" goal. For lifelong learning to take place—and by this we mean learning that occurs beyond the scrutiny of caring, teachers—learners must become habitually and consciously reflective, honest about their own abilities, and able to manage their own goals. These are traits of independent learning. Once learners have gained these traits and have experienced success, they will naturally seek new learning projects (both big and small), gain new skills, engage new knowledge, and create new understandings and self-identities.

But, without honest self-reflection learning beyond the classroom can grind to a halt. Learners need to develop the ability to engage in self-reflection and to identify the next steps in their learning. Often learning these abilities requires sagacious coaching by caring teachers who work to equip learners with a desire and capacity to take charge of their learning. Coaching is different than teaching or different even than providing regular insightful feedback; coaching asks questions and helps learners find their own answers while also developing self-assessment skills. Assessment for learning teaches the learners how to ask themselves these leading questions and to how to find the answers.

9. Assessment for learning should honour a wide range of learner achievements

Sometimes we forget how difficult and complex learning can be, especially if almost everyone we know seems able to learn. Learning can be especially complex for those who have experienced little success with learning. For learning to occur, the head is obviously involved—but so too are the heart and the stomach, perhaps especially for adult learners. The heart is a seat of the will and involves following through on long-term goals and holding onto the will power to work toward achieving them. As the saying goes, "if your heart's not in it," achievement of any intellectual goal is often challenging. But the stomach can rule too, as in the case of the ancient Hebrew story of Esau, who traded his inheritance to his younger twin brother Jacob for a bowl of lentil soup—such was his hunger. Learners can make similar short-sighted decisions if they become frustrated, embarrassed, or experience what seem to them to be devastating defeats on their learning path. They grow hungry for a sense of satisfaction and can make poor decisions as a result.

Good teachers know there is more to learning than moving content from books to brains. Thus, assessment for learning should become an opportunity to enhance a learner's opportunity to learn in a wide area of educational activity. The goal is simple: learning independence. Assessment for learning should help all learners find the intrinsic motivation and self-knowledge to achieve their best and to celebrate their efforts and their accomplishments.

Models for Assessment *for* Learning

Two models seem appropriate for assessment for learning and will be discussed briefly. One model comes from the thinking of Richard J. Stiggins (2002). This model is organized around four big ideas, adapted here for adult learning.

Idea 1: There is a difference between assessment *of* learning and assessment *for* learning. Teachers should learn and practice the difference.

Idea 2: High quality assessment is assessment that yields accurate (and helpful) results. Teachers should come to understand the results they are seeking.

Idea 3: Learner involvement in their own assessment improves motivation and learning. Teachers must ask, "How can I best involve my learners in their own assessment?"

Idea 4: Learning is a team activity. The goal of a learning team is to work together to (a) think about assessment, (b) consider new ideas, (c) shape these ideas into applications, (d) try new things, always observing and drawing insights from what works or does not work, and (e) work together to synthesize and share tentative conclusions with all those involved in the process.

A second model comes from the work of Grant Wiggins and Jay McTighe (1998) who have aligned assessment with learning by what they call "backwards" design. They suggest that educators be led through a three-step process:

1. Identify the desired results (enduring understandings, essential questions, knowledge and skills).

2. Determine acceptable evidence (performance tasks, evaluations, self-assessment, and a wide variety of prompted and unprompted evidence).

3. Plan learning experiences (sequences of experience with instruction).

Wiggins and McTighe see a difference between knowledge and understanding. They see the goal as understanding, which includes six activities: explanation, interpretation, application, perspective, empathy, and self-knowledge. And, they ask teachers to engage in three questions that lead toward this "Understanding by Design." The questions are:

1. What is worthy and requiring of understanding?

2. What is evidence of understanding?

3. What learning experiences and teaching promote understanding, interest, and learner's goals?

A Final Thought...

Assessment *for* learning is based on different principles that seem to help learners become better able to move towards appropriate learning goals and eventual independence in leaving. Assessment works best when it acts to support learners' personal learning and improvement. Teachers take an active and dynamic role in such assessment by posing questions that encourage learner's consideration, thoughtfulness, and self-assessment instead of encouraging the seeking of "right" answers. The self-assessment that results helps learners gain control over their own learning.

Assessment *for* learning works best when it is given regularly, over the breadth of the learning experience. Good feedback is not always grades. Formative feedback without grades helps learners know that they can succeed. Finally, teachers need to ask: "How is what I am doing helping learners become better able to learn?" This central question places the focus of assessment where it should be—on the learners. Successful learning is, after all, about teaching learners how to learn, not about teaching content to learners.

16

Assessing Online Distance Learning

Working Together When Apart

The Internet has changed the face of learning, and learning institutions have adapted their courses to follow these changes. This chapter offers a variety of suggestions both about teaching and evaluating online learning. We say "teaching *and* evaluating" together because, perhaps even more than in face-to-face learning (where over time we have developed ways of being together as teacher and learner), online learning requires teachers' concerted efforts to connect learners with content and process. If learning is to be successfully evaluated, much time is needed to set up the learning space online.

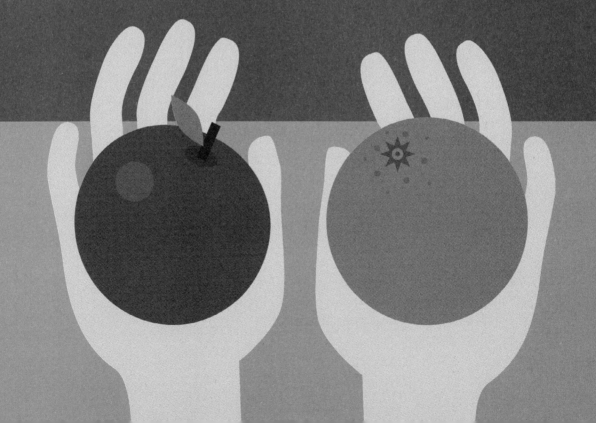

Adult education is changing, even at our most traditional academic institutions. Many colleges and universities have invested financial and human resources into alternative-delivery programming. Often called online teaching, distance education, or *online delivery*, these academic programs or courses are generally offered to learners using computer technologies; therefore interaction between learners and teachers is not face-to-face. Online delivery's unprecedented popularity and growth in public and private institutions around the world attests to the competitive culture of our society where staying up-to-date in one's field demands that learners seek constant professional development, and where the cost effectiveness of quality programming for those learners is paramount to institutional survival. Innovations in responsive learning and assessment in online learning are essential. This chapter addresses the question: How does the emerging opportunity of online delivery shape assessment?

> "The great end of life is not knowledge but action."
> – Thomas Huxley

Online Distance Learning

A discussion of online learning requires a number of steps. First, it is crucial to define what we mean by online delivery of education—the field is vast and complex. Second, we need to identify the players in online learning and assessment—the institutions, the learners, and the teachers, and briefly explore how each might be affected by online delivery. Third, we will explore what can be assessed online and share some strategies that have worked for several institutions.

Online delivery refers to a learning institution's teaching of courses or programs over the Internet and sometimes at a *distance*.

How Do We Define Online Delivery?

Until recently, online delivery was generally confined to a few variations of text-based *asynchronous* activities. However, today the variety of delivery choices is great—including interactive self-study CD- and DVD-based courseware; computer-mediated communications, such as chat rooms, emails, and blogs; electronic online testing; instructor-led two-way global telecommunications; and group web-based forums using *synchronous* or *asynchronous* interactive media such as Blackboard or WebCT.

Using all or some of these tools, courses can be offered entirely at a distance, largely targeted to learners who cannot access traditional campuses or professional development resources. Other courses use

The term **synchronous** is used to describe events or activities that occur at the same time. In online learning, there might be events that are synchronous–where all learners are asked to meet online at a similar time.

The term **asynchronous** is used to describe events or activities that occur at different times. One advantage of online learning is that a learner can access an Internet course at a variety of times that suit his or her work, travel, or circumstances.

more "distributed" learning models that combine elements of an on-campus portion with online materials and discussion forums. Others use traditional hard copies of reading materials—texts or course packs with "drop boxes" where assignments are downloaded, completed, and then uploaded to meet an established deadline.

Clearly, online learning is a huge and dynamic project and worthy of an entire text unto itself. For our purposes, however, we will focus on the issue of assessment within web-centric *synchronous* (happening at the same time) or *asynchronous* (happening at different times) interactive learning, delivered exclusively online, where the teachers and learners may never meet face-to-face. Assessments in most web-centric programs focus on personal written assignments, online participation, group dialogue via threaded postings, and self, peer, and instructor assessments of each learners' contributions and reflections on readings.

Synchronous learning can occur in online delivery when students are asked to "tune in" to a learning format at the same time so they might interact. A number of different formats—Skype or Elluminate for example—allow synchronous learning to take place. The conversations that occur in synchronous learning occur within a specified time period—much like speaking on the phone. In asynchronous learning, learners are not required to be present to each other at the same time. For example, they might post a response that sits in WebCT until another learner—perhaps days later—responds to that posting. Conversations can be carried out, but over a longer period of time—much like writing letters or email to each other.

Some Problems with Online Delivery

Online delivery is not without difficulties. Some problems include changes to program structures, administrative support needs, traditions of knowledge, learner readiness issues (both psychologically and technologically), how learners must rethink their workspace and workload, unimagined logistical issues, technical infrastructure needs, and more specifically for the purposes of this chapter, other teaching issues relating to changes to evaluation processes.

With reference to evaluation, in the end the goals of all good alternative-delivery learning are strikingly similar to the goals of more "traditional" learning: it must employ high educational standards. Similar to other delivery systems, online delivery uses a variety of instructional assessment methods and materials to develop effective communication and to honestly and fairly evaluate a learner's progress toward appropriate educational goals. Online learning differs in the need to adapt to new contingencies, new learner–teacher relationships, and the new technologies employed in program delivery. The *distance* of online distance education must be consciously mediated, especially when delivering learner feedback.

Who Is Choosing Online Delivery?

The move to online delivery is not so much *away* from traditional higher education but *towards* using new technologies that potentially increase enrollments by accessing a new group of students with different learning needs and expectations. The institutional inducements are an increase in revenue without an increase in capital costs, program flexibility, and an increase in accessibility. But, the transition from traditional to online delivery of academic programs is not without growing pains and a steep learning curve when it comes to assessment. Issues currently surfacing in the literature question maintaining academic rigor and an institute's reputation for high standards; assuring validity and reliability in online testing and assessment; measuring learners' interpersonal contributions;

Why Learners Choose Online Delivery

1. Access to the course no matter where you live or when you work.

2. Freedom to self-manage the pace of completion and the timing of the work.

3. Opportunities to learn from and interact synchronously or asynchronously with online materials and with teachers, other learners, peers, and online experts.

4. A sense of belonging to a community of like-minded learners. Although one typically works alone, online learning is less isolating than traditional text-based correspondence courses or modules of the past. There are opportunities to interact with others globally.

5. Learning can be applied to one's context and discussed with peers. Learners might have greater ability to apply their learning in real-life contexts. Most face-to-face learning environments use simulations or case studies for instructional purposes instead of issues and contexts more personally relevant to each learner.

6. Online learning reduces a learner's financial and time challenges, such as reducing costs and expenses of travelling, taking time off work, or being away from one's responsibilities.

7. New library technologies promise to make research searchable, replicable, highly communicative, and fast.

and creating effective online learning communities that engage learners and make assessment clear and manageable.

One might ask: Why do this at all? The answer perhaps lies in one of the biggest reasons for pursuing online delivery of educational programs—the learner demands it. When universities and researchers poll online learners to find out why they choose online delivery, there are several common reasons including access and flexibility.

A New Role for Teachers

As a teacher, your experience has probably been in face-to-face teaching, but in online classrooms, a teacher's role is less focused on "teaching" and more on creating a learning space that enhances meaningful relationships and facilitates discussion towards learning goals. The teacher's main tasks centre on guiding learners by crafting good assignments (problems to be solved) and by asking questions to help learners develop their own insights about what is being studied. These tasks, because of the nature of online learning, include a great deal of *coaching* and *guiding*.

In addition to accessing coursework and postings, most learners can access learning materials and resources from the Internet no matter where they live. For example, in researching an assignment, a student can access almost any online university, email and dialogue with experts in the field, or tap into live video coverage of a given topic from anywhere in the world. In fact, one hazard of online learning is the sheer volume of those resources, which can overwhelm even seasoned web users. Online teachers have to scaffold course content and help learners become strategic as they critique, negotiate, and navigate online learning resources used for assignments. Part of a teacher's task, therefore, is to *help learners critically assess* valuable information from less valuable information.

Stodel, Thompson, and MacDonald (2006) noted that online learning and assessment requires teachers to consciously create and support a cognitive, social, and teaching presence. **Cognitive presence** includes an expectation that supportive structures guide and enhance critical thinking, reflection, and rigorous dialogue. **Social presence** means learners are intentionally connected using online conversations—they're encouraged to get to know each other so that they might build enough trust and courage to converse openly about academic disagreements. Finally, online education needs a **teaching presence** that includes designing a

Cognitive presence refers to a teacher's or another person's online and directive influence with learners.

Social presence refers to the close relationship that can be built between teachers and learners. Having a social presence helps bridge the distance of an online space.

The more a teacher can be "seen" in the online environment, the greater that teacher's **teaching presence**.

space with thought about those instructional and organizational course structures that facilitate learning most effectively. Teaching presence also means that teachers are present, provide timely formative feedback, thoughtful responses, and guidance when needed. In face-to-face classrooms, teachers can simply watch and listen; however, online environments work best when teachers are vigilant and responsive to learner inquiries and learners know that the teacher really is "there."

Assessment is always more effective when there is a strong relationship between teachers and learners. This is especially true in assessing online courses. In their model, Rourke, Anderson, Archer, and Garrison (2001) subsume teaching presence into three critical teacher roles. First, teaching is the design and organization of the learning experience that takes place both before the establishment of the learning community and during its operation. Second, teaching involves devising and implementing activities to encourage discourse between and among students so that successful peer assessment might take place, and between the teacher and the student in both formative and final assessments. Third, teaching goes beyond moderating the learning experiences when the teacher adds subject matter expertise through a variety of forms of direct instruction. Each of these three roles, when done well, helps establish an infrastructure that supports online assessment.

The Nature of Online Assessment and Learning

It would be true, but less than helpful, to simply state, "Online learning differs from face-to-face learning." The bigger questions are: how does it differ, and what needs to be done about these differences? One important difference is that online learning is *constructive*. Constructivism is a theory of learning that believes we construct meaning using knowledge structures we currently possess; in other words, any new learning fits into what a learner already knows. When constructivism grounds learning, learners are supported to learn and self-evaluate by setting their own direction. Constructivist teaching tends to be holistic, collaborative in method, and encourages, accepts, and builds upon learner initiatives. That is, the learner is charged with constructing personal knowledge—with the aid of a teacher. Because it is constructive, online learning is both learner-centred and community-centred, and therefore, so is online assessment.

Mediating the Distance

Clearly, this chapter is about online assessment—not about how to teach online. However, experience suggests that there is an important correspondence between teaching and learning. Second, as noted before, mediating the distance in online delivery is an extremely important issue. Third, there is a direct link between how learners understand an assignment and how learners respond to those assignments. Therefore, teachers are cautioned to be especially careful when teaching an online course. We recommend the following suggestions to help clarify assignments and create a positive space for online coursework and evaluation.

- **Establish clear expectations**
  Because you do not have the luxury of clarifying messages in front of the whole class, clarity at the outset is important. Be clear about course expectations, participation requirements, communication standards, and what students can expect from you as a facilitator online. And, be ready for questions. Remember that online work can be frightening; students, especially on their first assignment, have little idea what a teacher expects and don't have the luxury of checking things out until they reach a comfort level.

- **Establish rapport**
  If you have not met the learners in person, they will want to know what you are like. A common practice is to start with introductions as you would in a face-to-face course. These can be informal or "to the point"—the idea is to let learners know your expectations and the context in which your responses will be based.

- **Constructive feedback**
  Purposeful feedback is paramount in online courses. Learners must "get it" using only a few clues (without body language) to test their understandings. Nor can they look around the room and see if heads are nodding or people seem perplexed. Good feedback does more than encourage the student; it provides needed structures and invites them to probe, question, ask for clarification, etc. Model good communication, and learners will likely pick up the patterns and start using them with each other.

- **Gauging the group**
  Teachers must monitor the progress of online discussions as they would face-to-face discussions by summarizing, moderating, guiding, prompting, mediating, or problem-solving. Creating good discussion questions and clear expectations about the length of posts helps alleviate the need to constantly track learners. Online discussions can become especially rich if teachers or learners ask metacognitive, reflective, or evaluation questions.

- **Generosity of spirit**
  Assessment at a distance is difficult. Like any educational experience, learners want to know how they have done. It is helpful to begin all feedback positively, especially if the general tone of the feedback is positive. Often, learners misread what are meant to be positive comments because the teacher did not begin with sufficient praise. If an assignment has been done well, be clear at the beginning that the work was strong.

The Purpose of Online Assessment

In many ways, online assessment should follow the learning and assessment theories one would expect in face-to-face classrooms. Both require sound pedagogical reasons for choosing a method of assessment. Second, teachers must be explicit about what learners are expected to produce. Providing examples, modelling appropriate standards, and collaborating on outcomes with learners are assessment practices that work both online and face-to-face. Quality work must be expected: including appropriate grammar, punctuation, sentence structure, and communication of ideas. Sadly, cheating—often copying from another online source—can occur and must be watched for. Finally, good assessment must consider the diverse learning styles and learning needs of students.

Because the purpose of assessment is to motivate learning, online teachers must ask and answer three assessment questions: (1) assess *what?* (2) assess *how?* and (3) assess *how often?* The distance between learners and teachers makes the *how often* an important consideration. There is a direct relationship between how present faculty members are in online courses and how willing students are to post and engage their work. If online courses are to work well, teachers need to have a course presence—that is, they need to interact often with learners, through formative assessment and through ongoing conversations.

While online assessment should follow the same theories, it does differ from face-to-face assessment. First, assessment opportunities are more frequent online because learners can simultaneously communicate with each other and with the instructor. Second, online courseware provides tracking tools that allow instructors to tally the number of times learners login to a course, post, and engage others' posts. These necessary actions are easy to observe and simple to count. Third, it is difficult for instructors not to be swayed by personal biases when grading, biases based on factors such as status indicators and interpersonal communication style—these biases are often less pronounced in online settings. Fourth, the decentralized nature of computer-mediated communication classrooms shifts the focus from teacher to learner by demanding greater learner interaction and participation.

What Can Be Assessed Online?

Quality online learning provides opportunities for both formative and summative assessments that involve the teacher, learner, and peer expertise. Perhaps, most importantly, these assessments encourage learners to assess their own learning reflectively. Unlike traditional face-to-face classrooms, few assessments in an online course include test-taking where learners produce "correct" answers. In online teaching, the space and process of gaining knowledge is viewed as crucial to the product. Assessment is based on learner observation, learner work, and the willingness of learners to participate and to communicate well.

Online assessments can be sorted into four categories: (1) social and communication skills, (2) literacy skills, (3) content knowledge, and (4) work skills. Translating these into grades depends upon a teacher's priorities. Essentially, four things can be assessed online:

1. Traditional assignments: because high standards are crucial to both face-to-face and online courses, the quality of learner work should not change to fit this different format. In other words, teachers assess research papers posted online as they would grade them in hard copy. Obvi-

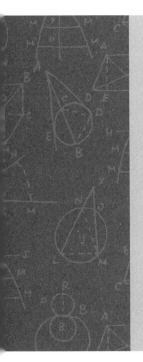

An Example of an Online Program's Assignment

The University of Alberta's Masters of Educational Studies (MES) in Leadership and Educational Improvement program was started in 2003. Learners are usually post-secondary teachers, leaders, or management—although a number of other working professionals take the program (nurses, medical doctors, pastors, etc.). The program begins with an intensive three-week summer residency, followed by an online course during the Fall term and another online course during the winter term. A second summer residency is again followed by online courses in the fall term and winter terms.

The first online course, is a traditional "History of Education Curriculum" course. One course assignment asks learners to read an article from a course pack, and post a 500-word review of their thoughts about this article. Postings generate online discussion that engages other students and faculty. The results of these discussions differ from face-to-face courses, perhaps because in a face-to-face course teachers somehow lead and shape responses.

Specifically surprising to the first-time online teachers were the learners' postings after reading a theory article by Maxine Green, a philosopher of education. Rather than engage the article philosophically, as one might expect in a traditional setting, the learners posted a series of "practical" classroom suggestions from Green's writing. The learner's were doing what they knew how to do—as constructivist adults, they framed what Green wrote in terms of their own experience, insights, and needs. Their practical, pragmatic classroom insights organized Green's thoughts in practical, pragmatic ways. Such an experience shows one way an online environment is shaped by learners.

ously, a teacher using a revision tool in a word processing program works through a different process than a teacher who grades a paper at the kitchen table. But, good work is good work. As a result, critical thinking and other high-level skills can be assessed using essays or critiques of readings, and comprehension can be demonstrated via online postings and other written assignments. A teacher can assess grammar, organization, sentence structure, the accuracy of citations, the correct use of borrowed material, etc. Because essays have the potential to elicit complex intellectual behaviour, they are recommended to online instructors. It is wise to develop suitable rubrics to guide learners and to communicate expectations.

2. Communication: quality online learning depends upon good communication patterns. Students need to "post" assignments; they need to email others; they need to share their ideas in conversation with colleagues; and they need to be present in different ways than in face-to-face courses. It is possible to hide in a face-to-face class—attending but not truly participating. Hiding is not so possible online. One has to put one's ideas "out there" for others to read and respond to and these posts are assessed on several levels. Assessing the quality of dialogue, scholarly arguments (utilizing the readings assigned), or the ability to flesh out concepts and ideas provide evidence that a learner has read and understood the text. A successful online dialogue requires teacher facilitation, starting with examples of quality assignments. The quality of communications can also be measured by self-evaluations, peer-evaluations for individual and group projects, and instructor evaluations. A good thing about online dialogues is that they remain on the course management system, as an archive of student work *and* feedback offered.

Giving clear and complete directions and modelling effective online postings is critical for creating effective teaching presence. If participation is a formal and assessed course requirement, developing and using an explicit assessment framework is essential. However, such assessment can be time-consuming. Teachers might ask learners to create a portfolio of their postings as evidence of their growth during the class. This assessment helps learners make quality postings and moves the responsibility from teacher to learner, a solution that saves teacher time and helps learners.

Rubrics for Online Assessment

Assignment	Assessment
1) Learners individually read an article and post a response to that article.	1a. Was the article read and a response posted?
	1b. What was the quality (form and content) of that response?
2. Learners read community postings and engage in collegial conversations about the topics addressed.	2a. Did the learner address the topic rigorously?
	2b. Did the learner post appropriate and community-building responses?
	2c. What was the quality (form and content) of the response?
3. Learners individually research a topic and write a paper. This paper is submitted via an online drop box.	3a. Was the paper well-researched?
	3b Was the written work of high quality (formal conventions and content)?
4. Learners contribute to class discussions.	4a. Did learners participate?
	4b. Were contributions constructive to colleagues?
	4c. Did comments add content to the dialogue?
	4d. Were contributions frequent enough?

Example Rubric for Posting in an Online Course

5: Postings reflect thoughtful engagement with course readings and colleagues' postings

Postings consistently show reflection on and critical response to colleagues' postings

Postings are relevant, of high quality, and contribute to class understanding of course content

Postings show regular and consistent engagement throughout the length of the module

4: Postings reflect engagement with course readings and colleagues' postings

Postings show reflection on and response to others' ideas and questions

Postings are relevant and contribute to the class's understanding of the course content

Postings show consistent engagement throughout the length of the module

3: Postings generally reflect engagement with course readings and colleagues' postings

Postings generally show reflection on and response to others' ideas and questions

Postings are usually relevant and contribute to the class's understanding of the course content

Postings show generally consistent engagement throughout the length of the module

2: Postings reflect some engagement with course readings and colleagues' postings

Postings are sporadic and/or inconsistent—"last minute" participation is common

Quality and relevance of postings is inconsistent

1: Postings reflect very little engagement with course readings and/or colleagues' postings

Minimal participation in the discussion

Postings seldom contribute to class learning

Adapted from rubrics developed for the MES program at the University of Alberta.

3. Community-building skills: communication between strangers differs from communication between friends. Online conversations require an especially considerate posture because face-to-face relationships are not present. An online comment misunderstood or offered thoughtlessly can be devastating. Somehow, the online nature of communication can empower a word with increased "hurtfulness."

Contributions to one's community and other's learning can either be counted for frequency or rated for quality. When rating online contributions, clear criteria and quality exemplars are required to copy from or this gets messy during evaluations—not all students are equally skilled at peer assessment.

4. Learning Independence: online learning doesn't work well if learners do not engage in their work independently. No one is there—except perhaps one's immediate online colleagues—to force a learner to post or to respond to a posting. As a result, learners need to be independent. For example, if learners are absent due to experiencing "technical difficulties," it is up to them to contact help desks or others to solve their issues. Online delivery, in many ways, requires a self discipline and accountability that isn't always required to succeed in face-to-face classrooms.

In summary, traditional academic skills remain important in assessing online learning. These skills include literacy, writing and editing, finding and accessing articles, following directions, and the established documentation style guides. However, community-building and knowledge-building skills are as important if online learning is to work smoothly. These skills include the will power to work to deadlines, the ability and desire to be collaborative and respectful in postings and other online interactions, and the will to act with responsibility for one's own learning.

How to Assess Online Delivery

Providing Feedback to Students Online

Thanks in part to the growing phenomenon of technology in our lives (instant messaging, email, VoIP, and cell phones) many of us live and learn with expectations of both giving and getting "instant responses" to our electronically submitted inquiries and learning needs. The same is true of online learners. However, because online courses lack the informal

Time Management in Online Assessment

Creating "teaching presence" is a challenging and important task. One challenge for teachers is the weight of time. Online delivery simply takes more teacher time and energy than face-to-face teaching and assessment.

Although timely feedback is important to help learners grow academically and stay motivated in online courses, striving to provide instant assessment feedback on assignments leads to unrealistic learner expectations.

It is wise to post and adhere to reasonable timelines so learners gain realistic expectations. As a teacher, posting realistic timelines helps you avoid the trap of feeling guilty that you do not provide 24-hour-a-day feedback.

Although it is wise to regularly check online activity and to support learners, it is possible for online teachers to lose their personal lives to the activity of online monitoring and assessment.

"quick" comments between teachers and learners, almost every communication about assessment seems formal. Students rightfully expect quality feedback—regular feedback that allows them to assess, at a distance, how they are doing in the course. Adult education, particularly at the graduate level, has a tradition of providing quality feedback, even if that feedback required patience to wait for a face-to-face appointment. Today, however, adult education is no longer immune to the demands of a culture of instant response. Since the advent of online programs, learners expect teachers to give prompt feedback.

Providing feedback to learners in an online environment presents a challenge. With complicating elements such as shifting demographics, distant geographical locations (and time zones), diverse ethnic, cultural or contextual backgrounds, a broad range of technical expertise and levels of accessibility among one's students, providing meaningful feedback in a timely manner requires a great deal of skill. Fortunately, there is a variety of ways to respond quickly to learners. The most predominant strategies for providing feedback to online learners are:

- Email
- Chat rooms and discussion boards
- Postings
- Assignments
- Telephone calls

Email: Perhaps the most commonly used and preferred form of online communication between learners and teachers is email. Email has many benefits, but also some downfalls. Benefits include privacy of feedback, time to form thoughtful responses to questions, an ability to include helpful links and informational pages online or to attach documents and learning materials, and an asynchronous nature that allows teachers and learners to answer emails day or night from any Internet connection. Emails also provide ongoing records of conversations and student progress.

One downside of email as a feedback tool between teachers and learners occurs when a teacher is working with large numbers of learners. Learners can generate volumes of email, especially if they are truly engaged with the work. Often faculty members dislike teaching online courses because they are expected to respond to each email and, because a course has deadlines, to respond quickly. As a result, the volume of emails can overwhelm instructors. Creative strategies can include:

- Automated email responses to acknowledge receipt of the learner's email, note that the teacher is away, or note when a response might be expected—these help avoid learner frustration or uncertainty that he or she is being "received."

- Sorting, delegating, or forwarding certain emails to an assistant or a designated responder.

- Moving to a more "one response hits all" type medium such as online discussion boards, chat rooms, or online postings, or group emails. This is very helpful if many individual students are emailing with very common questions.

Chat rooms and discussion boards: Chat rooms or discussion boards can be exceedingly useful for giving general information to an entire class and can be a space for informal communications such as news about learners, introductions, announcements (birth, engagements, etc), photos, and work-related questions (looking for advice from other learners). The variety of information on discussion boards is endless, and they help keep non-work related aspects of the community from "littering" the work space of a course management system.

Older Learners, Younger Learners, and Social Understandings

The differences between older learners and younger learners show up online. In general, older learners are more inclined to traditional learning styles, which include narrower and deeper communication patterns and social networks. Specifically, older learners are at home with individual assignments, individual assessments upon those assignments, and often are more inclined to keep to themselves. It is perhaps how they have been "raised" academically.

Younger learners are more inclined to group work, group assessments, and have broader and shallower communication patterns and social networks. They are inclined to work in and be at home in groups.

Often we think of culture as a function of nationality or even race or gender; however, it would be unwise not to account for cultural differences in learning histories. The inclinations of learners towards particular social patterns will be constructed online and will show themselves through social interactions and behaviours between people. All these behaviours are based conditioning, social positions, and roles. In short, different people will experience online learning in different ways.

As a collective unconsciousness between learners grows, learners will build shared meanings through communication. Our communications, even online, reveal everything we are and subconsciously come to identify us with those people we understand better. An understanding of these socially-constructed relationships can help teachers understand what they see online and consider this in their assessment choices.

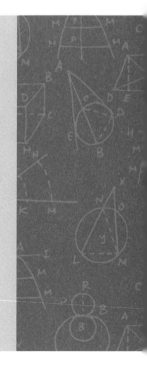

Postings: Most asynchronous and synchronous e-learning environments utilize some form of online interaction software/courseware known as course management systems (i.e. WebCT/Vista or Blackboard) where postings can be made at any time of day or night and others can respond to these conversation "threads." Using community postings to provide online information is effective because other learners directly or indirectly gain from the feedback as well. The more present an instructor is on these postings, the more energized these posted discussions will become.

The teacher's job is to monitor, prod, and synthesize discussions. If a common theme or question emerges from emails or a point is made that would benefit all learners, it makes sense to post the question in a public forum. Important information deserves a new general posting or thread as opposed to tucking it among the threaded conversations where some learners may not find it. Having someone—the teacher or a group of learners—summarize key points online after a lengthy discussion helps "close" a conversation thread so learners can move to other topics. One aspect of asynchronous postings is the "on-going" value of conversations. Peers can offer insights or helpful information beyond what a teacher can provide if questions are posted for feedback in the public domain. Learners also learn by teaching others and asking for learner feedback (with instruction on providing constructive feedback) which helps reduce teacher workload and encourage learners' skills of synthesis.

Assignments: Once assignments have been posted on a course management system or have been sent as email attachments, they are graded in ways similar to any assignment. However, the format of working with computer files changes grading. Usually, academic papers submitted online are graded using a *comments and revision tool* such as Microsoft Word's Track Changes feature, and written comments are embedded on learners' documents and assignments. These comments and highlights are usually editorial and substantial. A teacher is wise to self-schedule multiple shorter times for grading online assignments. Working on a computer screen can become uncomfortable and is best done in short periods.

Phone calls: Phone calls, if appropriate, are useful when there is confusion or frustration. It is often easier to simplify a complex issue over the phone than risk escalating emails or online postings. Sometimes the written word, with its lack of dynamic range, cannot alleviate complicated situations. If emotions are high, it can be difficult to get to the heart of an issue in a written (and somewhat public) forum.

Guidelines for Online Feedback

Teachers need to consider how students will "read" feedback or make sense of a lack of feedback in an online environment. Typically, because the online environment lacks visual clues and is open to misinterpretation, more consideration is needed to keep learning moving forward and to help learners feel empowered and not frustrated. A number of guidelines apply to providing online feedback:

Guideline 1: Feedback is needed. One of the biggest issues in online delivery is a "perceived" lack of feedback. This is especially true when giving or grading assignments. Learner's most common complaints centre on the following question: How can I improve when I don't get feedback on what needs improving? Instructor presence online helps online learning work well.

Guideline 2: Feedback must be prompt. Because assignments are time sensitive and learners often balance work, home, and learning, waiting for feedback is painful for learners who may be on a tight timeline and need clarity to move on.

Guideline 3: Feedback needs to be constructive and instructive. Because online learning lacks the clues present in face-to-face learning, it is necessary to *consider sensitivities first* and *content second*. Receptive learners are more willing to consider critique than those who feel thumped. Instruction must include substantial instructive feedback—suggesting positive improvements or leading learners to online resources or other sources for their learning is very helpful.

Guideline 4: Clarify that learners have understood—silence does not mean a message has been received and comprehended. Because it is easy to "lose" learners (in several ways), it is wise to double check that messages have both been received and understood. In all assignments, it helps when teachers provide direction for learners—necessary links, resources, clear directions, and rubrics that outline how assignments will be graded.

Strategies for Providing Effective Online Feedback

The use of tone and language in online learning is a key element in its success. In addition to cultural issues that must be attended to (learners may literally be from other parts of the world or from a variety of social or professional contexts), a positive tone is essential in emails and postings. We might be wearing out a theme, but using "encouragement-first" postings is a thoughtful acceptance that learners do not have non-verbal communications to mediate differences. Using all CAPS looks like you are yelling at your reader, for example. Informality and humour can help, but humour can be misunderstood. The best way to avoid misunderstandings is to involve learners early in the feedback process.

Three Assessment Questions for Online Delivery

1. Assess *what*?

2. Assess *how*?

3. Assess how *often*?

The distance between learners and teachers makes the how often an important consideration.

Celebrating Improvement

Receiving assessments of assignments is a concern for all online adult learners. Most course management systems allow learners to receive grades online in privacy. Focusing on improvement by highlighting "before and after" examples of work can help learners see progress and better understand the criteria against which their work was or will be measured.

Assignments and assessments that build toward a final quality product help learners accept critical feedback and encourage them to see both the process of learning and that learning is a team effort. For example, telling learners that you will be including their final essays in a course anthology allows them to work from initial draft to publishable final draft in a way that helps them see edits and critique as manageable and reasonable. Asking learners to save the first version of assignments and compare it to the final assignment helps them notice and celebrate improvement.

Creating Online Learning Communities

The simple act of showing up and sitting in the same classroom often creates community in face-to-face environments. It is human nature to cluster around classroom commonalities. However, it takes a concerted effort to break the ice, build community, and connect learners when creating online learning communities—you can't see each other and you know little about others unless questions provoke responses. Introductions are absolutely needed to build trust between people who cannot see each other, especially if peer evaluations will be part of a final assessment.

In an online learning context, the creation of an effective online educational community involves the three critical components described earlier: cognitive presence, social presence, and teaching presence (Garrison et al., 2000). Teachers whose actions incarnate flexibility, consideration, and empathy help create a safe space where learners can fully engage an online course. Like face-to-face courses, timely and detailed feedback motivates and enhances learner performance. Learners at a distance, especially if they feel they are working alone, can easily lose motivation if they are not included or invited into discussion.

Although the practice of assessing participation has been debated, online learning works best when a community of learners actively com-

Assessment Frameworks

Terry Anderson (2004) uses Susan Levine's (2002) example of expectations for student contributions to asynchronous online learning courses. She posts the following message for course participants.

1. The instructor will start each discussion by posting one or more questions at the beginning of each week (Sunday or Monday). The discussion will continue until the following Sunday night, at which time the discussion board will close for that week.

2. Please focus on the questions posted. But do bring in related thoughts and material, other readings, or questions that occur to you from the ongoing discussion.

3. You are expected to post at least two substantive messages for each discussion question. Your postings should reflect an understanding of the course material.

4. Your postings should advance the group's negotiation of the material; that is, your contributions should go beyond a "ditto." Some ways you can further the discussion include:

   - expressing opinions or observations. These should be offered in depth and supported by more than personal opinion.

   - making a connection between the current discussion and previous discussions, a personal experience, or concepts from the readings.

   - commenting on or asking for clarification of another student's statement.

   - synthesizing other students' responses.

   - posing a substantive question aimed at furthering the group's understanding.

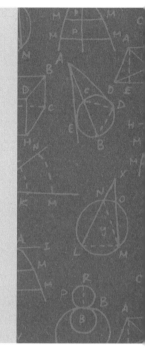

municates. Palloff and Pratt (1999) argue that the social emphasis at the core of constructivist learning demands learning participation, and pragmatics suggests that such participation must be evaluated and rewarded. Furthermore, adult learners are practical. They work hard to balance their time and are unlikely to participate in activities supplemental to core goals and assessment. In our experience, adult learners are not shy to tell us that, if participation is graded as only a minor part of the course, they will simply concentrate on other weightier activities. And yet building an online community is an important skill to learn.

In assessing postings, it seems fair to ask learners to use proper etiquette, including language, typing, and spelling. Requiring high standards of written communication helps learners get into the habit of communicating effectively both online and in an academic or professional world. Asking learners to demonstrate criteria such as responsiveness and understanding helps motivate online discussion and the completion of course readings, while it creates a sense of shared learning and growth.

It is possible at the end of an online course to ask learners to provide self-reflective assessments as part of a course evaluation. A portfolio of online postings helps learners illustrate their contributions to others and the community as a whole, which serves as evidence of their own learning. Such an assignment serves as a synthesis. They could ask colleagues to help them collect illustrations of their contributions. Obviously learners who do not participate will be unable to provide evidence from their own postings.

Whether you assign value to online community building or not, it is important to explicitly state the benefits of participating in online discussions in respectful, articulate, and supportive ways. It is not uncommon for learners who have met in online classes to become lifelong friends and professional colleagues, who continue to support each other in their learning.

A Final Thought...

Perhaps it is sad that formal assessment is needed in online learning. However, without assessment, learner motivation and collaboration withers. Assessment improves engagement and performance and encourages procrastinators and those who lack the natural ability to stay on task. With the increasing number of online classrooms, the question of how to consistently assess online learning has become increasingly pressing. However, providing such feedback through online delivery presents complex challenges that teachers must understand to successfully teach and dialogue with their learners.

As a discipline we must adapt to great technological changes facing our society. Learners and instructors must put forth effort to maintain an effective level of communication. On the plus side, online courses provide a level of confidentiality between learner and instructor that may not be present in a face-to-face course. For a teacher and a learner, online delivery demands thoughtful consideration and mediation if assessment is to be done well.

17

Evaluating Your Practice

Scrutinizing the Scrutinizer

This chapter begins with a pointed question. We encourage you to be honest. Do you regularly set aside time to deliberately and systematically evaluate your own practice? If you are like most teachers, you might have to answer, "No." Read on.

> "Habit is habit, and not to be flung out of the window by any man, but coaxed downstairs a step at a time."
>
> – Mark Twain

Although most of us think about what we do by replaying past incidents and imagining future scenarios, the pressures of adult education often divert us from the investment of time that produces truly reflective teaching. Perhaps we think it's easier to justify using what little free time we have planning new sessions than reflecting on what's past and done.

The irony is that we ask learners to do precisely what we so often fail to do—assess ourselves. If you subscribe to the underlying theme of this book, that our efforts when evaluating learners should be primarily directed at helping them become more self-sufficient, discerning, and committed to evaluating their own performance, then you need to become committed to evaluating your own practice.

In Chapter 2, you spent time exploring your philosophy of teaching and learning as a starting point for planning evaluation approaches best suited for your context as an educator. Now we encourage you to complete the cycle. What new insights await you about growth in your thinking and practice?

This chapter presents suggestions to help you engage in personal, critical reflection of your instructional practice, including evaluation methods. We have borrowed especially from ideas presented by Stephen Brookfield because instructors tell us they are provocative and valuable. You will probably find many of these exercises useful for the learners you work with, and as you make a habit of self-assessment in your own growth, you will uncover more ideas to share with others trying to grow through self-evaluation.

Expanding Self-Evaluation and Growth

When you evaluate yourself, first clarify the purpose of the evaluation. Is it to provide statistics for an institution? To punish or encourage yourself? Or to move towards further growth?

Joe Heimlich and Emmalou Norland (1994) have written a practical, thoughtful guide for instructors interested in self-evaluation: *Developing Teaching Style in Adult Education*. They argue that educators experience two kinds of growth. First, they grow towards congruence; they examine what they've said and done and attempt to align their behaviour with what they believe and value. Second, educators expand; when they achieve competence and internal consistency between actions and beliefs, they expand their style and repertoire. They try new things, which might include rethinking their rationale for doing particular skills. They try different things, which might mean attempting new techniques in familiar situations. They try challenging themselves, which might mean questioning basic approaches. Expansion does not mean the continuous striving to reach an impossible ideal, but growing by spiraling upwards, outwards, or inwards.

In the process of self-evaluation and the resulting growth, there are two cautions—beware of inertia and panic. Inertia comes from familiarity, boredom, feelings of being trapped, or a sense of helplessness in the face of overwhelming information or momentous change. Panic is fuelled by a sense of extreme urgency. This urgency overwhelms many businesses, government departments, and academic institutions. The rush to manufacture and measure "quality" or "total continuous improvement" can throw an institution or person into a madcap frenzy to learn more and faster, to perform better and sooner, to think in the short-term not the long-term, and to think less and do more.

When we understand how inertia and panic block our own growth and that personal change takes much more time than we expect, as educators we can help others to slow down, breathe deeply, and ask essential questions, such as: Why do I do what I do?

Returning to Your Beliefs

When self-evaluating, start by re-focusing on your educational beliefs and philosophy. Here are five quick questions that can help get you started.

1. What is the most important reason you work with learners?

2. What is the most important knowledge learners should be helped to develop?

3. How do you think learning happens? And what role do you play in this process?

4. What does an ideal relationship between the learner and the educator look like? What are the responsibilities of each?

5. What is your vision of the ideal environment for learning and the community of learners?

Six Ideas for Short Notes

1. Describe one concern and one positive response you have to what is happening in class.

2. Describe a connection you've just made or an insight you've just had.

3. Write down the most interesting idea you've heard so far.

4. Describe one thing that's happened that is meaningful to you. Explain why.

5. Write down one question with which you are struggling.

6. If you could make one change right now (to this workshop, your office, your home, and so on), what would it be?

Three Methods for Evaluating Learner Satisfaction

There are several informal methods of collecting learner feedback for individual training sessions.

◆ Have learners write an open letter about what is working well and what isn't.

◆ Ask them, after an activity, "What did you think of it? Were there parts that didn't work for you? Would you like to do it again? What would you change?"

◆ Check in with learners throughout the instructional period by asking, "How are you feeling? Do you want a break now or later? Do you have any comments?" Make sure to give learners time to respond.

Examining Seven Elements of Learning

Learning is an exchange. It is not an educator "doing" something to a learner. Learning is an intermeshed web of at least seven elements: educator, learner, content, environment, institution, learning community, and culture. To evaluate your own practice as an educator, understand how you function within this web. Imagine a specific context in your practice at some point in the recent past. Mentally conjure an instance in which you worked with learners. Step back from it and examine what you see.

1. **Content:**
   Look at the prescribed curriculum and the materials you use with learners. What content are you actually teaching? How important is content in your work with learners? Why do you teach the content you do?

2. **Environment:**
   What are the characteristics and climate of your workplace? How do you influence this sense of place? How much do you believe the environment affects your work with learners?

3. **Teacher:**
   Look at where you stand and how you move among learners; listen to what you say and how much you talk; watch yourself respond to learners; pry into your thoughts and judgments about learners. What is your predominant role in the learning process? To what extent are your own needs the focus of planning, implementing, and evaluating learning? What relationship do you strive to build with learners?

4. **Institution:**
   Look at your institution's traditions, current structures governing the flow of communication and authority, its learning mission, its resource allocations, its standard operating procedures, and its philosophical constraints. To what degree are your beliefs about teaching consistent with the institution's policies and approaches to learning?

5. **Learning Community:**
   Look at the sense of community among the learners. What creates the bond? What kind of learning community is your typical group of learners? What characteristics do they share? How does the sense of community affect their learning?

6. **Learner:**
   What do you expect of the learner? What balance do you achieve between meeting individual learning needs and working with the whole group? How well do you know each learner? What kind of relationship do you have with each? How do you interpret learner responses? How much do you like or respect each learner? How important is it that learners like and respect you?

7. **Culture:**
   An institution is marked by a distinctive culture, defined as behaviour patterns, customs, subtle rules and norms of social interaction, beliefs about what things mean, values about which objects, people, and knowledge are most important, and objects that have their own particular meanings. Within the institution there are sub-cultures, small distinctive groups that share meanings among themselves and expect particular behaviours. Outside the institution is a dominant culture, marked by general understandings and behavioural expectations.

Ask yourself which cultures influence how people act and communicate in your work with learners. Are there colliding cultures in your learning community? What is the dominant culture within your learning community? (What behaviours are rewarded or punished?) What culture does your own behavior belong to and uphold? What cultural behaviours are silenced or excluded in your work with learners?

These seven elements are entwined together and influence one another. Teasing them apart for analysis is not an easy task.

Your answers to these questions reflect your beliefs and values. The next step is to make your actions reflect your enacted beliefs and values. Try to visualize a specific teaching situation in your recent past, then ask yourself to what extent your practice matches your vision of education.

When you have begun to analyze your practice, your beliefs about teaching and learning, and the way you actually work with learners, inevitably you will confront areas you would like to change or enhance. The following are some ways to look at these areas and move towards solutions.

Evaluating Learner Satisfaction

When should we evaluate learner satisfaction? The answer is simple: throughout the program. Too often learners are asked to hurriedly fill out evaluation forms in the closing minutes of a session.

There are three advantages to asking learners to report their thoughts and feelings about what is happening early in the session.

- You remove learners from the rather intimidating position of being summative appraisers for the whole course. They realize they are giving feedback for authentic purposes—to improve the instruction and to report how the instruction is working for them. They can see that their feedback is a valued contribution to the design of the learning experience. As a result, they are likely to provide thoughtful and honest feedback.

- As an instructor, you become more responsive to the learner and less worried about your performance. Frequent evaluation helps you become more used to both positive and constructively critical feedback as an ongoing part of your practice. You become more skilled at interpreting and using feedback, rather than reacting to it as a judgment on your own personal style, effort, and choices.

- Instruction becomes a collaborative partnership between learners and facilitator. You adapt learning activities to the participants' needs as you discover what these are. Participants take more responsibility for owning and voicing their needs. Together you communicate to make decisions about the learning as it unfolds.

Dilemmas Teachers Work Through

Here are general problems that keep some teachers awake at night. How do you work through them? There is no right answer, because every situation is unique.

- How can you find out what your students really think?

- How might you interpret final learner evaluations of your course? How would you deal with negative learner evaluations of you as an instructor?

- How might you interpret and respond to apparent learner dissatisfaction, anger, or resistance to course activities or the learning process?

- How can you work to continually improve your practice? Specifically, how can you best learn from your mistakes and from your successes, using them to plan your future actions?

- How do you balance focus on process and learner growth, with rigorous standards for product and performance outcomes?

- How do you manage the tension between promoting collaborative work among learners, with a structure promoting individual achievement and competition?

Learner Reports to Instructors

Many instructors ask learners for quick responses to the instruction during class meetings, lectures, or small-group discussion. Some variations are:

- Ask learners to write a one-page summary of what they've learned in a particular session, and how they responded to it (what they enjoy, things that are surprising, things that are troubling) in prose or point form, addressed to the instructor.

- Ask learners to describe, in writing, an area of the course that is difficult, troubling, or confusing.

- Brookfield (1990) suggests you ask learners to write a short note to the instructor on a slip of paper or index card. The instructor may ask a participant to collect the notes, then read them to the class. Or the instructor can flip through them during a break, select a few to read aloud, and talk about their instructional implications. At various times in one change management workshop, we asked participants to write down one change they'd like to make to their work environment, two questions they'd like to ask the administration, and one wish they had for the organization. We typed up all the anonymous responses and distributed them to workshop participants, at their request, a month after the workshop conclusion. This list formed the basis for this staff's further work.

- Have participants divide a page in half. In the left column, they record course content from the class: notes, quotes, and instructional activities. On the right, they record personal responses to the class: feelings, hunches, connections, reminders of past experiences or past ideas, ideas for future application, questions.

Questioning Your Own Practice as an Evaluator

Below is a list of questions to ask yourself when you are reviewing how you evaluate learners.

1. *What is your most important evaluative role?*

- Are you primarily a gatekeeper for a particular institution, firm and assertive in your judgment, sorting people into levels, winnowing out the excellent performers from the poorer performers?

- Are you primarily an encourager, looking for what the learner is doing well, and using evaluation as an opportunity to cheer on learners and help them truly believe they can succeed? Do you use grading as an opportunity to reward and help demonstrate learners' successes?

- Are you primarily a coach, offering practical suggestions, viewing learner performance critically to see what areas could be enhanced? Do you de-emphasize the final grade and focus on evaluation as a never-ending process of feedback towards continuous improvement?

- How much time and energy do you allocate to evaluating learners in planning, during in- and out-of-class interaction with learners, and when reviewing final products and performance? Are you receiving maximum learner benefits from the time you invest in evaluation?

2. How clear are your criteria?

- Can you state clearly the criteria you use to make decisions about a learner's performance or piece of work? Even when you respond intuitively, can you verbalize the dimensions of learner performance you are responding to and the criteria guiding your judgment?

- Can you state why you use these particular criteria? Can you link them to the purpose of the learning and a defensible set of standards?

- Do the questions you ask the learner, the tasks you assign, and the products generated by your assignments genuinely match the criteria used to judge the learner?

3. How flexible are your criteria?

- Do you apply the criteria consistently when making value judgments about each learner?

- Do you allow learners to alter the criteria or assignments to further their own needs?

4. What are your reference points?

- Do you look at the range of class effort on a particular task and determine the high and low marks accordingly? Do you encourage learners to compare their performance to the performance of others (normative referencing)?

Evaluation Advice Memo

This exercise has been adapted from a reflective process suggested by Stephen Brookfield in *The Skillful Teacher* (1990).

Imagine you have been entrusted with the orientation of a new college instructor who has never taught before. You want to help this person avoid some problems and stresses of instructional evaluation and you want to share some of the wisdom you have gained through your own experience, trial and error, and fine tuning. You decide to write a memo to this person that contains your best advice.

Here are the topics to cover:

- The most essential things to know in evaluating learners.

- What you know now about evaluation that you wish you had known when you started this job.

- The most important things to avoid thinking, doing, or assuming in evaluating learners.

Write your memo honestly. Then choose the most important piece of advice in this memo. How do you know it's good advice? Write down the most convincing piece of evidence you know to support this advice.

Self-Reflective Teacher Questionnaire

As you answer the following questions, consider the evaluation strategies you have used during the past year—what you planned, what you actually found yourself doing, and what you observed.

1. Compared to what I knew about evaluation last year, I now know …

_____

_____

_____

2. Compared to last year, I am now more able to …

_____

_____

_____

3. Compared to last year, I now realize that my learner evaluations …

_____

_____

_____

4. The most important thing I know about students is …

_____

_____

_____

5. The most important thing I know about evaluation is …

_____

_____

_____

6. The most important thing I know about myself and how I teach and work is …

_____

_____

_____

When you look at your responses, ask yourself: What do I value? That is, what knowledge about teaching are you drawn to most, as reflected in your self-analysis? Is this knowledge truly where your heart is?

Traditional Training Model for Evaluation

- Do you have a vision of the potential standard for a task, or do you invite learners to develop a personal vision to strive for and encourage learners to reach this goal despite what others are doing (criterion referencing)?

- Do you consider the amount of growth a person has undergone in the learning process, even if the final achievement is less than satisfactory (self-referencing)?

- When you begin to evaluate student assignments or performances, do you think in terms of deducting marks for errors, or awarding marks for the things they do well? Do you tend to approach learner work more as an optimistic appreciator or a pessimistic critic?

Mirror Image Exercise

This exercise has been adapted from a reflective process suggested by Stephen Brookfield (1990) in *The Skillful Teacher*.

Think of the problem, difficulty, or dilemma that has bothered you the most in your planning for evaluation. Visualize it as concretely as you can, noting details of situations related to this problem, the consequences for you and your students, and your feelings.

Consider your responses to the following probes as you think about this problem.

1. What is the best response to this problem or dilemma that you've observed in a colleague?

2. What is the worst example of this practice you've observed related to this dilemma or problem?

3. If you've lived through this situation as a learner, what was the situation like from that point of view?

4. Of all the responses and solutions you've tried related to this problem, what's the one you think was most inappropriate or unhelpful?

5. If you could watch yourself as a colleague, what responses or advice would you offer yourself?

Think of something you do very well in evaluation or instruction. Try to imagine a specific time or situation when you were very pleased with your effort and the results. Visualize it as concretely as you can, noting details of the setting, your actions and thoughts, the consequences for you and your students, and your feelings.

1. How did you learn how to do this?

2. How do you know it works very well?

3. How frequently in your planning work do you employ this concept, skill, or attitude? (Would you like to do it more? What's stopping you?)

Think of colleagues whose teaching you particularly admire. Or you may prefer to imagine a teacher you've had the opportunity to work with as a learner. Ponder the characteristics and actions of these role models you've remembered. If you can, try to focus on the way they planned and conducted instruction.

1. Is there any characteristic of this teacher's instructional planning that you believe is important to his or her success as a teacher?

2. Which of the qualities and skills of this teacher do you most wish you could exemplify better?

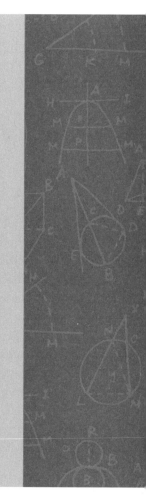

- What is your primary emphasis when you evaluate a group of student assignments? Which one or two things are you looking for most? Do your grades reflect this emphasis? Do your comments show learners this emphasis?

5. How do you foster learners' independence and responsibility for their own grades?

- Do you take responsibility for making all judgments about learner performance?

- Do you trust learners' ability to judge their own and others' performance?

- Do you actively show learners what to look for? Do you discuss standards and criteria with them?

- Do you provide models to demonstrate work that is good or less than good, performance that is more desirable or less desirable?

- Do you show learners strategies of continuous self-monitoring and encourage them in the practice of it?

An excellent resource for further deep reflection on your teaching practice is Stephen Brookfield's *Becoming a Critically Reflective Teacher* (1995).

A Final Thought...

It seems fair to us that teachers should evaluate themselves as thoroughly as they evaluate their students. Yet, often the last people to be thoroughly scrutinized are the teachers. If we believe that evaluation is an important task that may benefit all, we should be more serious about our own evaluation. Being serious, however, does not mean criticizing ourselves unmercifully for mistakes or errors. Instructors often fight feelings of self-doubt, "impostership," discouragement, even shame. As with learners, excessive criticism can stop us from acting and growing as educators. Self-evaluation is good, but only when it encourages positive movement, progress, and growth. This is why we need to keep returning to our philosophy, the passion and heart of our practice. Self-reference can ground us amidst the ever-expanding systems in which we participate. Be as compassionate with yourself on your learning journey as you are with your students.

TOOL BOXES

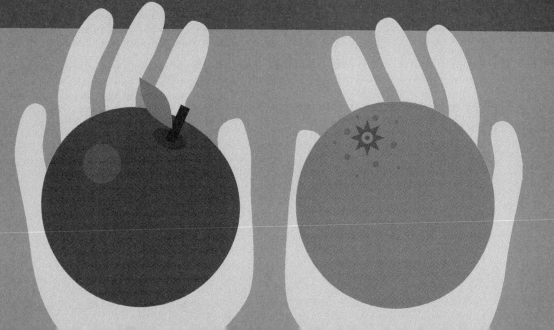

Toolbox 1—Assessing Portfolios

What Is a Portfolio?

A portfolio is a folder assembled by the learner that contains samples of the learner's work collected over a short period of time, such as a particular course of instruction, or a longer period, such as a two-year post-secondary program. The kinds of items will reflect the nature of the course content. An art portfolio may contain sketches, photographs, and paintings in various stages of completion. A portfolio for a management development program may contain written case studies describing aspects of the learner's workplace situation, a leadership style inventory, personal written reflections completed at various points, a plan for implementing a new program, an analysis of a particular management problem, a videotape showing a presentation or a chairing of a meeting. Any of the following items are commonly collected in learner portfolios.

- formal written papers, articles, descriptions, case studies, problem solutions

- assessment inventories (such as personality or learning style inventories)

- photographs or drawings of learner-created products, artwork

- videotapes of learner presentations

- journal, memos, or personal responses

- written reports/attestations to learner performance by others (peers and colleagues, or supervisors)

- test papers and results

- written observations of performance contributed by the instructor

Examples of Portfolio Assessment in Actual Practice

Lendley Black (1993) offers the following examples:

- Emporia State University (ESU) uses portfolios extensively to assess students' basic skills, knowledge, and values that are difficult to evaluate—integration, critical thinking, analysis of issues, values clarification, multicultural issues, and so on. A limited number of items was chosen to avoid assessing voluminous folders, and because staff feel that much information can be learned from relatively few items. Students submit nine products. Regularly scheduled reviews of the portfolios between instructor and student take place at key points in the student's academic career. The process of developing a portfolio required staff discussion of program goals and development of a statement of what students were to learn. A meeting of general education faculty and interested students was held to communicate this information. Course instructors then explained to students the intentions of the course, how it fit into the general education program, and how it helped achieve the broad goals of the program. Curriculum modifications have been made as a result of portfolios. The staff is now developing scoring protocols with descriptors, and exploring the use of electronic portfolios.

- At Western College (Miami University) staff first summarized portfolios by types—papers, lab reports, projects, in-class writing, exams, quizzes, and computer exercises—then broke down the categories further (papers: research, essay, reaction, creative, journal, and so on). Staff then together reviewed portfolios in a workshop setting, finding exemplar pieces (showing evidence of an important goal such as critical thinking, for example). When the focus shifted to finding out what students were doing rather than how well, staff report that defensiveness was reduced. The workshop review helped each staff member know what to look for when assessing portfolios in individual classes.

- Many institutions of adult learning, such as Sheridan College and Mohawk College in Ontario, Canada, have implemented formal Prior Learning Assessment Recognition procedures. One of the most common tools is a portfolio of items demonstrating the learning derived from life and work experiences. The college grants course credits for knowledge and skills represented in the portfolio.

Sample Portfolio Assessment

| Name: | Date: |

1 = Dependent   2 = Limited   3 = Adequate   4 = Competent   5 = Proficient   6 = Superior

Preparation of Portfolio	**1 2 3 4 5 6**	**Weighting** ___
Portfolio is complete—contains all required material Items are appropriately dated, identified, organized Portfolio contains Table of Contents Overall presentation shows care and thought **Comments:**		
Documentation of Growth	**1 2 3 4 5 6**	**Weighting** ___
Work samples reflect growth in particular areas Portfolio items chosen thoughtfully and purposefully Portfolio demonstrates achievement in significant outcome areas of knowledge, skill, and attitudes Portfolio organization and presentation demonstrates awareness of identified audience needs **Comments:**		
Evaluation of Selected Item(s)	**1 2 3 4 5 6**	**Weighting** ___
Overall quality Thoughtfulness: detail, clarity, originality, development Appropriateness of form for message and audience Relationship of form and content Use of details in presentation to enhance … (meaning, audience appeal, mood, design, unity, emphasis, voice, clarity, or whatever criteria are relevant to the item) **Comments:**		
Quality of Reflections/Self evaluation	**1 2 3 4 5 6**	**Weighting** ___
(demonstrated at closing conference) Comments examine products as well as learning processes, strategies Comments show evidence of revisiting specific work samples Comments show self-awareness and insight into behavior, attitudes, values, and beliefs Comments identify areas for further improvement and set directions for action and learning **Comments:**		

How Do I Use Portfolios?

Portfolios require careful forethought. Following are the four most important issues to consider in the planning process, according to experienced portfolio users.

- Decide what is to be collected, by whom, and when. Determine where the portfolios are to be kept and how disparate items can be evaluated fairly.

- Use portfolios in conjunction with other methods of assessment—surveys, standardized tests, and formally graded assignments.

- Limit the number of products required in a portfolio.

- Arrange periodic student-instructor conferences to discuss the portfolio.

Developing a portfolio approach is challenging and refining the program takes time. There are no prescriptions that transfer easily from one context to another. Each staff or individual who decides to use a portfolio approach must develop their own expectations, guidelines for content, and criteria for assessment. Samples of student work can be used to establish benchmarks for scoring, and to generate descriptors and numeric grades for each level of scoring. Some instructors have found that if they do not attach numeric grades to the portfolios, the institution does not grant credibility to the portfolio as a valid assessment tool.

Here are a suggested series of steps to follow when beginning to use portfolios.

- Spend time introducing portfolios to learners. Experienced portfolio users suggest that you give as much help to learners up front as possible. Be as clear as you can about what kinds of things can go in a portfolio, being careful to balance your directions with the essential theme of learners' freedom to create and choose from their creations. If possible, show samples. Share with learners the specific benefits of the portfolio approach. Help learners know what to expect in the process. Feelings of ambiguity and a sense of unclear goals are natural, and everyone needs to be open to the trial-and-learn process of building portfolios. Let them know you will adapt your expectations as the portfolios grow.

- Work with learners throughout the process. Even if you have outlined your general expectations for portfolio contents, learners need help focusing and selecting. Most simply need confirmation that the items they are creating and selecting for their portfolios meet your standards. You can help by providing time for learners to share their portfolios with one another and talk about the process of collecting items.

- Hold conferences with learners. Some programs build in two formal portfolio conferences, one midway through the program and the second at the end. At the conference, the learner chooses samples of work and discusses them; the background of the items, reasons for their choice, and his or her learning in the areas demonstrated by the portfolio.

- Grade portfolios holistically. It is difficult to grade each item in the portfolio and then add up the marks for a final grade. Different program contents dictate different needs for items in the portfolio. Items in one student's portfolio often differ in kind and number from items in another portfolio, so an item-by-item grading process will be counter-productive. In addition, such a grading process is very time consuming. Finally, the point of the portfolio is to demonstrate overall growth in learning. Item-by-item grading assesses early items against the same sorts of external criteria used to measure final items.

Instead, try a grading system allowing a holistic mark that blends different aspects of the portfolio process—grading of particular items in the portfolio (perhaps the learners' choice of the best), kinds of learning growth demonstrated, evidence of the learners' insight and self-assessment of their own learning process as evidenced in the conferences, and balance and range of skills represented in the portfolio items. As you see the kinds of portfolios that are developing, you can work out, ideally with the learners, the criteria for assessment and the sorts of indicators that will be most helpful. The process is an emergent one. In some institutions, instructors meet to decide general guidelines for the contents and assessment criteria of student portfolios; specific details are determined in each class or with each learner.

- Spend time responding to learners. Either orally or in writing, provide learners with thoughtful responses to their portfolios and the self-evaluation evident in their rationalizations for items chosen. Feedback throughout the process of collecting items is essential to help learners focus and clarify the purpose of the portfolio in their own learning.

What Are the Benefits of Using Portfolios?

- **Portfolios show learner growth over time.** They work well to track a student through a program from course to course and year to year, providing continuity, integration, and a record of overall progress.

- **Portfolios involve learners directly in their own learning and evaluation.** When learners can exercise more control over what is evaluated, their sense of responsibility for and ownership of the learning increases. The act of creating a portfolio also helps move learners towards self-evaluation.

- **Portfolios show the process of learning, not just the outcomes.** Samples are collected at various periods throughout the learning process, thus reflecting incremental stages of development. Learners find out more about their own learning process, and motivation for following through any learning project usually increases when learners can see visible evidence of their progress accumulating.

- **Portfolios build learner confidence.** One of the most common reports from instructors using portfolios is the powerful effect they have on student self-esteem. The folder is visible, concrete proof to students of their own ability and mastery of the new learning.

- **Portfolios are holistic measures of learning.** They contain diverse samples of work that demonstrate a variety of learner knowledge and skills. Thus they reflect more authentically the capability and achievements of learners.

- **Portfolios are a learning experience.** To assemble a portfolio, learners must reflect on their learning, evaluate it, make selections representing their competencies, and rationalize their choices. This process is a powerful way to raise awareness of the learning process. As the portfolio grows, it begins to shape the learner's goals. Meanwhile the student's insights about the learning process, revealed through the selection and reflection involved in assembling the portfolio, continue to shape the student's approaches to learning experiences and assignments.

- **Portfolios are useful for learners seeking employment.** The materials in a portfolio can be easily translated into a resume. Some employers now require applicants to provide portfolios of their work, and others are willing to use them in the hiring process. For example, many local school districts throughout the United States now accept portfolios from student teachers applying for teaching jobs. Lethbridge, Alberta, is an example of a school board in Canada that accepts portfolios.

- **Portfolios are useful indicators of gaps in the program.** At Miami University in Ohio, portfolio assessment revealed that students had little skill in using the library and conducting research. Faculty obtained resources and made a commitment to increasing instruction in these areas. At Emporia State University in Kansas, student portfolios demonstrated that they weren't integrating knowledge of different discipline areas. Key courses were refined to emphasize individual responses, connections between areas, and integration of the discipline with society.

- **Portfolios are an effective means of faculty development.** Portfolios require staff to work together to develop criteria and scoring tools, agree on items for inclusion, and make changes to programs and instruction based on portfolio results. Developing a portfolio approach requires staff to re-examine instructional goals and communicate these clearly to one another and to students. Because portfolios reach across courses, they promote collaborative teaching.

What Are Some Potential Concerns with Using Portfolios?

- Some wonder how a portfolio can be a valid or reliable measure of learner achievement. This assumes that learning outcomes should always be pre-determined and measurable against an external standard. Using portfolios acknowledges that learning unfolds in different ways, with different outcomes, for each learner. Portfolios allow learners to reveal skills, creative abilities, and understandings that are unique and possibly not anticipated by the instructor. In programs and courses where specific performance standards must be met, portfolios can be supplemented with other kinds of assessment tools (such as testing and student demonstration of a particular skill).

- Learners may choose samples of work that reflect different outcomes and performance standards than what have been pre-determined for them. For instance, in the case of trade or professional accreditation, particular standards of achievement must be demonstrated. The learner's own creative products reflecting a particular direction of learning may be admirable, but they are not always helpful indicators of the extent to which the learner has achieved the minimal standards.

- Portfolios are time-consuming for instructors to evaluate.

- Portfolios contain disparate collections of items, which makes evaluation an ambiguous process. The more wide-open and flexible the specifications for the portfolios, the more thought must be given to ways of fairly evaluating different students' work. How can a portfolio containing several pieces of personal reflective writing, one containing a professionally published article, and one containing a few items of business correspondence be compared as final submissions in a college writing course?

- Students are sometimes initially skeptical about the whole idea of portfolios. They don't know what to do, and wonder about the time involved. Some are unaccustomed to self-evaluation, and are uncomfortable with the decision-making process required. Give them lots of time to experiment and become comfortable with the process. Provide supportive help, suggestions when asked, and as much early feedback as possible.

Six Strategies to Maximize the Effectiveness of Portfolios

The following six strategies can help maximize the effectiveness of portfolios in evaluating students.

- Define the purpose of the portfolio.
- Teach the students to self-reflect.
- Structure portfolio reviews by the students.
- Make time for peer evaluation.
- Share portfolios with students regularly.
- Give yourself time to master portfolio use.

Overall ...

Portfolios can provide a history of learning, a structured record of learner accomplishment, a vehicle to engage learners in active reflection on their experience, a way to develop self-evaluation habits and skill, as well as a method for assessing progress.

Because they can be time-consuming to compile and assess, and criteria for judging portfolios can be difficult to develop and apply consistently, some instructors avoid using them. However, the benefits of portfolios, even when used to evaluate a small portion of learner development, are irrefutable in educational programs that must demonstrate difficult-to-measure qualities such as critical-thinking abilities and attitude. The keys seem to be good planning, involving students and staff, and patience.

Toolbox 2—Assessing Learner Journals

What Is a Learning Journal?

Journals are a learning tool. Journal writing is a powerful way for learners to clarify their own experiences and connect them to new concepts. Through the act of writing, learners often discover things they didn't know they knew. Connections often unfold almost magically in the writing process, as learners experience those wonderful "Ah-ha!" moments through the free writing a journal invites.

Journal writing is first-draft. It gives learners an opportunity to explore their personal feelings, hunches, half-formed thoughts, questions, and flickering associations without fear of how it sounds or worry about spelling and sentence structure. Learners should be encouraged to write in paragraphs rather than point form (paragraphs allow the flow of thought to be released), but these paragraphs might be sloppy compared to the standards of formal writing. Learners should not have to revise or rewrite journals. The point is to give them a place to work through their experiences in their own words.

Be clear about the journal's purpose. Some journals are meant to help learners give voice to their own responses, exploring their feelings and personal experiences or connecting these with the course materials. Other journals are meant to help learners develop as critical thinkers, beginning with personal experience but gradually moving outwards to explore different perspectives and to assess assumptions and beliefs. Some journals are meant to accomplish both purposes. Communicate the journal's purpose clearly to learners. Assessment of the journal is based on its purpose.

Examples of Journals in Actual Practice

Content will depend on the type of learning experience and the purpose of the journal. Below are some examples.

- In a political science course, learners are asked to write personal and critical responses to each of the readings in the program. They are encouraged to decide their own starting point for response, perhaps choosing from a list of suggestions such as those on page.

- Participants developing their conflict management skills in a series of seminars keep a daily journal recording what they did and said in key interpersonal interactions, and what they thought and felt but didn't say. They also write their interpretations of their own behaviours—what it reveals about the beliefs guiding their actions—and they record how well they're doing in using some of the conflict management skills they learn in the group seminars. Periodically participants are encouraged to review their journal and write about their overall progress.

- Managers participating in a company's new "action-reflection" program keep a personal journal of the process. The program teams each manager with others from different departments in the firm. Their mandate is to devise and experiment with solutions to a particular problem the firm is experiencing. The managers each record in their own journals any observable events related to the progress of the implementations, as well as their own hunches and interpretations of these events. At the monthly meetings, the managers summarize some of their findings for the team. Then the team members give critical feedback to one another. They help point out each other's blind spots, faulty assumptions, and personal beliefs, and offer different perspectives. After the meetings the participants record what they have learned in this reflective journal.

How Do I Use Journals?

There are many ways to evaluate journals. Some are not only inappropriate, but can be damaging in personal ways for learners. Choose the method which best matches the purpose of the journal, and the type of writing involved. You may want to discuss evaluation with participants. Share some of the options below, and have learners give input as to which method of evaluation they would find most helpful.

The issue of disclosure needs to be managed very sensitively. If a journal is to be submitted in its entirety to another reader, whether a peer or an evaluator, learners must be made aware of this before they begin writing. If the journal is a confessional record tracking a period of personal growth, like the second example on the previous page, it is probably inappropriate for an instructor to even read the learner's writing. It is certainly unfair to place a grade on such a personal journal.

Descriptive feedback should be given whenever a learner's journal is submitted to a reader. Trust is involved when sharing personal writing with another human being, and only a very insensitive or rushed instructor would respond simply with a numeric grade. With learners using journals for the first time, responses should be given early in the process to help guide and focus the writing.

Respond personally, honestly, openly, and humanly, but remember that what you say and how far you nudge the writer depends on where the learner is in his or her development. Evaluators sometimes offer examples of their own experience to help a learner feel more comfortable with personal writing. Sometimes they write questions in the margin or point out a focus to help the writer develop a particular line of thinking. Some write encouraging comments, or note which parts of the journal really strike a reader as insightful or powerful writing. Some write nothing in the journal pages, but write a personal letter at the end of the journal. Here are some further specific suggestions for responding to learner journals.

- Be an active reader.
- Encourage the learner to share excerpts from the journal with colleagues.
- Suggest future topics. Notice profitable digressions.
- Ask for permission to publish good stuff to share with other learners.
- Write an extended response, a short poem, or ask questions.

Journal Starters

Personal responses might use starters such as:

- A central point to remember here is…
- An example from my own experience of one of the key points here is…
- Some questions raised for me are …
- A quotation that is important for me is … because …
- It is ironic that …
- Some things I didn't understand in this reading are …
- A new insight I had in this reading is …
- Some useful ideas from this material that I can apply to my own work are …
- Some implications of this article for issues I care about are …
- Some things I already knew that this article reinforces are …
- A pattern I notice is …

Critical responses to readings might use starters such as:

- A point I particularly disagree with in this article is … because…
- I agree that … because…
- The purposes seems to be …
- The context of this article is…which affects the message that …
- The author's point of view is …
- My reply to the author's point of view is
- One assumption the author makes is …, evident in …
- The target audience for this article seems to be …
- Some limitations or problems I see in this article are …
- This material is similar to or different from … because …

- Avoid empty comments like "interesting," "nice," or "good idea."

- Always be honest. It is better to say nothing than to "blow smoke."

- Look for something good.

- Avoid sarcasm—even offhand humorous comments in writing can be hurtful.

- Take breaks—respond to just a few journals at a time.

Self-Assessment of Journals

Try having learners review and evaluate their own journals at the conclusion of the course. Here is a sample format used in an adult drama course. In this course learners responded in writing during each class after dramatic activity, and also wrote responses to the dramas being studied. At the end of the course learners used the format below as a template on their word processors. Many wrote two or three pages using these suggestions. Learners submitted the complete journal as well as the evaluative summary. Instructors skimmed through the journal, read the summary, then completed the section at the bottom.

Feedback only: a journal can be read and responded to (see the suggestions for feedback, above) without being given a grade. An instructor can do this or learners can swap journals with their colleagues. In graded courses some instructors grant automatic credit, say 20 percent of the course grade, to learners who complete the journal requirement.

Partial Assessment of Journals

Selected passages submitted for assessment. Journal writers select a limited number of passages from the journal to be submitted for assessment. They might rewrite these passages to make them easier to read. An advantage of this approach is that the learner controls which parts of the personal writing are disclosed to the evaluator. The passages might be assessed using a holistic scale like the one below.

Reflective summary submitted for assessment. Journal writers read through the journal and prepare a brief summary, using guidelines suggested by the facilitator. For example, the conflict management course (second example on page 205) might require learners to submit a three-page description of the learning process that is evident in their journals. The description might

Journal Assessment: Holistic Scale

Score	Explanation
5	Thoughts and feelings are purposeful and insightful. The content is either detailed or philosophically approached. The unique voice of the learner is present and sustained. Significant risks in thought may be evident. Readers can follow the presentation easily.
4	The thoughts and feelings expressed are purposeful and either insightful but general, or detailed but conventional. The expression is clear, easy to follow, and appropriate for the context.
3	Thoughts and feelings are present but not always clearly connected to the purpose for language use. Language and thinking may be very conventional and lack development. Readers can follow the writer but may need to work a bit to do so. The language is generally appropriate for the context.
2	Thoughts and feelings are not consistent or connected but are related to the purpose and context. The content and expressions do not anticipate the audience. The writer knows what is meant but does not lead the reader through that intended meaning.
1	The content is very confusing or even conflicting. It may be only tangentially related to its intended purpose.
INS	Sample is too brief to score

note themes appearing throughout the journal, as well as turning points and critical incidents in their development. The summary might also present a critical self-reflection, analyzing the writer's own assumptions, inferences, and beliefs as evident in the journal. Writers could quote parts of their journals if they wished. Learners who have completed this sort of summary often remark that this reflecting and synthesizing process is almost as valuable as the journal writing itself.

Holistic Assessment of Journals

The entire journal is submitted to the evaluator, who skims sections of it and peeks through the entire thing, then gives the journal a holistic mark. This mark is based on fluency (how much the learner has written, and to what extent the writer has addressed the expectations), thoughtfulness (level of detail and creative thinking), and critical thinking (learner's ability to move away from personal experience and reflect on the assumptions and broader implications of the issues). The following scale is a sample, used to assess journals in a political science class.

Dan Kirby (Kirby and Liner, 1982) explains a different scoring system that he uses to grade and respond to learner journals in a writing class. The three criteria he checks for are *truthful, thoughtful*, and *thorough*. He collects the journals regularly and gives each a 1, 2, or 3 rating. Unusually good journals receive a five-star rating and "copious verbal praise in class."

What Are the Benefits of Using Journals?

- A journal offers a free-form space for people to explore new ideas. For many, the liberation from correctness and the stiff, restrictive form demanded by essays and other typical assignments allows them to reach new levels in learning and in writing.

- The free style of a journal can create new learning. As people struggle to put tentative ideas into words, the journal format allows them to put vague, cloudy, half-thoughts onto paper. In the process they make connections, find patterns, compare one idea with another, and reveal all the contradictions and messy parts of their thinking. The writing can also create a momentum of thinking that spins out new thoughts. Many people who write in a journal attest to the experience of finding themselves writing about something, creating a whole new pattern of thoughts, that they didn't even know was in their heads.

What Are Some Potential Concerns with Using Journals?

- They contain personal information. Be absolutely clear at the beginning of the process about the purposes and suggested content of the learning journal. Explain the difference between confessional, diary-like entries, and personal or critical response to discussions and readings. Above all, maintain the confidentiality of the journal-writer, and never share

journal material without the written permission of the writer to do so.

- They can be time-consuming. If you don't work out a systematic way to quickly score journals using some of the holistic methods suggested here, it is easy to become bogged down in reading and responding to them. Limit the amount you read, limit the amount of time you spend at one sitting reading, and you are likely to truly enjoy the startling fresh insights and vivid bold writing that journals so often yield.

- They may create learner discomfort. Prepare for and encourage learners through the initial period of frustration as they become used to the lack of structure, openness, and writing demands of journalling. Some learners will declare at the end of the process that they found it all a waste of time. Remember that you gave them an opportunity to sample a new way of thinking and learning, but often learners are not ready for in-depth self-reflection through journalling.

- Learners may have had negative prior experiences. Journals have been used extensively in learning settings, and not always with a clear purpose, models, helpful feedback, or care and sensitivity exercised towards the writer. As a result, many learners may be cynical about the process or self-protective about writing freely. Your opportunity is to present an alternative journal experience through sharing models of other journals, your encouraging and positive responses, and your demonstration of the integral role journalling plays in the learning process.

Overall ...

We have found over years of using journals in the workplace, in classes of various sizes and discipline areas, and in discussion groups that most learners who try them are enthusiastic at the end of the process about the benefits. If you are cautious about using journals, try incorporating them into just one section of the course, such as asking learners to keep a journal throughout the process of a research project or group activity in a particular course unit.

Journal Self-Evaluation

Name: _____

When I re-read my journal, I most felt/noticed:

One theme I notice recurring periodically throughout my journal that I believe is important is:

One part where I was making connections between my own life and drama is:

One part where I was sorting out my confusion or exploring many questions is:

What I learned about myself is:

What I learned about journal writing is:

What I learned about drama is:

Evaluation:	TOTAL _____/25
Relating to personal experience	1 2 3 4 5
Critical reflection on dramatic experience	1 2 3 4 5
Exploring technique	1 2 3 4 5
Exploring theme	1 2 3 4 5
Making connections among literature, dramatic activity, personal experience	1 2 3 4 5

INSTRUCTOR SECTION:

When I was reading your journal I thought:

One theme I noticed recurring periodically throughout your journal is:

One area of growth I see reflected in your journal entries over the duration of the course is:

One area you might be interested in exploring further is:

Evaluation:	TOTAL _____/25
Relating to personal experience	1 2 3 4 5
Critical reflection on dramatic experience	1 2 3 4 5
Exploring technique	1 2 3 4 5
Exploring theme	1 2 3 4 5
Making connections among literature, dramatic activity, personal experience	1 2 3 4 5

Rating Scale for Evaluating Journals

Name _____   Evaluation Period _____

1 = Dependent   2 = Limited   3 = Adequate   4 = Competent   5 = Proficient   6 = Superior

Criteria	Rating	Comments
Responses are complete.		
Responses extend beyond description and report to interpret, analyze, connect.		
Responses demonstrate close listening and deep reading.		
Responses link personal experience and other resources with the course material.		
Responses demonstrate ability to follow an idea.		
Responses reflect on significant issues and concerns.		
Responses consider various perspectives and viewpoints.		
Questions reveal insightful, perceptive reading/ listening.		
Responses demonstrate ability to compare and evaluate.		
Responses build on previous entries.		
Responses show growth in insight, risk, appreciation of issue complexity, understanding of patterns.		

Toolbox 3—Assessing Written Assignments

What Are Writing Assignments?

Written products are among the most common assignments that adult learners are asked to prepare and submit for assessment. Written products vary widely according to format, style, purpose, intended audience, and organizing principle. Here are some sample formats.

- Essays or articles: compare and contrast, autobiography or biography, opinion paper, editorial, character profile, personal memoir narrative and analysis, definition, critical review, argument of attack or defense, exploring an issue, theme, or phenomenon, speech, travelogue, and so on.

- Report writing: explaining procedure, describing events or people, technical reports, case study and analysis, problem analysis and proposal, research or lab summary, interview, resume, worksheet, definitions, itinerary, memo, letter, schedule, manual, and so on.

- Imaginative writing: poetry, written drama or scene, song, fictional character description, monologue, short story, imaginative memoir, imaginative dialogue, novel or novel chapter, and so on.

- Alternate or blended writing genres: prose poetry, fictionalized accounts based on a true story, instructional computer programs created through authorware, hypertext programs, photo-essays, scripts for video production or docu-dramas, storyboards, a series of correspondences between two learners, a series of email correspondence or an Internet homepage.

- Process writing: journal, diary, logbook, personal memo, list, quotation collage, note files, and so on.

How Do I Use Writing Assignments?

- **Show people the how-to's of tackling a written assignment.** The issue of helping people through the process of preparing written assignments extends beyond the parameters of this book. However, many adult learners flounder because an instructor assigned written work without offering any suggestions on how to get started, or any recognition of different

stages in the process. We have counselled adults who are on the verge of quitting a course because they are intimidated by the requirements for writing sophisticated essays or reports. Many of them completed high school before emphasis on writing instruction and writing process was introduced into the curriculum. Some well-educated folks have never been shown how to brainstorm ideas, how to focus and organize their thinking, how to find the flow, how to rework and revise, then finally, edit and polish. Many adults believe that elegant, polished, error-free writing flows magically from the pen. No wonder so many sit staring at a blank computer screen or paper!

Too often, instructors simply expect adults to know what to do, and focus all evaluation on assessing the final product of the writing. But the process of the writing is where the bulk of learning takes place. Little red marks on the final essay showing

Holistic Guide for Evaluating Writing

A reminder of characteristics of good writing:

Impact—*The reader's interest is engaged.*

The writer has something to say. The idea is conveyed with fluency or intensity. The writing is convincing.

Inventiveness—*The reader is surprised.*

The writer may have chosen a fresh, interesting angle on a significant topic, presented an unusual perspective or tone, or has chosen words carefully to be precise and create deliberate effects to enhance meaning. The writer may have embedded layers of meaning or introduced unexpected ideas or particularly interesting details.

Individuality—*The reader is aware of a distinctive speaking voice.*

There is a distinct, individual flavour in the expression or ordering of ideas. The writer may use a tone that enhances the meaning, or go beyond the ordinary to be expressive by expanding the resources of language (imagery, figurative devices, precise vocabulary, control and variation of sentence structure and syntax).

Sample Preliminary Writing Plan

In two weeks, please submit an outline proposal for your final essay. The outline should contain the following:

- the general topic area you want to explore, and why you chose it
- the specific question or issue you want to pursue
- the kinds of information you'd like to include
- a preliminary list of resources you have found and intend to start with
- your proposed timelines for various stages of the thinking-writing process
- an indication of the sort of format you think you will use (case study, proposal and solution, comparison and contrast, memoir).

many tedious corrections are fairly useless if the writer will not be revising the work.

All instructors who assign written work, not only writing teachers, should offer specific instruction in how to approach the assignment. This is true for any assessment activity, but instructors tend to believe that adults already know how to write an essay or report. There are many excellent resources available that can help you outline criteria for writing assignments. You can recommend them for learners' use; you might also read one or two yourself, if you are not familiar with the writing process and ways to help people develop their writing ability.

- **Show learners that writing is a process.** Each writer has a unique process. Adult learners often need to be reassured that writing is not neat and tidy but a messy, backwards-and-forwards process, and that it takes a great deal of time—a finished piece of writing doesn't happen in one evening. Consider including the process in your evaluation as well as the product. The writing goes through the stages shown in the adjacent chart.

- **Recognize and reward the process of writing.** Here are some ways to acknowledge the process of writing, and include it in your evaluation.
  - For an essay assignment, have learners submit a brief written outline of their topic. This gets them thinking and planning early, and motivates those who are intimidated by the prospect of an essay looming in the future. The outline is also useful in the future, for it displays the starting point of the process. When the learner reflects on the process, the outline provides an interesting reminder of earlier thinking. Here's a sample format.

The outline allows you to detect potential problems early and provide appropriate feedback. For example, learners often try to tackle a topic area that is too broad or are unable to focus on the central issue. Completion of the preliminary outline (you might stipulate that learners must revise the outline after receiving feedback) might receive a small amount of credit as part of the overall grade for the writing.

- Ask writers to hand in an early draft of the paper for response (you might award credit for completion and handing in an early draft). You can provide feedback for revision yourself, or set up peer conferencing activities. A sample format to guide peer conferencing for an early draft of a paper is found on page 215.

- When it's time for final editing of the writing, consider having everyone bring their drafts to class for an "editing clinic." One small group could read and mark all spelling errors, another might look for particular common slips in grammar or usage, another could look for sentence or punctuation errors, and so on. Or have learners pair up or work in trios, editing each other's pieces with the use of a good writer's handbook. Writers can then take the drafts home to correct errors. If you don't have time for this in class, arrange for groups of learners to meet outside class, or book a room where interested learners can meet on a weekend or evening. During this process, students can practise their editing skills and learn more about writing style and correctness.

They learn to work collaboratively. They have an opportunity to read closely a wide range of other learners' work, always helpful as models. Usually people find that they are much more able to see errors in unfamiliar text than in their own.

■ Involve learners in developing the criteria for assessing the writing. (See Chapter 4 for a discussion of read-around groups, another way to involve people in developing criteria.) Peter Elbow, a popular writing teacher who has authored many how-to-write books that adults find helpful, such as *Writing with Power* (1981), suggests a system where groups of five learners read a student paper. They respond by finding and noting words and phrases that work well and have a particular effect in the piece. They may also find words and phrases that are weak or empty, limiting these to only a few. Then the group summarizes the piece in the following steps. First, tell the main points, main feelings, or centres of gravity. Second, summarize the piece in one sentence. Third, choose a single word from the piece that best summarizes it. Fourth, choose a single word that is not in the piece that best summarizes it.

Fifth, give the piece a grade: 3 = strong centre of gravity and supporting detail; 2 = clear centre of gravity that is sometimes lost in detail or not powerfully stated; 1 = not centred—starts anywhere and goes nowhere. The result of this exercise is that learners quickly begin to understand the difference between a focused, well-argued piece using concrete, vivid, honest language, and a weaker, flabbier, more scattered piece. They also learn a vocabulary for critiquing their own and others' writing.

■ When final drafts are due, consider having learners present an oral, five-minute overview of their papers to a small group (four to six). The group members then respond by asking questions, sharing their own perspectives on the issues the authors tackled, and so on. In one class of 45 students we asked the group members to complete a formal written evaluation for each presenter. These evaluations were then submitted to us and credit was given to the writers. The peer evaluators tended to be quite rigorous and thoughtful in their feedback, knowing that we were examining their comments. The advantage was not only the amount of rich feedback the forms

PRE-DRAFTING
Thinking, brainstorming, collecting information, trying bits of writing.

▼

DRAFTING
Getting prose down in rough blocks.

▼

REDRAFTING AND REVISING
Sorting and organizing the blocks, working on clarity, tearing out chunks, finding gaps, polishing style of sentences, adding transitions.

▼

MORE DRAFTING
Rethinking, writing new bits, repositioning the focus, changing things, more cutting and more adding.

▼

EDITING AND POLISHING
Correcting spelling and grammar, adding more details, trimming away details, shaping up format and sub-titles, writing bibliographies and table of contents, finalizing diagrams.

provided to each author, but also the learning yielded by the evaluation process of making and justifying decisions. Each person also received in-depth and sometimes eye-opening exposure to different learners' approaches to the same assignment. When we skimmed the feedback, we found that in most cases it echoed the same sorts of comments we would have made on the writer's work. Thus we were saved hours of work making extensive written comments on 45 papers.

- Encourage learners to explore a variety of writing formats. There is more to life than the "formal essay" or the "five-paragraph essay." Overly formalized papers can stifle writers' voices and vitality, producing the well-known, lifeless, gray prose common among university term papers. Too often instructors assign artificial topics, or formal papers that have no other purpose than to be read and graded by a single person. Such conditions are anathema to creativity and motivation. There is no reason why writing assignments can't be selected to serve an authentic purpose outside the classroom. There is also no reason, other than perhaps format consistency and thus convenience in their assessment for instructors, why writing must be presented in formal, conventional formats such as essays. Consult the list of possible formats at the beginning of this Toolbox (p. 211) for suggestions. Encourage learners to dream up formats and topics that are linked with their own lives outside the class, at home or work.

- Adapt criteria for assessment according to the demands of the format. You can't assess poetry using the same criteria you use for a position paper. And there's no law that states you must be consistent in using the same assessment procedure and criteria from one learner to the next in any group of assignments. Here are some possible solutions.

  - Involve learners in developing criteria for assessing their own particular assignment, either individually or in small groups (each group tackling a different genre).

- Provide a list of three to five alternative formats for assignments in the course, stipulating that learners may choose a different format for each assignment. Then work out an assessment rubric for each format. For example:

  - two-page case study and three-page analysis

  - three poems

  - five-page position paper based on a focus question

  - narrative of personal experience, and exploration of its significance and meaning (five pages)

  - photo-essay: five photos each accompanied by one page of interpretation/description

- Try holistic or impressionistic grading practices in evaluating written products. Here is one approach for grading early drafts used by a writing teacher named Emily Gregory. She suggests reading papers quickly and using the guide on page 211 simply for direction in order to sort papers into three or four piles. Then go back through the piles, reading here and there to make some adjustments. At this point you could give each draft a preliminary grade and one or two specific comments. The focus is on getting a quick impression or "feel" for the piece, not on converting this guide into a scoring scale.

A more complete rating scale, with all levels of criteria furnished with descriptors, is helpful when grading large quantities of student writing. Each descriptor category furnishes the specific comments the writer needs to understand the numeric grade. Further comments written on a paper might respond to the content—questions and musings, personal responses to the writer's ideas, comments about other connections or related experiences, and resources. If a scale is provided to the writers along with writing samples to model the different descriptors, it can be helpful for people as they move into the late stages of redrafting and revising (see pages 217–219).

Peer Responses in One-On-One Writing Conference

The writer completes the top part, then the peer responder reads and completes the sections below.

Writer

My central purpose in this writing is:

The audience I have in mind is:

The parts I would particularly like your feedback on are:

Some questions I have for you are:

Responder

From my reading of your piece, I find the main idea to be:

Here are some specific strengths I liked in your piece:

A part(s) I found a bit confusing or unclear was:

Here's what I felt about the parts you wanted me to focus on:

Here are some responses to your questions:

Peer Feedback to Individual Presentation

Title:	Presenter Name:

Thought and Detail: (Interesting or fresh ideas. Original interpretations. Specific details. Critical thinking. Presenter goes beyond the obvious. Lots of material.)	POINTS: _____/ 20
Organization: (Well prepared. Focused. Introduction arouses interest, gives overview. Conclusion summarizes. Clear, logical, sequence of points made: 1, 2, 3, and so on. Presentation flows from one part to the next.)	POINTS: _____/ 20
Presentation Skills: (Ideas explained clearly. Confident, direct approach. Presenter knows material. Eye contact includes everyone in group. Enthusiasm for topic.)	POINTS: _____/ 20

Two things I learned that I found interesting:

One thing I'd suggest to the presenter:

Evaluator Name (print) _____	TOTAL _____/60

Scoring Guide for Opinion Paper

	Argument	1 2 3 4 5	X 6_____
1-2	Your argument needs to be more convincing. Develop your ideas more fully, using specific details, getting rid of logical fallacies and following through each idea.		
3-4	You've got a clear argument despite some points that falter or need substantiation. Explain your ideas fully, use details, and watch your assumptions. Show why you interpret the way you did.		
5	Your argument is convincing, well-supported, and offers insight about a significant issue. You show awareness of other interpretations and compare them to yours.		

	Evidence	1 2 3 4 5	X 4_____
1-2	Opinions are generally unsupported. Rethink your reasons.		
3-4	At least one of your pieces of evidence is strong. Support more completely.		
5	Good, solid support for all your ideas. Reasons are explained clearly, and include specific references.		

	Language	1 2 3 4 5	X 4_____
1-2	Be more forceful in your wording. Get rid of excess words. Clear up some confusing spots.		
3-4	Some words are strong. Be more specific, avoid generalization. Choose words that work to express exactly what you mean.		
5	Good, strong, concrete words. Honest, fresh language.		

	Organization	1 2 3 4 5	X 4_____
1-2	Create a new paragraph for each new point or example you discuss. Be careful not to lose focus.		
3-4	Sometimes the thread of your position disappears in detail or confusing arrangement. Check your conclusion or introduction: is it as strong and clear as it could be?		
5	Argument builds well throughout the paper. Each paragraph leads logically to the next. Arrangement of points and evidence is effective.		

	Punctuation and Spelling	1 2 3 4 5	X 2_____
1-2	Proofread please, or get someone to help! Too many errors that slow down the reading.		
3-4	Still some errors, or errors in significant spots, that detract from your meaning.		
5	Either the piece is error-free, or you have a few tiny errors that can be easily corrected.		

Scoring Guide for Argumentative or Research Essay

Thought and Ideas

Thought and Ideas	_____/5x 5
Organization and Focus	_____/5x 2
Voice and Style	_____/5x 1
Diction and Clarity	_____/5x 1
Control of Conventions	_____/5x 1
TOTAL	_____/50

1. Main idea difficult to discern. Includes minimal or vague information or detail. Little demonstration of understanding of issues, limited use of resources, minimal or no support for ideas.

2. Partially developed main idea. Issues discussed simply and concretely without detail or depth. Some unsubstantiated opinions, few resources. Some irrelevance or confusion.

3. Clear main idea that focuses on single dimension of issue. Strong development and discussion of issues although clarity sometimes wobbles. Variety of resources.

4. Well-developed, clear main idea considering more than one perspective of issue. Solid discussion and understanding of issues. Convincing support with details, using multiple resources effectively.

5. Well-developed, clear and original main idea integrating multiple perspectives smoothly. Sophisticated analysis and evaluation of evidence. Strong supporting arguments. Synthesizes and evaluates multiple resources effectively to present main argument.

Organization

1. Random or scattered ideas lacking focus. Difficult to follow. No apparent deliberate organization.

2. Minimal simple organization. Some orderly progression of ideas and a general focus, but some sections are confusing or unrelated to main idea.

3. Clear pattern of development in organization. General focus and coherence, logical sequence of ideas.

4. Clear, logical, sometimes complex sustained pattern of organization appropriate to the ideas and purpose of paper. Transitions between ideas are smooth and effective.

5. Elegant, subtle, seamless pattern of organization. Structure may be innovative. ideas flow naturally and smoothly, reinforce and support content.

Voice and Style

1. No sense of writer's voice. No rhetorical devices or imagery. Unaware of reader's presence. No attempt to involve reader. Little sense of impact of statements.

2. Point of view discernible in parts. Some voice, some awareness of reader. Simple style with minimal use of rhetorical devices.

3. Clear but sometimes inconsistent point of view. Clear voice and awareness of readers' responses and questions. Considers effects of statements on reader. Uses language to achieve a particular effect, or to express subtle meaning.

4. Assured confident voice and consistent point of view. Uses tone appropriate to purpose, attempts to create mood through language. Experiments with imagery or figurative language. Successfully attends to readers' needs.

5. Strong individual distinctive voice that may use successfully use humour, irony, or other tone to appeal to the reader. Well-defined point of view. Innovative or artful use of language evident in imagery, unusual combinations, figurative language, and so on.

Scoring Guide for Argumentative or Research Essay

Diction and Clarity

1. Limited vocabulary, simple sentence structure. Unconnected or wandering ideas.

2. Some inconsistency in flow of ideas. Simple, concrete vocabulary. Mostly simple sentences with some attempts at more complex structures.

3. Clear convincing diction, appropriate vocabulary. Smooth flow of ideas with a few disruptions.

4. Wide vocabulary used correctly. Tight, varied sentence structures. Clear and expressive language.

5. Mature vocabulary used correctly and appropriately to purpose. Sophisticated use of sentence patterns and syntax appropriate to purpose. Effortless flow of ideas.

Mechanics

1. Many critical errors in spelling, usage, grammar, punctuation that impede meaning.

2. Significant errors in spelling, usage, grammar, punctuation that sometimes create awkward constructions or confused meanings.

3. Evidence of control of written language conventions, with occasional errors in spelling, usage, grammar, punctuation that disrupt clarity or otherwise interfere with meaning.

4. Skillful control of written language conventions with some inconsistences or a few minor errors. These errors, however, do not interfere with meaning.

5. Effective control of written language conventions. Only minimal, surface errors that may result from occasional carelessness or experimentation.

Toolbox 4—Assessing with Video

What Is Video Assessment?

Video is one of the most effective ways to help learners see their own level of performance, learn how to evaluate themselves, and attend to those subtle details of performance that are so much easier to show than explain. Seeing oneself on video produces powerful and almost immediate change. A student teacher has been trying to remember to move among the students more when she's explaining something. She sees herself once from the eye of the video camera at the back of the room, standing far away against the blackboard at the front of the room, and her lessons afterward are instantly more interactive. Videotaping is also a powerful reinforcer and encourager, showing students who may feel frustrated with what they believe to be slow progress that they have actually mastered many new skills.

Being videotaped is also one of the most threatening experiences many learners can imagine when they are learning something unfamiliar. Would you want your inexpert, clumsy efforts at trying something new put on record for all to see in embarrassing detail? Evaluation is stressful enough for most adult learners, and a video camera simply raises the tension a notch. As video cameras become more popular, people are getting used to seeing themselves and others recorded in live action, but there are still many who are afraid of being in front of a camera. One participant in a train-the-trainer session flatly refused to allow her oral presentation to be recorded and quit the course when the instructor tried to persuade her otherwise.

How Do I Use Video Assessment

Prepare Learners

Be sure to warn adult learners that videotaping is a planned part of the course. If the course is a short workshop, indicate in the course write-up that learner performance will be videotaped. Before using the video camera, discuss the reasons for its use and explain the kinds of things learners should look for when examining their own videos.

If possible, don't restrict videotaping to a one-shot session. For some people, the first occasion that they are videotaped is marked with anxiety, and their first viewing of the playback focuses on their glaring mistakes. When videotaping becomes a regular occurrence, people can focus more precisely on specific aspects of their performance, and note improvement over time.

In some settings it may be appropriate or even necessary to allow learners to opt out of videotaping if they do not wish to participate. Some people may suffer low-esteem or phobias about cameras or pictures of themselves. Some may have religious, cultural, or personal reasons why a videotaped record of their actions is not permissible. Be sensitive to other's feelings in this area, despite your own enthusiasm for the benefits of video playback. If you force videotaping on a person who is extremely uncomfortable with it, he or she will derive little benefit from watching it. First, the performance will be influenced by anxiety and thus may not reflect accurately what that person truly can do. Second, people who suffer severe discomfort in the filming will not likely be able to comfortably watch and analyze their performance, or they may be hypercritical of what they see.

Plan Practical Details

Familiarize yourself with the operation of all equipment, and with the proper ways of using a video camera. Be sure that anyone videotaping another is familiar with the operation of the camera. Check equipment carefully before the taping session to ensure that glitches don't interfere with the proceedings. Test sound levels. When using a hand-held camcorder, it's sometimes appropriate to ask another participant to manage the camera so that the instructor remains free to facilitate and/or evaluate. (Be sure to rotate the duties so that one participant doesn't always get stuck behind a heavy camera.)

Creating videos of all learner performances can be impossibly time-consuming in a large class. You don't necessarily need to videotape people individually. A small group discussion, a two-way conference or interview, or a group performing a skill together can also be videotaped.

Viewing videotapes of all learners is time-consuming. Video playback of individual student performances should never occur in front of the whole student group unless learners are very comfortable with each other and with seeing themselves on video. If learners are used to viewing themselves on video and are comfortable with their peers, have them watch the videos in small groups of three to five. This requires a lot of equipment unless you schedule out-of-class sessions for small groups to view and discuss each other's videos. With smaller classes you might be able to arrange to view a video privately with each learner and talk together about the performance. Another option is viewing one small clip of each learner's performance in front of the whole group, discussing the performance together. The best method is often to have learners bring their own videotapes, which they can take home to view (or arrange to use your playback equipment after class) in privacy.

Help Learners Review Their Performance Both Critically and Kindly

Before sending learners home with videotapes of themselves, teach them how to observe their performance. Make sure they are aware of the limitations and distortions of the camera. Give them a list of positive things to look for in their skill performance. If possible, develop with them a checklist or rating scale to use. Always encourage them to look for those specific aspects of their performance that are desirable, as well as those that can be improved.

You might demonstrate how to respond and give feedback by showing a clip of another learner or an "expert" performing something on video (be sure to secure written permission from the person for doing so), and leading a discussion about what has been observed.

What Are the Benefits of Using Video Assessment?

- Video learners focus on and become aware of detailed aspects of their performance that might be improved. The camera can show things that are sometimes difficult for a coach to articulate. Coach and learner together can analyze a video again and again for subtleties of performance.

- Watching oneself on tape is a powerful, instant teacher and persuader. For some people, change

Suggested Protocol for Group Analysis of Performance Video

- ◆ Before the viewing, discuss the characteristics of a desirable performance of the skill to be observed. If appropriate, draw up a simple rating scale for the performance and some of the indicators that viewers expect to see.

- ◆ View the video clip once. Have viewers jot down what they observe and their impressions. Then compare what they saw to their pre-determined criteria.

- ◆ Start by noting aspects that were "positive," that matched the characteristics of a desirable performance.

- ◆ Then note characteristics that were lacking, or seemed to be unsuccessful attempts at particular skills.

- ◆ Finally, note surprising aspects of the performance, things that the pre-determined criteria did not anticipate. Adjust the rating scale as necessary to reflect this analysis.

- ◆ View the video clip a second time, asking viewers to systematically apply the rating scale as they watch.

- ◆ Debrief this second viewing. Start by analyzing the performance again, beginning with its positive aspects, then noting areas needing improvement. What things were noticed the second time that weren't noticed on the first viewing? How did viewers' value judgments of what they saw change or stay the same? Compare the ratings completed by various viewers: Where are the differences? How can these be accounted for? Finally, ask viewers to decide what one or two suggestions they might offer to enhance the performance.

happens almost immediately after being confronted with their actual performance.

- Video helps learners track aspects of their progress over time.

- Video demonstrates mastery. It reveals what learners are doing well, in a way that for many is more believable than simply being told.

What Are Some Potential Concerns with Using Video Assessment?

- The logistics of videotaping take careful planning. Equipment is sometimes difficult to arrange. Videotaping and playback time is also time-consuming in a large group. If you want to break the group into smaller clusters of five or six, you need a camcorder for each group. However, you may find in a large group that several participants own their own camcorders and do not mind bringing them in to the session. Even so, if you want to allow people to view and analyze the results in large or small groups, you need to plan your time and equipment carefully.

- The issue of individual anxiety about the videotaping process must be approached sensitively. Some people are so critical of themselves that they find it impossible to see the positive aspects of their performance on video.

- Most people become accustomed to the process quickly, especially if it's introduced as a simple, useful tool, and learn to focus on their performance rather than their personal image. But some will never be persuaded to try it. If you allow some participants to opt out of videotaping, you must make alternate arrangements for them to be observed and receive fair assessment.

Overall ...

Video assessment must be planned carefully and used with sensitivity. Learners must be taught how to review and analyze what they see on video. But once people actually see their own skill performance, they often understand immediately what areas need improvement and how to do so.

Videotaping is a powerful tool for assessment, but it ultimately reduces reality. The video camera focuses only on what can be observed—actions and speech recorded by the small lens of the camera. Imagine someone judging the atmosphere, rapport, or teacher choices in a class by watching a videotape of the instructor—much of the energy, multiple dynamics, and "feel" of the class are missed on video. Also, there are many aspects to learning and masterful skill performance that simply cannot be observed by watching what a learner actually does moment to moment. Some things transcend observable behaviour.

Toolbox 5—Assessing Through Performance Observation

What Is Performance Observation?

Whenever you observe a learner performing a skill, and you purposefully compare that performance with a set of desired criteria, whether in your head or on paper, you are using performance observation to make a judgment.

If you ask a learner to perform a task for the purpose of assessing a skill, you need to decide five things.

1. What is the purpose of the assessment (final testing or improving)', and who will use the results?

2. What skills or strategies should be emphasized, and what task will best elicit these?

3. How should the performance be arranged? (What conditions are most appropriate, given your constraints in time and resources? How many performance samples will yield valid results?)

4. What features characterize an effective performance? (How do these need to be adapted to accommodate different situations?)

5. How detailed does the record need to be?

Too often the observer assumes the position of an all-knowing authority who parachutes in to watch people perform, then makes a judgment based on what he or she believes should be done. But the observer may not recognize some considerations that are very important to the learner and shape the choices the learner makes. As observers, we need to ask what situational factors affect the learner's actions. People take shortcuts under pressure, they adapt regulations for efficiency, they adjust their actions to please or resist supervisors, they invent ways to make do with equipment malfunctions or inadequate tools. The observer's own presence changes a situation. The criteria or standards we use need to be applied flexibly, considering the particular situation and individual.

Here are three additional questions to ask when you observe and judge another person's performance.

1. How does the learner view this performance?

2. How is the learner's performance (or lack of performance) being shaped by the situation?

3. What standards are being used to make this judgment, and are they completely appropriate for this learner in this particular situation?

The important thing is to work collaboratively with the people you are observing. Before observation find out what's important to them. Afterwards, listen to their perspective on their performance and communicate clearly your own perspective, including the criteria you are using. Together explore areas for further development. It is easier to accept feedback when your own view has been heard.

There are two kinds of performance observation assessments: summative and formative. Performance observation for formative assessment is used informally and frequently in skill-based instruction to provide feedback to learners. Ideally learners have many practice opportunities and are given feedback frequently and immediately after their performance. This is a coaching style of teaching. The purpose of formative assessment is to show learners areas for improvement. For summative assessment, performance observation is used to make a judgment about the learner's progress.

How Do We Use Performance Observation for Assessment?

Plan Performance Observation Carefully

Observers must decide:

- what to look for and how to look for it (focus)

- what particularities to consider (the situation and individual)

- how to record what you see (record)

- what standards against which to compare it to make an evaluative judgment (assess)

- how to communicate the results of the assessment (communicate)

Focus Your Observation of a Learner's Performance

One difficulty of holistically observing a learner is that there are many things to see. Watching a new teacher facilitate a discussion, for instance, presents an almost unmanageable amount of data, some relevant and some less important. Even watching someone perform a prescribed sequence of skills such as closing out a cash register can be difficult to evaluate if you don't have a clear focus, because everyone approaches tasks in a different way.

When planning the observation, start by deciding this focus—both for your own observation and for your feedback to the learner. When the learner performs several skills simultaneously, such as facilitating a discussion or making a presentation, you may choose a few skills to attend to, such as helping all audience members become involved or using eye contact. Will you choose the crucial skills to observe? Or will you ask the learner which skills he or she wants some feedback on? When the learner is to perform a prescribed sequence of skills, such as installing a power transformer, which aspects of the performance will you focus on? The correct sequence? Particular crucial steps in the process? What will the indicators be for some of the steps the learner should perform, such as "troubleshooting after installation"?

Consider the Particularities of the Situation and the Individual

Be sensitive to the context in which the learner is using the skills. It is far different facilitating a discussion in a simulated classroom micro-lesson with a predictable audience and familiar environment than it is in a one-day management workshop in a hotel room, or with an audience containing some resentful or angry people, or with cultural groups who prefer not to participate in discussion.

Many skills, especially in the workplace, must be performed when other, sometimes conflicting, demands are being placed on the learner. A newly trained receptionist can rarely focus completely on simply answering the telephone using the prescribed procedure. It must be done while also handling, often simultaneously, many other unforeseen tasks such as clerical duties, requests, emergencies, and difficult people. If you are observing a learner in the workplace, modify your expectations. The prescribed procedures may not be appropriate in some situations. If you are observing a skill in a controlled classroom environment that the learner must later perform in the workplace, adjust your evaluation. Here are three suggestions: find ways to simulate the actual environment in which the learner will be performing the skill in the world, follow up the classroom evaluation with on-site evaluation, or teach the learner how to follow up using self-assessment in the actual situation.

When planning and conducting performance observation, take into consideration the individual learners and their particularities. What is this person's idiosyncratic approach to the task, and to what extent is it acceptable within the range of practice allowed by your standards? When something doesn't appear to be quite right, can you tell by watching which of the learner's choices of action are problematic?

Record Carefully During Performance Observation

Records provide evidence to help communicate the assessment, and a trail of raw data to retrace when checking the validity of the interpretation. A record can be a written description, noting as much of what is said and done as possible, a checklist, or a quick anecdotal note.

Decide how detailed the record needs to be. Who will be the audience for the record? How will the record be interpreted? How much time will you reasonably have to create the record?

- **Scripted description.** Scripted description is a comprehensive, moment-to-moment account of everything that happens, attending especially to the focus for the observation. The emphasis is on description—of the various little events, observable behaviours, and interactions in a period of time. Simply write down as quickly as possible what is heard and seen. The script does not usually contain evaluative comments. An alternative is the double-column script: in the left column record the events and what people say and do; in the right column record evaluative comments, questions, intuitions, or feelings.

Before the observation period, explain the process to the learner being observed, assuring him or her that after the observation period you will review the script to make sense of it and evaluate what happened. Ideally, talk through the script with the learner, asking questions, listening to the learner's perspective, and offering insights from your perspective. Together you can decide what can be improved in the performance, and generate suggestions for change. Note what worked well in the session—something that some adults have trouble seeing in their own performance. Scripts often yield very interesting data for the person being observed, helping them to acknowledge positive aspects of their practice and style that they might not be aware of.

Scripted description is time-consuming and requires one-on-one concentrated observation. It is therefore most appropriate for formal assessment,

Example of Summative and Formative Assessment

Summative Assessment
Medical Testing

A medical examiner observes an interning pediatrician perform a diagnosis on a sick baby. The examiner is sitting at one of twenty stations set up to assess the practice skills of the interns. The examiner has a checklist of items that are ticked off when the intern mentions a key word or performs a particular step in diagnosing the baby. The list is weighted for priority. In this case, the intern must sooner or later decide to perform a lumbar puncture on the baby in order to pass that station. Each intern performs a particular five-minute operation at each station: some are diagnostic, some are treatment-based, some are communication-skill situations ("Break the news to the parents that their child has leukemia").

Formative Assessment
Teacher Training

Jacob, a student teacher, is about to be observed teaching his third lesson in a junior-high unit on poetry. Before the lesson, Jacob talked through his lesson plan with Marla, the class's regular teacher who is observing, showing what he hoped the children would accomplish in the 40 minutes. Jacob asked for particular feedback on his questioning skills during the whole-group discussion.

During the lesson, Marla writes constantly, jotting down everything that is said and done by the children and Jacob that pertains to his general purposes. During feedback, Marla first describes everything she saw happen in the class, referring to the detailed script she developed. Then she interprets the script, inviting Jacob to talk through his own impressions of what happened. Together they note strengths and weaknesses of Jacob's performance, comparing what Marla saw and what Jacob remembered to Jacob's stated goals. They focus on his questioning skills.

either summative or formative. This type of record is helpful especially when the performance outcomes are uncertain, or when a person's performance is interlinked with other things. And practically any performance in a workplace setting is unpredictable because there will be interaction between the learner and other people or circumstances which cannot be controlled, laboratory-style. Marla's comprehensive notes of everything that happened as she observed Jacob teach a class is one example of scripted description.

- **Checklist or rating scales.** In cases where the skill performance is more predictable or follows a prescribed routine or sequence of steps, the record might take the form of a checklist or rating scale (consult Toolbox 6: Assessing with Rating Scales, on page 231 for further information and samples). Think of the checklist used on driving tests. The list is thorough, broken into categories of skills (parallel parking, left-turn, changing lanes), itemizing individual skills within each skill area. The list is precise, clear, and extremely comprehensive. Specific descriptors identify the standards the learner must demonstrate (car is slowed to 10-15 km/h on right-hand turns). The list is communicated; most learners are familiar with the kinds of criteria that will be used to measure their performance. The preparation of the list must be as inclusive as possible, without being so detailed that the observer cannot find examples of all the items.

Checklists are helpful for learners, too. They can sometimes be involved in preparing the checklist, and in using it to evaluate their own and others' performances to give informal feedback.

The drawback of using a thorough checklist is that usually one-on-one observation of an individual learner is required to complete the assessment effectively.

- **Anecdotal descriptions.** When observing people during a practice session to learn a skill, or when watching people in the workplace to see if they are integrating newly learned skills into their practice, neither scripted descriptions nor comprehensive checklists are usually practical. Instead, simply make an informal observation, then write a brief anecdotal description that is then analyzed.

Focus comments and observations on specific and important aspects of learning. One way to set up this kind of observation is to first select skills the program is attempting to develop, then look for the demonstration of those skills. Jot down what is observed, noting where required skills are not demonstrated. Analyze the observation: what are some of the contributing or inhibiting factors?

Use a consistent format to record your observations. It's a good idea to create key words or symbols that you can locate quickly when you need them later.

- **Group checklists.** Another quick way to circulate through a group of people practising a skill or integrating it into their workplace is to record your observations using a group checklist. List individual names in a column. At the top of the page write down some of the skills the group is trying to develop. Record, for each person observed performing a particular skill, its relative degree of development. This is a technique that people can use to observe each other as colleagues. The checklist should be developed through a process of dialogue, and used only with consent of all participants. Results should be openly shared with all. An example used by a college instructor to assess learners' work in a laboratory is found on page 228.

- **Formative feedback notes.** When observing a learner during a practice session, you can act as a coach. The object is to compare the learner's stage of skill development with a clear sequence and standard performance level, and give further coaching as required. A form such as the one on page 229 can help guide you. Use the form periodically to note learner progress. (Note: while useful for feedback, this form is not appropriate for formal assessment because it lacks attention to criteria, context, and learning level.)

- **Analyze carefully.** Compare the data to the criteria you have chosen and make an evaluative judgment.

Consult Chapter 4 concerning criteria for detailed information and suggested procedures for developing criteria.

- **Communicate clear and precise feedback to the learner.**
  - *Be selective.* To be most helpful, focus on one or two specific things that can be improved. Correcting many things at once is impossible. People learning new skills need to gradually internalize new behaviours so they become automatic. This happens through practice focusing on a particular skill at a time.

- *Be immediate.* Learners tend to remember and internalize the feedback that occurs soon after their performance. The most effective learning situation is when learners can practise soon after feedback.

- *Be relevant.* The most valuable feedback is directly related to whatever aspect of the skill the learners are focusing on in a particular performance.

- *Be precise.* Put yourself in the learner's position. It's easy to become overwhelmed. General comments are frustrating for someone struggling to understand exactly what they should be doing to improve their performance. Use fewer words, and focus your feedback on a very specific area. Think backwards from the visible indicators of what you observe to figure out what the source of a problem might be. Skilled observers know through experience how to target a particular behaviour to produce an difference in the performance.

Don't just evaluate, suggest what to do next. All feedback should include specific, concrete suggestions for the learner. Imagine a student pianist having problems with a difficult passage that requires sweeping up the keyboard. A list of problems are evident to any observer: scrambled and uneven rhythm, wrong notes. But a gifted coach-observer suspects that the problem lies in general tension, and in a lack of initial momentum. She helps the student relax, then shows him how to lift his arm high off the piano while inhaling, then swoop down and pretend he is pushing an iron up the piano while letting his fingers "find the way." Almost magically, the whole problem of the passage is solved.

What Are the Benefits of Performance Observation?

When assessment is focused completely on the product of a learner's effort, it is difficult to pinpoint the source of problems. Focused observation during activity helps instructors see exactly where students may struggle or have difficulty.

Observation can occur frequently, over time, with different people and tasks, in many different contexts and activities. This gives a much wider base of information for making an judgment about learner ability, knowledge, and progress.

Observation includes the whole person, not just a product outcome. The observer-evaluator watches not only what learners do but how they do it, how they respond to and interact with others, and how they respond to the consequences of their decisions during the process. Observation can reveal the individual obstacles, personal challenges, and unique work style and personality of each learner. This information provides a significant context for understanding and interpreting the competence of each learner.

What Are Some Potential Concerns with Using Performance Observation?

The personal bias of the observer is an issue. We all perceive and interpret events according to our own values and priorities. We don't ever become "objective" in our observations, just more sensitized to the particular way in which we view the world. The best way to learn more about our own idiosyncratic perspectives is to compare what we see to what others see. In some testing situations, inter-rater reliability is achieved by training testers. People training to evaluate teachers, for example, watched video clips of classroom activity, then independently described and evaluated what they saw. When they compared their responses, one discovered that she was searching for evidence of surface order and teacher knowledgeability. This was of marginal importance to the other raters who were focusing on evidence of the relationships the teacher had cultivated with each learner, and the initiative learners were taking to participate.

It is difficult to assess performance of a skill for which there are many equally effective methods. Observers need to be aware of the allowable variation. For example, every facilitator manages a discussion differently. These differences are not necessarily more or less effective, just variations. The observer herself, like Marla, may have a preferred style or method that a learner like Jacob does not use and never will use with his own groups, a style that might be effective for Marla but wrong for a different personal style of relating to a group. In the pre-planning stage of a performance observation, the observer needs to think about what is most important: the final outcome or the things the performer does to get to the final outcome. This is like assessing someone's drive in a golf lesson: is it more important to rate various aspects of the physical swing, or to look at where the ball drops? Naturally both are important. But normally the observer only corrects particular aspects of the swing that are directly preventing the golfer from achieving the accuracy or distance desired.

"One-shot" observation is a problem. No summative assessment of a learner or worker should ever be based on a single period of observation. Each observation is confined by the context in which the activity is performed, the interactions of the people involved in that period, and the learner's and observer's ways of perceiving and responding. Only if the evaluative report is careful to describe all of the known limitations and assumptions governing both the learner's performance and the observer's assessment is a one-time observation acceptable.

Many aspects, such as changes in a learner's attitude or the development of new concepts, are difficult or impossible to observe. Unless a situation is artificially constructed to compel a learner to produce evidence of certain things, much of what people learn cannot be translated into behavioural indicators. Even learning that eventually may produce new ways of acting and behaving in the world, such as beginning to appreciate multiple perspectives, is often not evident for a long time. Conversely, many things that are easily observable, such as stating information that has been learned, do not represent deep, internalized learning.

Overall ...

Evaluation through performance observation is simply making a judgment based on what we see a learner say and do. If we become sensitive to all the factors influencing the learner's actions, and, most important, if we are thoughtful and humble about our own limitations as observers and aware of our own idiosyncratic ways of perceiving and valuing, we are more capable of providing helpful feedback to learners. A performance observation evaluation should involve learners as much as possible in the design of the evaluation protocol and in the post-observation analysis and interpretation of the performance. And finally, as observer-evaluators of a learner's performance, we need to be extraordinarily cautious in deciding exactly what can be concluded about learning from certain behaviours or the lack of certain behaviours.

Group Checklist: Informal Skill Observation

Date: _____

Observer: _____

Names:	Skill A	Skill B	Skill C	Skill D	Skill E	Skill F

Skill A =	Prepares equipment, reviews procedures, determines purpose before commencing lab work.
Skill B =	Follows safety procedures throughout lab experiment, as specified in the lab manual.
Skill C =	Follows directions carefully, and uses equipment accurately.
Skill D =	Records data systematically using protocols outlined in manual.
Skill E =	Cites limitations and/or assumptions involved in the experiment.
Skill F =	Develops conclusions based on data.
Skill G =	Cleans lab area after finishing, rinsing, and properly storing away equipment and chemicals.

Ratings:

1 = Competent, consistently demonstrated.

2 = Improving, needs further practice or reminder.

3 = Incomplete, skill not demonstrated or unsuccessful.

N/A = Not applicable

Formative Feedback for Practice Session

Name: _____

Task: _____

Date: _____

Place: _____

Observer: _____

Sequence of skills to be learned	Rating	Helpful Comments
_____	1 2 3	_____
_____	1 2 3	_____
_____	1 2 3	_____
_____	1 2 3	_____
_____	1 2 3	_____
_____	1 2 3	_____

_____

Ratings:

1 = competent

2 = needs some more practice

3 = unsuccessful, needs further coaching

Anecdotal Description

Skills to be observed:

1._____	Generally present Generally not present
2._____	Generally present Generally not present
3._____	Generally present Generally not present

Date and time: _____

Place: _____

Group being observed: _____

Observer: _____

Comments:

Follow-up action:

Toolbox 6—Assessing with Rating Scales

What Are Rating Scales?

A rating scale measures learner performance against predetermined criteria, often using a three- or five-point scale to show where, on a continuum, the learner behaviour falls. Rating scales recognize that learning is continuously developing, and emphasize the element of change. Rating scales can also be used to record judgments about observable features of intangible qualities such as risk taking, listening, enthusiasm, confidence, resourcefulness, and appreciation of multiple perspectives.

Holistic rating scales focus on general impact and make a judgment about the overall quality of a learner's observable performance or product. *Analytic* rating scales break the performance into individual components and rate each independently.

Analytic scales are more complex to use and take time for the evaluator to internalize. One danger is fragmentation: breaking something into too many discrete parts can sometimes destroy its essence. On the other hand, holistic scales do not provide specific information for the learner as to why a performance received a particular rating.

How Do I Use Rating Scales?

Designing the Rating Scale

- Be selective. Choose only those behaviours and dimensions that you have come to understand are important.

- As much as possible, choose only observable behaviours, or find valid observable behavioural indicators of other learner qualities.

- Allow sufficient space for comments. Numerals alone do not convey much helpful information to learners struggling to improve.

- Express behaviours and criteria in positive terms: "the presenter makes frequent eye contact with people in different areas of the audience," not "the presenter avoids eye contact with certain parts of the audience."

Using the Rating Scale

- Establish and internalize criteria for rating each dimension on the scale. If, for example, you are observing the organization in a learner's presentation, decide what each number you assign represents. If you will be using the rating scale several times or for several learners, jot down descriptors for each point on the scale.

Organization:

- 1—No clear focus. Provides no organizational pattern. Provides no supporting evidence or clarification. Does not use transitions.

- 2—Often strays from central focus. Provides discernible opening and closing. Uses inappropriate supporting evidence and fails to clarify main points. Transitions are weak and inappropriate.

- 3—Provides a reasonably clear and consistent focus. Provides a definite opening and closing. Uses adequate support and clarification. Uses mainly mechanical transitions.

- 4—Organizes material with a clear focus. Uses a clear organizational pattern with an opening and closing. Provides good and sufficient support and clarification. Uses appropriate transitions.

- Be sure to communicate to learners the characteristics of a desirable performance and the dimensions on which they will be rated.

- Rate what you see, not what you hope or expect to see.

- Include written comments as much as possible to clarify a rating, to emphasize a positive aspect of performance, to point out a very specific suggestion for improvement, or to encourage a learner when ratings are low.

- If you have trouble making a decision about a part of the learner's performance, you likely have insufficient information. Arrange for more periods of observation.

- If you are creating a score from the scale, be sure to consider carefully how you will weight the various dimensions. For example, on page 233 is the scoring guide used by teachers to grade a final essay in a first-year college English course.

Reviewing the Rating Scale

- Check your judgments and the criteria underlying them to be sure you are applying the rating scale consistently.

- Check the dimensions to be sure these are the most significant aspects of learner performance. If you frequently observe aspects not on the rating scale, adjust it accordingly.

- Check the validity and reliability of an analytic scale by periodically making a holistic judgment: the results should be the same.

What Are the Benefits?

- Rating scales express learning as a developing process, not as a fixed destination.

- Rating scales can show specific areas for learner improvement.

- Rating scales are consistent and thus useful for assessing groups of learners who need to achieve a pre-determined standard in their work.

- Rating scales help evaluators to be discerning, focusing on specific dimensions of the learner's performance.

- Rating scales that are not too lengthy or complex can be used quickly to give feedback to learners, or to evaluate a large group of learner performances.

What Are Some Potential Concerns with Using Rating Scales?

Three- or five-point rating scales can encourage "centralizing tendency": the evaluator chooses the mid-point rather than committing to a judgment above or below the center. However, when judging someone else using subjectively-based criteria, many raters avoid the lower ends of the scale except in exceptional cases. In four-point rating scales used to evaluate a learner's performance, for example, some evaluators select mostly from the upper two scale points because the lower two tend to be interpreted as indicating a generally weak performance rather than a generally good (or strong) performance. The point is that rating scales must be interpreted very carefully and used cautiously in any evaluation of learners.

Rating scale descriptors can be demeaning to learners. Often they reflect value judgments without elaboration.

> 1 = Weak
> 2 = Poor
> 3 = Satisfactory (a word many adults hate)
> 4 = Good
> 5 = Excellent

Such descriptors can invite defensive reactions from learners or encourage raters to stay within the higher ends of the scale. Alternative descriptors for lower ends of the scale might be "Skill is developing," "Basic level," or "Skill needs some practice"; a mid-scale descriptor might be "Competent" or "Meets all basic requirements." Some scales remain neutral, simply designating the performance of a skill as "level 1" or "competency 3." The best descriptors provide specific statements of performance to show as specifically as possible what a number represents. Refer to some of the rating scale samples provided throughout the Toolbox section for examples.

Rating scales that are complex can be impossible to apply; for a single-learner activity, any more than six items is difficult to manage. Even when there is the luxury of time when analyzing a learner product, such as a video-tape or article, most evaluators can't assess more than one to three dimensions at a time. So, if possible, consolidate the items on the rating scale to a few of the most crucial.

Rating scales often do not allow for inventive or unique learner performances. They have many of the limitations of standardized measurement instruments: they are normalizing, unforgiving, and don't take into account the humanness and idiosyncrasies of learners.

Overall ...

When there are clear, predetermined standards against which to measure the learner and when time is limited, rating scales that are carefully constructed to be selective and focused, used by raters who have a clear sense of the indicators for each part of the rating scale, can be used somewhat effectively to evaluate observable performance or products.

Rating scales are efficient tools for instructors, and helpful for learners who want to see the assessment of different aspects of their performance or product to demonstrate learning. Like all evaluation tools, however, rating scales are limited and subject to misrepresentation and misinterpretation. They should be used in combination with other evaluation methods, and supplemented with verbal explanation or written feedback to learners.

Scoring Scale for Formal Writing

Thought and Detail Depth and breadth of thought, clarity, originality of argument, precision of distinction between ideas. Presence of critical perspective. Development using examples and/or references to literature to substantiate main ideas, clear details, specific terms and references.	1 2 3 4 5 ____/5 X 4
Organization Evidence of a central organizing principle appropriate to the content and used consistently. Writing reflects a central purpose. Ideas and their supporting examples are controlled and shaped according to this purpose.	1 2 3 4 5 ____/5 X 2
Choices of Style Degree of eloquence, care and consistency in expression, presence of voice, and appropriateness of diction.	1 2 3 4 5 ____/5 X 2
Use of Conventions Spelling is correct, punctuation and usage and grammar adhere to accepted conventions of formal English language (or a style appropriate to the paper that is used consistently).	1 2 3 4 5 ____/5 X 1
Overall Impression: Originality in thought or expression, comprehensiveness, convincing views, consideration for the reader, maturity.	1 2 3 4 5 ____/5 X 1
TOTAL	_____ /50

NOTES

Toolbox 7—Using Participant Course Evaluations

"I hate bad evaluation forms—and everyone gets them!" So said a trainer to one of us in frustration. And probably with good reason. Many human resource departments and consulting firms base personnel decisions about training staff on results they achieve from participant evaluations. We have heard cases of instructors in certain organizations who throw away negative participant evaluation forms for fear of nasty consequences. Even in supportive environments, most instructors find that learner criticism can be hard to cope with.

According to Donald Kirkpatrick (1982), participant course evaluation forms, or what are commonly known as "smile sheets," are often the only form of evaluation that many learning programs undertake. Learner satisfaction, says Kirkpatrick, is only the first level of evaluation. His "Return-on-Investment" model of evaluation shows evaluators how to go much further to assess the value and outcomes of instruction. But in our rush to develop more comprehensive evaluation methods, we'd better be sure not to overlook the value of participant evaluation of the instruction. Nor should we shortchange the time we spend designing useful ways to invite participant feedback, and the need to interpret this feedback to produce what can be valuable information for revising instruction.

What Are Participant Evaluation Forms?

Almost all courses, credit or non-credit, offered to adults should provide some way for participants to respond in writing to questions about the program's effectiveness. Usually a participant evaluation form is brief (5 to 20 questions answered with a rating scale), standardized for all similar courses, and completed at the conclusion of the course. Most colleges and universities have clear policies regulating the procedures. They are often exceedingly formal to protect the anonymity of participants, stipulating that the instructor must not be present while participants complete the evaluation forms, and that an appointed person, not the instructor, must collect, seal, and submit the forms to the teaching department.

Why find out what learners thought of a course of instruction? Because learners can jar us from our comfortable assumptions about how things are going. Learner reports about their experiences, their responses and difficulties and triumphs, are rich sources of information when we are trying to make choices about content, instruction, and activities to help guide their learning.

How Do I Use Participant Evaluation Forms?

Determine the Purpose of the Forms

The design of participant evaluation forms depends, like all evaluation planning, on the purposes for the feedback. Does the instructor want to build a case for his or her effective teaching? Does the program coordinator want to know whether participants think they've learned anything useful? Do the course planners want to know if participants are comfortable and having fun?

Remember that Forms Are Limited to the Perceptions of Individuals at a Particular Time

Perceptions are affected by emotions: people who have just received an "unfairly" low grade will likely respond differently to a question about their overall satisfaction than people who have just received feedback that builds their self-esteem. Perceptions are affected by physical state: people will respond differently at 3:50 p.m. after a long intense day to questions about their level of enjoyment and the extent to which their needs were met than they will after a rousing enjoyable activity. Perceptions are affected by expectations: participants who go into a discussion-oriented course hoping for information-packed lectures may reflect disappointment on the evaluation form, despite the value of the session. Perceptions are affected by previous experience: participants who have experienced training workshops that are fun-filled, entertaining, and active may be puzzled by a workshop that is intensely reflective or otherwise challenges their beliefs. Perceptions are affected by interpersonal relations: people who feel a connection to the group or experience positive interpersonal relations tend to perceive that the course's effectiveness is higher than those who feel isolated.

Consider When to Distribute the Forms

See above for some obvious implications for timing the delivery of participant course evaluation forms. There's no reason to wait until the final ten minutes of a day-long workshop, or the final session of a course when graded assignments are handed back, to have learners complete forms. Find a time to distribute forms when learners feel fresh and positive about their progress.

Ideally, you'll also build in opportunity for participants to respond in writing to the course earlier, at least by its mid-point (see Chapter 13 for examples of continuous evaluation). Early feedback allows you to address the concerns of participants and reinforces your commitment to try, where reasonable, to meet their needs.

If possible, find a way to invite learners to respond much later to the helpfulness of a course. One consulting firm mails a self-addressed, stamped questionnaire to learners three months after the conclusion of the workshop, asking them about the ways they are currently applying specific skills taught in the session to their work. One training department visits or phones employees who have taken a training session periodically in the year following the course to ask about their progress. The advantages are many: participants are reminded of the course content, they are able to report on learning that has had time to become internalized and concrete, they have a more balanced perspective when distanced from the rush and intensity of the course experience, and they see that instructors are interested in their long-term growth.

Make Sure the Questions are Appropriate

Don't ask participants to assess areas they aren't able to evaluate (such as, "Were the objectives for this course appropriate?"). Don't ask questions that invite participant response to issues that are irrelevant to the course purpose ("Rate the quality of refreshments …"). Don't ask standardized questions that were formulated for a conventional course design but may be wrong for your course ("Were the objectives clear?" is not useful in an emergent course; "Did the instructor present information clearly and in an organized manner?" is not useful in a discussion-based seminar course). Do ask questions to which you really want to know the answers. Do ask questions that help reveal participants' perceptions and feelings, and that ask them to describe their experiences with instructional activities, climate, pace, feedback, and materials. If possible, design questions that will show the context of participant response: their expectations, their criteria for making evaluative judgments, what they consider to be a "high" or "low" educational experience.

Keep a Balanced Perspective When Interpreting Results

Many instructors tend to overlook the positive and even glowing course evaluations they receive and dwell upon the one negative comment. Too easily we forget that many internal and external personal factors influence participant responses on course evaluations. We also forget that participants may find new concepts and skills uncomfortable. A course that doesn't meet their expectations won't be welcomed. Unfamiliar learning activities or content that challenges cherished beliefs may produce a negative response immediately after the course is over. This is not to minimize the significance of participant responses, only to suggest that instructors must look carefully at the people who are responding and ask why they are responding in this particular way, and what it means.

A defiantly negative participant response, even one that seems to indicate general anger, is a sign of a problem and should not be dismissed. The problem may or may not be rooted in exactly what the learner has pointed out, and there may be underlying messages that are important cues to help improve instruction. Perhaps a learner is sending a signal about a problem with the institution, course structure, peer community, or instructional delivery that can be remedied. Any negative response deserves sensitive interpretation and possibly personal follow-up.

Positive responses also need interpretation. If someone indicates a preference for a particular activity or piece of course content, ask yourself why it was singled out. Most importantly, what are the implications for improving the course and the instructor's approach?

Other Ways of Gathering Data about Participants' Responses to the Course

Quick Vote

Lynn Davie (1997) handed out a red card to every audience member who entered a lecture. At the end, she set up five boxes at the back of the room marked, "Excellent," "Good," "Fair," "Poor," "Not Worth My Time." The audience was asked to deposit their red cards in the box that represented their judgment about the worth of the experience.

Participant Response to Course Experiences

1. What ideas and activities in this workshop were most meaningful to you?

2. What ideas and activities in this workshop were least meaningful to you?

Circle the number that represents the overall value of the workshop to you:

1	2	3	4	5	6	7	8	9
No help		Some help		Helpful		Considerably helpful		Extremely helpful

3. How could we make this workshop even better?

4. If this workshop were made available again, with the goal of helping your staff, how would you like to see it done? What should be changed?

Thank you for your suggestions.

Sample Participant Course Evaluation Form

PLEASE COMPLETE THE EVALUATION FORM AND DROP IT IN THE BOX AT THE DOOR. THANK YOU!

		Strongly Agree	Agree	No Opinion	Disagree	Strongly Disagree
1.	Were you greeted at the door and provided with all materials you require for the seminar?	❒	❒	❒	❒	❒
2.	Did you have sufficient opportunity to interact with other participants?	❒	❒	❒	❒	❒
3.	Did you find the information presented in this seminar helpful for your work?	❒	❒	❒	❒	❒
4.	Did you find the speaker to be entertaining, dynamic, and knowledgeable?	❒	❒	❒	❒	❒
5.	Did you enjoy the learning activities?	❒	❒	❒	❒	❒
6.	Are the materials useful for you?	❒	❒	❒	❒	❒
7.	Overall, did this seminar meet your expectations and help you achieve your objectives?	❒	❒	❒	❒	❒

Follow-Up Interviews

By telephone or face to face, a one-to-one conversation with a random sample of participants some time after the course can reveal content that is most or least pertinent, their reflections on instructional methods after a period away from the course, and perhaps even some interpersonal issues related to the participant and instructor dynamics that are sometimes easier to describe after the pressure of learning and performing is over.

Follow-Up Opinion Surveys

Wait for three or six months, then send out a short questionnaire asking participants to rate the usefulness of the course in terms of its long-term benefits. Participants are generally more able to assess which are the most valuable skills as these have become integrated into their daily lives over time. You might provide a list of the focal skills or concepts of the course and ask participants to rate them: 1= can't remember; 3=concept is still familiar but I could use some refresher; 5=I use this frequently in my practice. You might also ask questions. For instance: list two things you remember vividly from the course; describe what the most useful thing is that you obtained from this course in terms of your own growth.

Open Communication Paths During the Course

Don't wait until the end of the program to find out how participants are feeling and responding. At the very least you can ask people frequently during the course how things are going for them. One course instructor closes every class with the question: What changed for you today? Make yourself available at coffee breaks, during group work, and before and after the class sessions to chat informally with participants. Encourage learners to jot down "Reflection Notes" (see page 119) and share some of these with you.

What Are the Benefits of Using Participant Course Evaluation Forms?

Participants should always be given the opportunity to respond to an instructional program in writing. Even if the participant course evaluation form is not perfectly suited to the feedback that learners might want to offer to course planners and instructors, its very existence shows that the learners' voices are important.

A course evaluation form also helps instructors and course developers to listen to learners' experiences. If analysis of these forms is approached with humility, respect for learners' perspectives, and a genuine commitment to instructional improvement, the resulting data is invaluable in revising instructional content and methods.

Course evaluation forms help instructors accept their courses and their teaching practice as constantly evolving, always open to reinvention and revision. Learners can offer surprising perspectives that help instructors break free from self-reinforcing ways of viewing the teaching–learning process. Thus, course evaluation forms help prompt critical reflection and self-questioning towards better teaching practice.

What Are Some Potential Concerns with Using Participant Course Evaluation Forms?

Such forms, while representing useful perspectives, are limited. Not all learners complete these forms conscientiously and thoughtfully. Sometimes learners project blame onto the instructor for a negative experience resulting from factors such as unrealistic expectations, outside stress, or difficulty in completing assignments. Sometimes a learner will generalize negativity about the whole course from one bad experience, such as having a weak group member. A popular folk belief among some college instructors is that course evaluation forms should not be given out to students just after an exam or assignment has been graded and returned, for some learners may vent their disappointment or frustration at their results on the forms.

For many instructors, the sting of one angry evaluation can outweigh all the positive comments offered by all the other students. The point is not to ignore negative course evaluations, but to avoid taking them personally. Distance yourself and ask, "Why is this person making this comment? Is the negative evaluation my responsibility? If so, what could I do differently to enhance the learning experience?"

Course evaluation forms designed by an institution to serve all instructors and courses are inherently problematic. Generic questions such as "Were the course objectives clear?" are not appropriate for certain instructional approaches such as holistic courses using emergent curriculum methods. Students struggling to apply questions to such course contexts may give low ratings, which can skew the data. Each instructor ideally should design a few questions that are tailored to a particular course and that reveal the information the instructor most wants to know.

One school of thought claims that students can't possibly evaluate a course because they cannot know its full benefits, nor understand the changes they have experienced, until much later in their lives. If a particular learning experience is designed to help move learners into a transformation of their beliefs, their responses to the process when the course concludes may not be valid indicators of program or instructor effectiveness. Learning is change, which is often painful.

When insufficient time has been allotted for participants to complete course evaluations, the results may not be valid or helpful. Sometimes the most useful feedback learners offer is their written comments, and quiet class time is needed for the required concentrated reflection.

Some instructors need to learn how to view negative course evaluations. Low ratings and negative comments sting, and too often instructors dwell on the one negative response while ignoring the 29 positive responses.

Participant course evaluations must be used extremely cautiously in formal instructor evaluation. The context of the course delivery, the particular learners and instructors must be carefully considered when interpreting course evaluation results.

Overall ...

Participant course evaluations are an important part of the overall evaluation program for any learning experience. This section has focused only on written forms, partly because this is currently the most common and convenient method of eliciting formal participant response to the instructional experience. Written forms should be supplemented by talking to learners, one-on-one or in small groups, about what worked for them and what they learned. Or have them scan their learning logs or journals, and write or draw a depiction of their learning journey. Chapter 13, presents many ideas for finding out what learners are experiencing. Don't wait until the end of the course to ask them.

Toolbox 8—Using Learner Contracts

What Is a Learner Contract?

A learner contract is a document designed by the learner in collaboration with the instructor before the assessment process. Usually a contract is between one independent learner and one supervisor, although a small group of people might propose a contract.

A contract can state the main purpose and specific goals of the learning experience, the learning activities; the function and responsibility of the instructor; the responsibility of the learners, the period of time bounding the contract, the grade to be awarded for completing different kinds of assignments, and tasks to demonstrate learning. Both learner and instructor sign and date the contract and keep a copy for their records.

A contract can be used with a group of learners. For example, a university undergraduate course allows each student in the class to contract for a grade: to obtain an A, the student must agree to read and review ten of the books on the course reading list, participate in all classes, write an essay, and present a philosophical argument to the class. For a B, a student agrees to read and review seven books, participate in all classes, and write an essay. For a C, a student agrees to read and review five books and participate in all classes, and so on. Many students report that they like the system, for it gives them control over their own assessment and workload.

In a life-skills course, learners are invited in the first few classes to design a contract for their learning that lists the particular skill areas they will focus on, and the resources they will use to develop these. Then individual learners design three assignments, with the instructor's assistance, to demonstrate skill development. The assignments are described on the contract. The learners may also specify the sorts of criteria they would like used as part of the assessment of their assignments.

A contract can also be used with an individual. For example, a person wishing to pursue independent studies in a formal learning institution may contract with an instructor to study and summarize selected articles and books, attend seminars, view instructional videos, or collect data through a research project. The student usually agrees to complete some kind of product(s) that synthesizes and shares the learning: produce a videotape or article, prepare a report, give a presentation, mount a display, or design or implement a program.

How Do I Use Learner Contracts?

There are three distinct phases to a learning contract that are related to the evaluation: getting started, monitoring the process, and evaluating the products.

Getting Started

- **With the learner, clearly establish the purpose of the contract.** The purpose should be consistent with the learner's personal interests and should benefit the learner in achieving her or his own goals. A clear purpose can help provide focus and direction throughout the learning process and create the foundation for evaluation.

- **Choose outcomes that are authentic, not just easily measured.** The activities of the contract should be enjoyable for the learner, or provide a chance to learn something he or she is interested in. Products should be directly related to and useful in some area of the learner's life, such as work, family, or community involvement. Help the learner be imaginative.

- **Spend time to design a contract that is feasible given the constraints of time and access to resources.** Some people are ambitious at the beginning of a project, but become overwhelmed when unforeseen circumstances frustrate their plans.

- **Work with the learner to decide how the contract should be evaluated: criteria, weight of various parts, and products or demonstrations to be assessed.** Of course, this criteria must be flexible, because the learning process inevitably alters the details of the contract. Some general discussion about evaluation criteria when designing the contract is important, especially concerning bottom-line standards, or aspects of the project that must be adhered to. However, don't squelch the student's creativity—allow room for shaping or modifying specific criteria to judge the project as it emerges. All criteria must be discussed with the learner as soon as it is practical.

- **Put all terms of the contract in writing, and revise them as appropriate.** The contract may state any or all of the items that follow.

Monitoring the Process

- **Have periodic contact.** Some supervisors establish benchmarks as part of the project, with a formal meeting scheduled for each one to discuss the progress of the project. You may also meet informally to help work through problems. Be aware that some people have difficulty approaching a supervisor or instructor, and need to be encouraged or invited.

- **Suggest that the learner keep a log.** Many learners find that keeping a record is helpful not only to track the learning and the choices made throughout the process, but also to help them see their progress at the conclusion. A log can be simple, containing regular notes jotted about actions taken, questions raised, choices made, resources encountered. Or a log can be like a journal, describing the learner's feelings and learning and reactions throughout.

- **Be flexible.** The process of the learning and the kind of products that emerge are rarely as neatly defined as they are in the contract. Periodically, learner and instructor should adjust the contract, within reason.

- **Be prepared to give time.** For the supervisor/ evaluator, making time available for the learner is the most important part of the contract relationship. Initiate contact with the learner if necessary, ask for and give feedback on early work, suggest resources, provide encouragement and motivation.

- **Ask questions.** For many people, some of the most illuminating feedback comes through a question they hadn't thought of themselves. A thoughtful and penetrating question can open new dimensions, or suggest a new. A general conceptual question can help rescue people from becoming mired in details; a precise question can help a too-general thinker to move into more specific analysis.

- **Record contacts with the learner.** This is helpful if any part of your final evaluation focuses on the process of the project. You might keep a file containing the contract, in which you jot down comments after each meeting. Note the date, the progress of the learner, the learner's concerns, if any, and your own impressions.

Evaluating the Product

Decide ahead of time what will be evaluated. Consider evaluating both the products delivered by the learner, and the process through which the learner journeyed. Here is a list of possible suggestions for products the contractor might submit for assessment:

- a written or oral argument, or analysis of an issue

- a report or article summarizing or interpreting findings of research

- a narration of an experience and critical reflection on that experience

- a piece of literature: poem(s), script, story, memoir

- a presentation or videotaped presentation of information, procedures, or opinion

- a live or videotaped demonstration of a newly learned set of skills or way of practising

- a design for a new program, structure, creation, etc.

- a map outlining a concrete or abstract terrain, or tracing a pattern or process

- a description of a solution for a dilemma

- a description of a case, an analysis (perhaps from different perspectives), and proposed action

- a report describing something implemented by the learner, alone or with others

- a piece of visual or performance art, film, music, drama, slide presentation, photo essay

- a written response or set of responses to experiences

- a documentation of a series of dialogues or focus-group meetings

- a portfolio containing various finished products or rough artifacts, such as notes or correspondence

- a commonplace book—a combination of scrapbook and journal, containing significant items such as: quotes, portions of articles, poems, summaries of essays, notes from lectures, or brief reviews, as well as the learner's interpretations and reflections on the items

To evaluate the process of learning, here are some possible sources of data:

- your records of discussions with the learner

- the learner's journal or log (the learner might prepare a summary of this log describing the learning process, explaining any themes that emerged in the journal, pointing out insights along the way)

- a final conference with the learner about the process

If applicable, decide the dimensions that will be evaluated. You might evaluate in one of three ways:

- Evaluate each product separately for quality, effort, relation to the main purpose of the project. Each product of the contract will suggest its own criteria. (e.g. a written essay may be evaluated using criteria such as those suggested in Toolbox 3.)

- Evaluate the group of products holistically. (See sample of a holistic rating scale Toolbox 3.)

- Evaluate the group of products together using criteria common to them all. This is a suitable method when no one product must meet a particular standard. For example, Toby has completed an independent research project working with a focus group. He submits a written report summarizing the research findings and recommendations, and a literature review. Throughout the project Toby has met with his supervisor and explained the process of the project. Toby's report is not meant for publication, only circulation within his department. The quality of the recommendations he has produced will be assessed later as part of his job performance appraisal. But in the interim, the supervisor is preparing an evaluation of the learning Toby has demonstrated in the project. The overall evaluation will analyze the products and process all together.

To evaluate the learning process, written comments are probably the most appropriate. If you must score the process, try developing a holistic rating scale with the learner. Determine the dimensions you agree are significant, and the meaning of the various points on the rating scale. Try scoring the process independently, then comparing the results.

Involve the learner in the evaluation. Invite learners to suggest specific areas for feedback that would be most meaningful to them. Ask learners to write or talk through their own self-assessment of the contract (a log or journal kept by the learner throughout the project is helpful). Here are some sample questions for a learner:

- Describe the process of learning. To what extent did it follow your plan?

- What were some of the highlights or turning points of the process?

- What were the most significant things learned?

- How do you know you've learned them?

- What have you learned about yourself in this project?

- Where would you like to go from here to continue the learning process, or to integrate your learning into your way of living?

What Are the Benefits of a Learning Contract?

- Learning contracts are flexible, custom designed for learner needs, and thus hold great learning potential.

- Learning contracts help develop self-directedness in both the learning process and self-assessment.

- Learning contracts offer teachers and evaluators a wonderful opportunity to learn. Because the process is not fixed, the learning journey may unfold in any number of ways according to the relationship between the contractor and the supervisor.

What Are Some Potential Concerns?

Not all people find they are suited to working on independent projects. Some need a great deal of direction because they lack the competence to make their own choices through the process. Others lack the commitment or confidence to work on their own. Some are self-directing because they have sufficient experience and information, but they may need emotional support. Some miss talking with people and need relational support.

Overall ...

Contract learning assessment is used for formalized self-directed learning experiences. Like any independent learning project, contract learning is not for everyone. Learners must have a high degree of initiative, personal discipline, creativity, ability to learn in the midst of ambiguity, and tolerance for frustration and unpredictability. They must be ready to be accountable for their own learning. For those who long to challenge themselves and design their own projects while meeting institutional needs for a numeric grade, contract assessment can be liberating.

Learning Contract

Name: _____

Supervisor: _____

General purpose of contract: _____

Proposed objectives:

1. _____

2. _____

3. _____

Proposed outcomes (products and/or non-tangible outcomes):

1. _____

2. _____

3. _____

4. _____

Description of proposed process (learning activities or research methods, resources, timeline, and so on):

Suggested criteria for evaluation:

Signed _____ Date_____
                Contractor

Signed _____ Date_____
                Advisor

Independent Study Proposal

Name: _____ Date: _____

Project Timeline _____

Complete the following sections as fully as possible, using additional sheets if necessary.

Proposed topic:

Resources to be used:

Strategies for recording information:

Working partners and their tasks:

Target outcomes or assignments to be completed:

Project Schedule:

Task completed_____Date_____

Task completed_____Date_____

Task completed_____Date_____

Task completed_____Date_____

Conference Schedule with Instructor:

Conference 1 Date_____ Topics discussed_____

Conference 2 Date_____ Topics discussed_____

Conference 3 Date_____ Topics discussed_____

Rating Scale: Learning Contract for Focus-Group Research

1 = Dependent   2 = Limited   3 = Adequate   4 = Competent   5 = Proficient   6 = Superior

Ability to plan: 1 2 3 4 5 6 .   Weighting _____

Establishing and maintaining a focus that has demonstrated relevance. Predicting task requirements of the project and allowing sufficient time given constraints.

Use of resources: 1 2 3 4 5 6   Weighting _____

Initiative in locating current resources, breadth and/or depth in using resources, ability to select and synthesize information from resources relevant to the project.

Organization: 1 2 3 4 5 6   Weighting _____

Maintaining timelines, anticipating intervening circumstances, and managing details of the project efficiently and effectively: interpersonal, informational, and organizational.

Information processing: 1 2 3 4 5 6   Weighting _____

Originality, insight, ability to make connections and inferences, ability to discern ideas and draw conclusions with precision, relevancy.

Understanding of self: 1 2 3 4 5 6   Weighting _____

Awareness of own particular world-view and values and how these shape the process and findings of the project. Ability to articulate specific aspects of self revealed through the project.

Self-assessment: 1 2 3 4 5 6   Weighting _____

Ability to observe and assess own actions and decisions during the process. Ability and willingness to reflect on overall personal learning growth and determine areas for further growth.

General comments: TOTAL   _____

Evaluation of Learning Project: Process and Product

Name _____   Class _____   Date _____

Description of Project _____

1 = Dependent   2 = Limited   3 = Adequate   4 = Competent   5 = Proficient   6 = Superior

	1	2	3	4	5	6	Weight
Preparation and Presentation of Product							
Thought: originality, insight, interpretation							
Research: depth and breadth, accuracy							
Development: use of detail to support opinions							
Clarity: thought and expression							
Organization: focus and relations of ideas and information							
Style: personal, appropriate to audience and purpose							
Language: used appropriately for purpose and audience							
Processes of Research and Learning							
Selection and definition of topic							
Independent access and use of multiple resources							
Organization and selection of information							
Organization and selection of tasks							
Initiative, effort, commitment							
Problem-naming and solving throughout process							
Teamwork with others (if applicable)							

TOTAL GRADE:

Toolbox 9—Using Case Studies for Evaluation

What Is a Case Study?

Case studies are often used to illustrate concepts in real-world applications. Instructors bring case studies to the learners, who then analyze and problem-solve. To evaluate learners, case studies are useful in any of the following ways.

- Learners can work through a case study provided by the instructor, writing out their analysis, recommended action, and reasons for the action. Their analysis can be evaluated, by the instructor or by each other, applying criteria such as those listed below.

- Learners can construct their own case studies, using a problem they have selected from their own work or home experience, or from a situation they have read about in the media. Give very specific guidelines and provide samples for learners to use as models. Have learners bring their case studies to a group meeting.

- Learners analyze each other's case studies in small groups, one by one, using a protocol such as the one described below.

- Students can work in pairs to read and analyze each other's case studies.

- After each person has had the benefit of hearing other learners' perspectives on the case study, all learners prepare a revised version of the case study (if necessary) and a written analysis of his or her own case, using the guidelines below.

How Do I Use Case Studies?

There are three main parts to using case studies for assessment. First, the case study must be written. Then it needs to be interpreted and discussed (most learners need help to become skilled in case-study analysis). Finally, learners' analysis of the case study is usually evaluated to determine their ability to understand problematic situations and make appropriate decisions towards resolving them.

Creating Case Studies

Below are seven steps for writing good case studies for instructional uses. Choose a situation that ends with a particular dilemma to be resolved, choice to make, or action to take. Describe briefly the context (time, place, external and internal environmental factors that affect the situation) and the background incidents of the situation. Sketch only the facts most pertinent to the situation for the reader. Show the events by telling the story as a narrative. Some case studies tell the story from the perspective of a particular character, such as a supervisor who must make a decision to solve a problem. Name the people involved (using pseudonyms) and use dialogue to illustrate key conversations or meetings. Use description. Avoid using judgmental comments when describing the situation. Let the readers interpret the events. Leave the case open-ended. Some case studies end with the main character considering what to do next.

Some case studies are lengthy and comprehensive; others are one paragraph long. When you ask learners to construct a case study themselves, specify the length and level of detail required.

Consider having learners bring draft case studies to a class session to exchange, get feedback from peers and instructor, and revise for clarity. (Many learners, even adults who are quite familiar with reading case studies, have difficulty creating clear and engaging case studies themselves.)

Analyzing Case Studies

This is difficult for many people trying it for the first time. They often tend to identify the problem immediately then proceed to generating solutions before considering the process of framing the problem and understanding the complexity of issues surrounding the case. It's helpful to walk through a model analysis with learners to show them how to tease out issues underlying the obvious problems.

In a demonstration of case study analysis, you can help learners question their own perspectives by showing them how interpretations vary according to different value bases, power positions, and priorities. You can open discussion about the tricky nature of problem-framing, showing how different case study interpretations will produce different views of the essential issue and appropriate action to be taken. One way is to assign each learner a particular character in the case study, then ask the student to write out an analysis of what is going on, state the essential problem, and the most desirable outcome from that character's perspective. Another approach, sophisticated but very effective, is to

Five Steps to Case Study Analysis

1. List the most important facts of the case. Identify the key actors. List the assumptions and inferences you make to fill in the gaps in the case.

2. Discuss the various issues underlying the case. Go beyond the most obvious issues. Show the different perspectives of the key actors and how these are significant.

3. Pinpoint what you believe is the key issue of the case, the issue that must be addressed first before a decision can be made.

4. List alternative actions that might address this issue, and show advantages and disadvantages of each action.

5. Select the action you feel is most appropriate, and explain how you would implement it.

outline different perspectives (such as socio-political, feminist, ecological, psychological, and so on). Different small groups are assigned a particular perspective from which to analyze and solve the same problematic case study. Comparison of the results is illuminating for those who believe their own perspective is the only possible view.

Evaluating Case Study Analysis

Learners can submit their analysis of a case study in various formats.

- Exploratory essay: learners explain the various issues they uncover in the case study, or speculate about different motives of people involved, or illustrate possible consequences of different actions taken.

- Multiple perspective analysis: learners choose two or more contrasting perspectives from which to examine the case study, and explain the issues and desirable solutions from each perspective.

- Case study writing: learners use an experience from their own lives as a case study. (This often requires revision. One suggestion is to ask learners to share an early draft of their case study with the class and get a response, then write the complete draft. Some instructors take in this draft and offer substantive feedback, asking learners to rewrite and resubmit the final case study. This final draft is then distributed to peers for analysis, or kept on file for use in future classes.)

- Essay analyzing peer case study: learners analyze their own case study, or swap and analyze a partner's.

Encourage learners to make clear the perspective from which they are writing this analysis, whether it be a particular character or stakeholder in the case, or a theoretical perspective (feminist, human capital, or historical for example).

- Individual or group presentation of the analysis: the presentation can be didactic, explaining the steps and outcome of the analysis to the whole class, a role-play of the case after one or more solutions have been implemented, or a panel discussion analyzing the case from different points of view.

- Log or journal: learners can document, in a free-writing fashion, the case study analysis they do in a small group. The important part of such a journal would be each learner's own assessment of the process used by the group to analyze the case.

Each of these forms of analysis needs to be assessed in different ways. Be sure to adjust the indicators for assessment according to the learning context.

In the sample rating scales on page 248, there are two sets of indicators. Scale A evaluates a group of senior educational system executives analyzing a case typical of their daily work as part of their final projects in a certificate program. Scale B evaluates student teachers analyzing legal cases that illustrate principles that, for most learners, are completely theoretical.

What Are the Benefits of Using Case Studies?

Case studies help learners ground new concepts in concrete examples. By exploring the permutations and difficulties of issues in living contexts, learners come to understand and work through complex nuances of situations. Case study analysis allows instructors to evaluate learners' sensitivity to these complexities. It also provides a window into learners' problem-solving processes. Finally, case studies are an excellent way to assess learners' appreciation of multiple perspectives.

What Are Some Potential Concerns with Using Case Studies?

Case studies seem like real-world applications, but they are always highly simplified. It becomes easy to peel apart, in classroom discussions, complex situations composed of many power dynamics, emotions, intentions, and conflicting interpretations. Learners may need to be reminded that case studies are highly artificial exercises.

Two Sample Rating Scales: Case Studies

1 = beginning level and 5 = highest level possible

Sample Scale A—Evaluating case studies

Selects the key facts without becoming bogged down in too many details or missing important information.	1 2 3 4 5
Demonstrates reasonable interpretation of events presented in the case, attending to context and perspective.	1 2 3 4 5
Identifies and articulates clearly more than one issue underlying the case, both stated and unstated.	1 2 3 4 5
Selects and clearly articulates a key issue.	1 2 3 4 5
Builds a case to support the selection of a key issue.	1 2 3 4 5
Presents creative alternatives for action to solve the problem identified as key.	1 2 3 4 5
Builds a case to support selection of a particular action.	1 2 3 4 5
Constructs a practical plan to implement the chosen action, with consideration of situational constraints and available resources.	1 2 3 4 5

Sample Scale B—Evaluating case studies

Identifies key ethical issue requiring attention.	1 2 3 4 5
Views the case from different perspectives to interpret the case situation and suggest alternative actions.	1 2 3 4 5
Correctly identifies the teacher's legal responsibility.	1 2 3 4 5
Locates and applies relevant ethical, legislative, and professional regulations to interpret the case.	1 2 3 4 5
Suggests appropriate action, considering situation context and background, regulations, and constraints.	1 2 3 4 5

Awareness of perspective is sometimes neglected in classroom case study analysis. Students are often allowed to be the all-knowing experts, without taking into account their own limited views and the biases that shape their understanding of the case and recommendations for action.

Good case study analysis takes patience. Often the process is rushed when instructors feel compelled to get through the curriculum, and sacrifice the time required for critical thoughtfulness.

Case studies tend to reduce real-world practice to a series of problems that can (and should) be solved. In fact, many messy situations in the workplace, community, and family need to be worked through and made sense of, not "fixed." It's important not to perpetuate a fix-it mentality by using too many case studies in a course or insist that all case studies be brought to a "solution."

Overall ...

Like many other forms of assessment, case study analysis requires thorough preparation and planning. Many learners need to be taught how to interpret and work through case studies. Many instructors need to be reminded to slow down and have students analyze fewer cases with deeper comprehension of the inherent complexities and contradictions of such real-world situations.

But when rich case studies are constructed, analytical tools are taught, and people are given time for careful exploration, learning can be profound. Assessment tools for case study analysis must be designed carefully, and match appropriately whatever activity for analysis is chosen by the instructor.

Toolbox 10—Assessment in Online Courses

What Is an Online Course?

Distance education "online," using the Internet, is becoming increasingly common as the number of Internet users across North America continues to rise. Many instructors and institutions at the time of writing are just beginning to experiment with online course delivery methods, while others have been creating and modifying online courses since the early 1990s. As a result, there are a huge variety of online courses available now employing different instructional methods. Below are a few representative examples.

How Do I Assess Online Learning?

As you can see, assessment methods for online courses vary as much as they do for different classroom courses, to match the demands of the content, learning activities, and instructional process most favoured by the instructor. In fact, many online courses use similar methods of assessment to those found in a face-to-face classroom—with a few technical tweaks. This brief Toolbox can only address a few issues and methods.

The focus here is on assessment, not facilitating online learning. There are now some excellent resources about teaching online which can give you much more detailed information, and many are available online.

1. Participation in Online Discussion

Many instructors requiring students to participate in online discussion want to evaluate this participation somehow. Here are some suggestions for implementing and assessing online discussion.

- **Welcoming and building community.** Some students, especially those unaccustomed to online dialogue, may be intimidated by the requirement to post their "first draft" views publicly without necessarily knowing the audience or receiving an immediate response, verbal and nonverbal. For others, especially the less fluent writers, the onerous task of putting all their thoughts in writing is overwhelming. For everybody in online courses, writing becomes the major form of communicating ideas, arguments, affirmations of others, and

relationship-building comments. Here are some suggestions to help build an online community that encourages participation:

- Consider posting a welcome letter before the course begins inviting students into the virtual community. Talk directly about the process of online learning and establish some ground rules to make the community a safe and trusted place. This is different than a course outline.

- Consider having an informal chat about yourself personally before the course begins, and encourage learners to do the same. This should not be a formal biography, but an invitation to get to know each other better.

- Carefully prepare your responses to students online. Tone is important, and sometimes our more direct, quick replies can be interpreted as brusque and abrupt. Consider revealing some of your feelings and personal responses to what students write, beginning from an affirming position. Share some non-verbal responses you might be making if you were talking face-to-face in a class: "Susan, I was smiling and nodding as I read your comments about…"

- Encourage students to carefully read each other's contributions, answer each other's questions, affirm and build upon each other's contributions, and bring their own experiences into the discussion.

- Consider building in at least one teleconference during an online course to allow learners to share personal responses to the course, voice concerns, and talk about issues of particular interest.

- **Formal discussion.** In a formal discussion asking each student to post one response only to the week's discussion question, some instructors read through the responses and determine a quick holistic grade that is recorded beside each student's name. Let students know up front what criteria are used to assess their weekly contributions. Here is a set of criteria used for one graduate-level course:

- conciseness and clarity of writing
- focused argument
- use of literature to support an argument
- ability to synthesize literature
- use of specific examples from own experience to illustrate points made
- reference to others' postings to create a thread of dialogue

In such a discussion you might want to set clear guidelines for word length. For individual student postings, some instructors ask that responses stay within 300-500 words (approximately one screen). Also set clear deadlines for the conclusion of each week's discussion, and for the posting by the leader (whether individual or group) to initiate the new week's discussion. Some instructors post one weekly response themselves, both to model and to establish a presence in the discussions.

- **Informal discussion.** Some courses use informal discussion, where several students post responses throughout the week. Establish guidelines for such discussion, on length and frequency of postings. Otherwise some students may feel compelled to respond daily to earn their participation grade, which creates an overwhelming load of email for everyone to read. Also, one-line responses such as thank-you messages can clog students' inboxes.

Think carefully about the criteria that make most sense in assessing students' participation in a particular course. Margaret Haughey and Terry Anderson (1998) suggest that you may consider the following:

- frequency of a student's contributions
- extent to which the contribution adds to the discussion
- whether the contribution includes new information and/or information from required readings
- whether the contribution extends or synthesizes others' contributions

You can even set up an automatic log which tracks when each learner logs on or posts a response. In larger classes, such a chart helps you see at a glance the participation patterns for each topic or reading in the course

To track types of responses in smaller classes, you might want to use a simple symbol system. Dr. John Bratton of the University of Calgary sets up a chart for himself, with one column for each week of the course. Beside each student's name, he denotes the type of contribution made to the discussion. For example:

A/Ex   Affirmed or Extended another student's ideas

Q   Raised a useful question

CT   Showed critical thinking

RL   Referred to literature

OP   Presented an original/creative point or example

SR   Satisfactory response: conventional and clear

You can also keep track of your own responses, if you are concerned about giving equal amounts of attention and helping each student to feel included. You might try keeping a second chart like John Bratton's, jotting a symbol beside each student to whom you post a response:

A   Public affirmation

PA   Private affirmation

C/Q   Public question or challenge

PC/Q   Private challenge or question

PF   Private evaluative feedback to a student's response

M   Public mention

R   Public response to a point or question that student raised

IR   Informational response to question student has asked

2. Written Assignments

Many online courses still rely on written assignments submitted by students for assessment. In online environments your instructions for assignments must be detailed and crystal-clear, unless you want to deal with multiple student messages requesting clarification. For help with criteria and procedures for grading, refer to Toolbox 3: Assessing Written Assignments (see page 211).

Technical difficulties and tracking assignments are another issue. You might want to give some thought to how you will organize the incoming assignments. One instructor reports that as assignments came into her e-mail she carefully placed them all into a special file in her

Inbox labelled with the course title. Then, with everything neatly filed and out of sight, she promptly forgot that she had 20-some unmarked assignments sitting waiting for her in her virtual file! Now she keeps one file called Unmarked, and one called Marked. Organization also is easier if you instruct students to label their assignment carefully in the "Subject" box on their email: Course number, Module or Unit Number, Subject/Topic of assignment.

Some learners report a little anxiety when they post their assignments into the virtual blue yonder. Send quick messages to notify each student when their assignment arrives safely and "reads" with no problem, and ask for their response when they receive your "marked" copy of the assignment.

Students may email assignments as attachments that your software cannot open. We have found the easiest method is to ask students to cut-and-paste their entire assignment into the body of their email message. Then we paste it into a word processing document. Off-line, we write feedback directly on the students' document in capital letters or using asterisks to indicate the location of our own comments. We print or save a copy of this "marked" assignment. Then we paste the document into an email message and send it back to the student.

3. Tests

There is special software available for online tests that permits learners to enter only once, prevents them from accessing others' responses, and imposes time limits. This software also scores and records the test results.

If you don't use such software, your tests will be like open-book tests where learners have flexible time and access to other resources during the test.

4. Other Assessment Activities

As in a regular classroom course, choose from a variety of methods of assessment in your online course: written assignments, discussion, self-assessment, peer assessment, portfolios, journals, case studies, and projects. Toolboxes in this book providing details for these methods are applicable to your online course, with minor modification.

How Do I Implement Online Learning Assessment?

1. Be Clear About Expectations and Evaluation Criteria

- Spend time introducing the assessment methods to learners. In any online course, a "listserv" is a helpful tool for broadcasting messages explaining assignments and fielding questions that can be answered for everyone. A listserv encourages students to answer each other's questions too, so the load isn't always on the instructor. Some instructors keep a list of the most frequently asked questions, along with their responses, and create a FAQ link for the next time the course is run.

- Establish assignment structures carefully, thinking through the logistics of students connecting with each other and with you almost exclusively through electronic messaging. Be as clear as you can in explaining the assignments online.

- Let students know your expectations for grading as soon as you can (don't wait till the end of the course). Post the criteria for each form of assessment you will use. Show any symbols you may use to informally track their responses in discussions.

2. Use Frequent Communication to Build Relationships with Learners, Reassure Them, and Clarify Their Tasks

- Work with learners throughout the process, particularly if they are new to online course delivery. Use email to send private feedback messages to students, more frequently and more affirming at the beginning of the course when some students may feel intimidated and isolated from the group. When a learner is not contributing, contact him or her privately to check in.

- If you have a few learners who are afraid to contribute in the open class discussion, set up a mini-discussion between yourself and them until they gain enough confidence to "post public."

- Assess online learning holistically, especially weekly discussion. People grow in their confidence and their ability to express all of their ideas in public writing, and your assessment should allow for this developmental process to unfold throughout the course.

- Be prepared to spend a lot of time responding to learners. Provide learners with as much thoughtful response to their work throughout the course as you can.

3. Plan, Organize, and Manage Time

- It is worth the time to set up recording systems to track student responses and their submission of assignments. Many instructors also set up separate electronic files for different incoming and outgoing assignments, "formal" course dialogues, informal "café" discussions, and general instructor notes to students. Special software for online delivery allows such files to be set up easily.

- Decide how you will limit your online time. Many instructors become quickly deluged by the volume of student email. You don't need to respond to everything. Encourage students to ask and answer each other's questions. Refer students to other sources for some questions. Consider establishing personal limits to your time at the computer: Tammy allows an hour a day, and Tara alerts learners she will log on only Mondays and Thursdays each week (then limits each session to 3 hours).

  Some instructors set up a few weekly virtual office hours where they make themselves available for email questions, or "live chats" online. If necessary, revisit course norms with students to remind everyone of the need to be concise, to limit the amount and frequency of responses, or to break students into groups for the majority of their discussion.

  Some instructors build in breaks from online discussion throughout the course. Dr. Bruce Spencer of Athabasca University asks learners to "go away" for a week now and then. Read, think, write in a journal, but take a break from the continual virtual class discussion.

What Are the Benefits of Assessing Online Learning?

- **Large amounts of written data.** Analysis of learner understanding and progress is made easier when you have access to so much written data from each learner. You discover early in the course each learner's strengths, areas for growth, interests, special struggles, learning process, and ability to work within a group. Because you have access to transcripts of all class conversations, you can analyze patterns within the group—their understanding of content, and topics of particular interest. Some instructors look back at transcripts to determine which questions produced the most responses, and which comments sparked "threads" of online conversations that went furthest and deepest.

- **Continuous assessment.** Relieved of the difficulty of trying to observe learners while simultaneously facilitating the class, you can take your time in thoughtfully assessing each learner from the beginning of the course to the end.

- **Convenience.** Obviously this is one of the most appealing aspects of online discussion. You can participate when it suits your schedule, or when you feel freshest. Challenging issues and learner responses can be thought about before your response is demanded.

- **Data for learner self-assessment.** Learners have a written record of every idea and feeling they have expressed in the course, as well as all their interactions with their colleagues. This is a rich source for learner self-assessment along a variety of dimensions: growth in conceptual development, critical thinking, team participation, leadership, and writing ability.

- **Rich discussion.** Many learners report they participate far more, and with far more thought and preparation, in an online course than a face-to-face course.

What Are Some Potential Concerns with Assessing Online Learning?

- **Time.** Most online instructors will admit that the time required for the assessment is far more than for a regular face-to-face course. Even when there is no online dialogue, many instructors feel the need to provide more written response to learner assignments than usual, to accommodate the lack of face-to-face interaction. Check the suggestions for time management above.

- **Tone.** This point was raised in the section above about instructor posts in online discussion, but it bears repeating. Responses to learners should be carefully worded, and critical responses especially so. The typewritten word carries an appearance of official finality, and can come across very bluntly. We suggest taking time to introduce yourself at the course beginning, posting informal responses throughout the course, and providing large amounts of formative response before the summative evaluations on assignments. Critical responses need to be expressed as you would face-to-face: always beginning and concluding with affirmation, using precise language focusing on the item needing correction or improvement, limiting critique to just one or two items the learner can work on, and providing suggestions for the learner's actions in the next response or assignment. Critically assess your responses to learners, and invite your own colleagues to provide some peer assessment about the efficacy and tone of your more challenging responses.

- **Learner anxiety.** The anxiety some learners experience about participating in an online discussion can be allayed through suggestions offered above about welcoming and building community. Some learners miss face-to-face contact with classmates very much. This is another reason why it takes extra thought and work by instructors to present a personable and welcoming online persona, to create a warm and safe environment for dialogue, and to build trusting relationships with learners—all through writing.

There is a possibility that some students will find participation even more difficult when they know they are being assessed throughout the process of online dialogues. Check with them if you suspect this. Use frequent and formative feedback so learners don't wonder what you're thinking (and possibly judging critically) week to week.

- **Technical issues.** Technical problems range from some learner difficulty managing the equipment or software required for a course, to minor "glitches" occurring as part of the process of any online course. Most experienced online educators insist that for a course to run smoothly the instructor absolutely must have access to some kind of technical support service during the course, such as a specialized staff person, to trouble-shoot and help problem-solve. This, for many educators, is a non-negotiable item!

Overall . . .

Online learning is a wonderful way to link learners in very different contexts. It can provide access to courses for learners isolated by geography or busy schedules. It also offers a medium for learning which suits some people much better than either class gatherings or autonomous self-directed learning projects.

Even given the potential drawbacks, online learning is exciting and rich. There are new challenges posed to the educator regarding assessment in the online medium, and this Toolbox has tried to address these with specific strategies. Undeniably, more and more institutions and organizations turn to web-based environments to offer formal education and training opportunities. Therefore, we believe it behooves educators to learn how to become comfortable and competent in facilitating and assessing online learning. As relatively recent converts, our experience with this medium has opened our eyes to new educational possibilities and questions.

Toolbox 11—Evaluation Through Peer Assessment

What Is Peer Assessment?

Peer assessment involves the formative or summative assessment of a product, activity, or action by one's peer or peers. Although peer assessment contains inherent problems, including a re-structuring of power relationships and the breaking away from the tradition of assessment by experts, when done well peer assessment has great potential for improving learning. It is also an important way to help people develop critical learning skills, including the skills of evaluating oneself and others regularly, critically, and appreciatively, using defensible criteria, and forming follow-up action plans for further learning.

Peer assessment provides necessary alternative perspectives to balance the instructor's limited view. The potential result is richer feedback to the learner. In the workplace, the valuing of peer assessment is evident in the growing interest in practices such as "360 degree" feedback and employee evaluations of supervisors. In summative evaluation, peer assessment interrupts the top-down power flow set in place when the instructor or supervisor is seen as the sole evaluator. Peer assessment helps create more democratic spaces for work and education.

Peer assessment is valuable when a learner needs to tap experiences broader than the instructor's background; when insight about marking criteria would benefit learners; when critically examining another's product would help teach the peer assessor; when the evaluation of learners' work is needed but the teaching staff is already overcommitted; or, when learners' work within a group needs to be evaluated.

Peer evaluation involves two main activities: observing and communicating.

1. Observing

- learning to recognize one's own role and limitations as an observer
- learning to use criteria to observe, interpret, and assess what one sees

2. Communicating

- learning to express one's judgment in helpful ways to a peer
- learning to receive, interpret, and act on feedback provided by others

Following are common situations of peer assessment in educational evaluation:

> **Situation 1:** Individual: One person provides face-to-face or written feedback for a peer, either anonymously or with full disclosure
>
> **Situation 2:** Group: Together provide feedback for one individual through discussion
>
> **Situation 3:** Individual: Evaluates a group he or she has worked with, through written feedback
>
> **Situation 4:** Group: Evaluate themselves as a group through discussion
>
> **Situation 5:** Group: Evaluates another group, through discussion or written feedback

People develop valuable skills in observation, interpretation, and communication as they practise assessing their peers (see the section below describing Benefits of Peer Assessment). However, problems can develop when peer assessment is combined with summative judgment. For example, instructors may incorporate a peer-assessed grade with a grade they have given. Sometimes peer rating and instructor rating are discrepant: peers anxious to support one another may award "inflated" grades; or peers attempting to be honestly rigorous may award unfairly low grades. The practical question becomes how to use learners' perspectives as valuable input. Instructors of adults send a problematic message when they unilaterally adjust a peer's assessment to be more in line with the instructor's.

In our educational tradition, peer assessment is an unnatural communication relationship. Most peers are more anxious to sustain warmth and harmony than judge each other—regardless of the possible benefits. We often avoid making critical statements which can create tension and awkwardness. As a result, our skills as peer evaluators are often weak. But, if we do not evaluate our peers and allow our peers to evaluate us, we miss an important educational opportunity. Most of us just need a little help to learn how to participate in peer assessment effectively.

How Do I Implement Peer Assessment?

When implementing peer assessment, we recommend that educators first help learners become more conscious of the complexity of evaluating their friends. Second, learners need to develop the ability to see and describe experiences in specific detail. We suggest the following four processes for helping people develop greater awareness and competence as peer assessors: awareness of observer's limitations, observation and interpretation, honest and sensitive expression, and listening and action.

1. Learning to Recognize One's Role and Limitations as a Peer Observer

- Discuss with learners how the presence of an observer shapes the observed reality. The observer is never just a fly on the wall. Simply being present changes the everyday actions of the person being observed into a performance for an audience.

- Discuss how observers, no matter how attentive, can only see a fraction of the multiple processes going on as the observed person interacts with the environment. First, observers are influenced by what they consider novel or important. Second, observers are human, with limited sensory systems that cannot process the innumerable data available. Observers miss, or misinterpret, a great deal.

- Invite people to consider themselves and others as "critical friends." Each person has the capacity to offer knowledge to a peer—authentic responses based on unique and highly subjective perspectives. Critical friends can offer responses that broaden and enrich the information available.

- Try leading people through an activity that compares their own perspectives with their peers, and helps sharpen their sense of criteria. Following are three suggested activities:

  Activity 1: Taste-Test: In our evaluation workshops, we ask people in small groups to taste-test five different kinds of donuts or cookies. Each group must develop criteria, rate the items using this criteria, then present and defend their choice for "top pick." This exercise alerts people to how personal preferences and individual perceptions affect assessment.

Activity 2: Compare Ratings: Show a group of learners two or three short video clips of people performing similar activities that match the skills the learners are developing themselves. (Student teachers watch clips of teachers presenting information or working with students; managers watch chairs at meetings or staged samples of manager-employee interactions; employment counsellors watch clips of staged interviews, etc.)

Ask viewers to write evaluative comments after the first clip, then share their comments. Most viewers find points of agreement, but focus on different aspects, which influences their judgments. We also find that viewers offer different perspectives that alter their interpretations.

After the first video, give learners a simple set of criteria, or have them work together to develop a list of four or five benchmarks they consider important. Then watch all the clips, applying the criteria. The after-viewing discussion is usually rich in insight about the difficulties of observing, the dilemmas of comparing external criteria against the complexities of a particular incident, and the need for information about context and the performer's perspective that is crucial to understand what is being seen.

Activity 3: Read-Around Groups: To reveal one's inner sense of "what is good," the Read-Around-Groups activity described on page is helpful. People in groups quickly skim a pile of their peers' writings, rating each item. Then they examine their top picks to determine what made these best, and the criteria they used to decide. Using these criteria, they develop a rubric to apply to new cases. This activity can be adapted to any peer performance by having people recall or observe samples of different work skills.

2. Learning to Observe, Interpret, and Assess What One Sees, Using Criteria

Attentive, focused observation is difficult. We are all susceptible to assumptions that blind us to significant details. Some of us build perceptions more through our intuition than our senses, interpreting so deeply from within our own rich, inner worlds that we are not fully present to other insights. Learning to compare a list of criteria against what is being observed is difficult—it's hard to attend to different facets of performance at once. Peer evaluators need practice observing and interpreting their peers' ideas and actions.

Perceiving and describing details takes practice. Emphasize the need for clear, specific descriptions of peer performance. People often leap to interpretation and evaluation before carefully noting the evidence.

- **Note-taking.** A useful exercise when learning to observe a peer's performance is to take longhand notes. First establish a focus for observation, then record everything seen and heard. Verify these notes with the observed person, attending to the "critical incidents" upon which our assessment might be based. Ask, Did you and I notice the same critical incidents? What did I miss in my observations that you (as performer) felt was important? Then we should check our interpretations with the person we observe. Ask, What did it mean for you when…? Why did you…? And we share: This is what I thought was going on when you…. Here's what I felt when you….

- **Inter-rater reliability.** Take a group of people through the process of establishing inter-rater reliability for a particular rating scale. First discuss the items on the scale, and talk about the expectations for each item. Give examples and benchmarks for each item. Then have them view and assess examples of performance, using the scale. Compare their ratings. Have raters present reasons for their ratings, and discuss discrepancies. Finally, view more samples, working to make their ratings consistent with one another.

- **Ladder of interpretation.** Chris Argyris created an exercise to help people uncover their assumptions when interpreting what they see—a helpful reminder of the interpretive biases operating when we assess a peer. Jot down a brief description of a "critical incident" you have observed. Then focus on a small piece of that incident. Draw two columns lengthwise down a page. In the left column write, in sequence, exactly what was said and done. In the right-hand column opposite each item, write how you interpreted the speech or action. Then—and this is the hard part—talk it through with the observed person. Share your interpretations, and find out what that person was thinking during the same words and actions. This activity immediately shows how much meaning we automatically construct from very little observed evidence, working through our own expectations, assumptions, and personal understandings of what things mean.

- **Rating scale practice.** Review the rating scales throughout this book that can be used when observing a peer. For example, refer to Peer Feedback to Individual Presentation, page 216.

3. Learning to Express One's Judgment Honestly and Sensitively to a Peer

- Remember that until a comfortable, mutual trust is established, people will not disclose their opinions honestly. They must feel assured that their ideas will be received with respect, and without retaliation. This takes time. Trust unfolds in conversations where people test their ideas, assess the consequences, and gradually risk disclosing more and more.

- Peer assessment is effective when it unfolds in a caring relationship that preserves the other's dignity while sharing honestly. In such a relation, the attitude of the assessor to the one being assessed should be one of appreciation and value for the unique contribution (friend). The task is to discuss the observed experience (critical). Remind people that the concept of critical friend is one part friend and one part critical, with the friend part key.

- To provide helpful summative assessment for a peer, learners need clear criteria, clear indicators, and clear rating scales to use with the indicators. For example, there should be distinct differences between the indicators describing an "A," a "B," or "C" level performance of a particular skill. For examples, refer to the system used at Royal Roads University shown on page 43.

- Discuss openly with learners the power dynamics circulating in any group of people that make expressing truly open, honest feedback difficult. It is naïve to pretend that everyone in a group enjoys equal voice, status, and respect. People in any group affect one another. We are attracted to some and resist others as we build relationships—these relationships naturally shape how we observe and respond to each other. We sometimes struggle to establish identity and recognition in a group. This creates dynamics that affect our observations and responses. Talking through these issues, with a focus on the goals of the exercise of peer assessment, may help raise some "ground rules" that everyone is comfortable with.

Evaluation Guide for Cooperative Groups

Rate your team's effectiveness on each of the items below, using the following scale:

4. **Outstanding:** A consistent strength of the team
3. **Competent.** Our team is usually effective in this area
2. **Developing:** Some problems in this area, but we're improving
1. **Weak:** Help! We had problems we were unable to solve

___ 1. All members shared their ideas freely.

___ 2. We offered support and encouragement to one another.

___ 3. We asked each other questions to make sure everyone understood the ideas and information we were working with.

___ 4. Our group was energetic. We welcomed new ideas, showed enthusiasm, and laughed with each other.

___ 5. We questioned and criticized each other's ideas, but didn't make personal attacks.

___ 6. We shared the workload fairly.

___ 7. We tried to make sure everyone in the group was comfortable with our plans and decisions.

___ 8. We often probed for new ideas or deeper understanding by asking questions.

___ 9. We tried to come up with many ideas and alternatives before we settled on a solution.

___10. We were satisfied with the report our group shared with the class.

One area we have decided to work on in future group projects is:

Some things we are each going to try doing to improve in this area are:

- Make the difference between "personal response" and "criteria ratings" clear. In criteria ratings, raters compare what they observe to a set of external criteria. In personal response, raters offer "I" statements, expressing personal feelings and understandings in response to what they see. Both kinds of feedback are valuable. State clearly which kind of feedback peer raters are being asked to offer in a particular situation.

- Remind peer raters to avoid giving prescriptive advice. Stick to describing the observed, either offering personal responses to this observation (I felt..., I thought..., I assumed...), or showing how the observation compared to external criteria. The point is to share observations and personal responses, then show how these observations compare with the agreed criteria.

- When beginning peer evaluation start with low-risk situations, gradually moving to more high-risk situations. Low-risk situations include anonymous evaluations, or expressing formative feedback to a peer. The following examples can help learners develop the ability to express honest opinions:

  - **Rate-the-argument.** Pose an issue to the group, then ask everyone to form an opinion and write down two arguments to support it—each on a separate yellow "stickie." Post the stickies on flipcharts. Give each learner a coloured marker or gummed coloured dots. Have learners circulate around the flipcharts, reading the arguments. Each person marks what they believe are the "best" four arguments and jots their reasons why the argument is "best." Groups re-congregate and examine which "stickies" received the best marks, then discuss the criteria used to assess these arguments.

  - **Ink-shedding.** Ask people to "free-write" for 10 or 15 minutes, scribbling down honest ideas about a relevant topic. Depending on the situation, for example, people can argue a particular issue, assess a problem, recommend a solution, respond to an experience, etc. After ten minutes, have everyone pass their writing to someone else in the group, without signing it. That person reads the page, then "free-writes" a personal response. The responses note areas where readers agree or disagree,

ideas they appreciate as original, and ideas they would challenge. Papers are passed on to one more reader, who reads both the original and the first response, then writes a second response. The focus is always on honest personal response, and no one signs their names. After people are given time to re-read their original writing and the two responses, discuss insights and other learnings.

  - **Writing conferences.** In pairs, have learners respond to each other's written drafts of assignments or reports. First show them what to give feedback on (refer to "Peer Responses in One-on-One Writing Conference," page 215). Ask writers to state a few things they want feedback on. Ask responders to restrict feedback to personal responses like: I liked this part because.... I found this part unclear because....

  - **Group self-assessment.** After completing a group activity, have each person note an honest, private assessment of how the group worked. Provide a simple list of criteria before these assessments. Then invite group members to discuss their individual assessments, talking through areas of discrepancy. (See the sample form for group assessment on page 257.)

- Peer assessment becomes more risky when it is face-to-face and/or involves summative evaluation. The most difficult assessment task may be delivering "bad news" to a person whose confidence may be already low, who is easily hurt, or who becomes defensive.

- Peer feedback should be expressed in a dialogue, sharing meanings about what happened. Feedback should be straightforward and matter-of-fact, focusing on observed behaviours and the observer's experience of those behaviours. The observer should check perceptions frequently with the one who was observed. If discrepancies exist between observer's and the observed's perceptions or interpretations, explore them together.

- Help people develop a method for expressing feedback after observing a peer completing an activity. Here is one suggestion:

  - First ask the other how the experience went for the person being observed. What did this person notice most? What would he or she most like feedback about? Listen carefully.

- Explain the experience as you understood it: what happened and how you reacted to what happened. Tell what you were looking for. As much as possible, explain "where you're coming from"—the values and assumptions through which you observed and interpreted.

- ALWAYS start and end by communicating those things you wish to celebrate. Explain why you interpret these observations as positive. Avoid generalizations. Be as specific as possible.

- To express critical feedback, stick to what you observed or what you were looking for but did not see. For example, "I did not see/hear you _____," or "I saw/heard you _____, when _____" Use the benchmarks of the criteria.

The following activities may help ease some of the risk from high-risk situations of peer assessment:

- **Bouquets and beefs.** Peers write a note, signing their name, providing personal response to a peer's performance. One thing I appreciate … One thing I learned … One thing I wish had happened … Emphasize the need for specific description. General, vague responses are less helpful to a peer.

- **Practise giving critical feedback.** Working together, view a videoclip of an unsuccessful performance. Using simple criteria, note your responses, what you observed, and your judgments. Discuss these in pairs, as well as strategies for delivering feedback. Make new pairs and practise delivering the critical feedback to the new partner. The partner's job is to provide personal response to the peer assessor by discussing his or her feelings during the feedback and further actions he or she might take.

4. Learning to Hear, Interpret, and Act on Feedback Provided by Others

- Remind learners that peer assessment is only one small piece of data available as they move towards deeper self-knowledge. Discounting the feedback refuses a gift of valuable information.

- Some learners assume that assessment is either right or wrong. Remind them that all judgments are framed by particular, limited perspectives (their own included), and all perspectives help illuminate the truth.

- Learners may have difficulty listening to peer assessment. Some magnify critical comments, ignoring appreciative observations. Others hear only comments which echo their own opinions. Encourage learners to take notes as they receive feedback, jotting down everything they hear for later review. To clarify the feedback, invite learners to ask questions and to paraphrase what they think they are hearing.

- Remember, people may choose to "own" the feedback that makes most sense to them. Ultimately, learners decide what makes sense.

- Both the observer and the observed need to realize that it's okay to leave discrepant perceptions "unresolved." If one person interprets an experience differently than another, allow both perspectives to exist together rather than insisting, outwardly or inwardly, "I'm right and you're wrong."

- Invite learners to focus on what they can learn from the feedback, not on what others think of them. Learners might ask themselves these five questions when receiving peer assessment:

  - Did anything make you feel defensive or hurt? Why?

  - What thing that you already knew or suspected did this feedback confirm?

  - What new insights and lessons did this feedback open for you?

  - What responses surprised you? Ask yourself why, and what you can learn from it.

  - What one thing will you act on? What will you do first to improve it?

What Are the Benefits of Peer Assessment?

- People sharpen their ability to observe their own actions and others' thoughts and actions critically and appreciatively.

- People become more aware of their own personal biases and begin to see how these biases influence their judging processes, both when they assess themselves and when they respond to others.

- People are opened to a wide variety of perspectives and observational styles.

- People develop the ability to judge what they observe more by using particular standards and criteria, and less by personal preference and emotional appeal.

- People become aware of complex issues in establishing defensible criteria for judging the quality of work and thought.

- People learn to express their evaluative opinions in non-offensive ways.

- People gain confidence that presenting honest feedback to someone else need not be a negative experience or break trust. Thus, people learn the regular routine of providing constructive feedback to one another.

- People learn how to accept constructive feedback from others without viewing assessment as a personal attack.

What Are Some Potential Concerns of Peer Assessment?

- There are definite risks in peer assessment. Some adults need to fine-tune their skills in diplomacy; others need to learn to accept feedback without viewing it as personal attack.

- Humiliation can occur if a learner's dignity is not preserved throughout the assessment process. To avoid this, frame peer assessment within the framework of a caring, appreciative relationship. Emphasize the need to stick with observable behaviours in the here-and-now and personal responses to these observations. Feedback is best communicated in private; "negative" feedback should never be a public event. Peer assessment should be confidential, between the observers, the observed, and the instructor.

- In an assessment situation, power is always an issue. A learner is asked to temporarily become an object of scrutiny to a peer. The evaluator, temporarily, has the most power. This dynamic should be acknowledged openly. Participants should understand that peer evaluation is a voluntary and temporary relation. Difficulties can be allayed when the evaluator affirms his or her peer, offering feedback within the context of "critical friendship." Both observed and observer can find that assessment is an opportunity to dialogue about different experiences and perspectives—to learn from one another.

- Sometimes peers are afraid to be honest, perhaps because our society attaches negative connotations like "overly critical" and "judgmental" to constructive criticism. The "critical friend" approach can help. Clear criteria and specific descriptions of indicators can also help people observe with attention to detail and describe with precise phrases. This removes the focus from the "personal," placing it on sharp observations and careful, valid interpretations of behaviours.

- Communication styles vary. In *You Just Don't Understand* (1990) Deborah Tannen describes two main styles: indirect and direct. Direct communicators may appear abrupt and even rude to indirect speakers, while indirect styles use so much nuance that a direct person doesn't "get it." People must be aware of their own communication style and how it's received and possibly misinterpreted by others. They also need to be resilient and allow elbow room for other communication styles. Check perceptions and interpretations!

- Peers may provide different feedback to instructors. This is problematic if peer assessment is an important part of a program's summative assessment. We believe that providing learners with clear criteria (they may develop these), models, and specific descriptive indicators to help them visualize what these criteria look like, and practise applying the criteria, helps alleviate this problem. The relationship dynamics of offering critical feedback must also be recognized openly. If these elements are in place and significant discrepancies between instructor and peer assessment still exist, these should be discussed. Perhaps instructors and learners are applying criteria differently. Or, relational issues may be interfering with simple comparison of criteria to observations of peer performance.

Overall . . .

We believe the advantages of peer assessment outweigh potential disadvantages. The key is to help learners develop the skills of observing their peers and interpreting these observations, then communicating their perceptions with compassion and respect. Distinguish carefully between personal response and criteria ratings. Be clear which feedback is requested, and help people develop the skills of preparing and presenting the feedback with specific description. We believe "critical friendship" helps make peer assessment a positive learning experience for participants.

Toolbox 12—Using Objective Tests to Evaluate

What Are Objective Tests?

Objective tests usually refer to paper-and-pencil tests containing closed questions, where very little deviation is permitted from the "right" answer as determined by the test designer. These typically include multiple-choice questions, short-answer, true-false, matching or labelling activities that students complete under timed conditions with or without access to resources to assist them. Because such tests may focus mostly on recall or limited application of information, many instructors prefer to use more authentic or holistic assessment activities. However, objective-style tests offer some benefits that will be discussed below.

The word "objective" is a bit misleading. Such tests are subjective because they reflect the test designer's (usually instructor's) view of the world. The instructor decides what is true and what is false. In making up questions the instructor chooses what knowledge is most important, what questions are most worth asking about that knowledge, how that knowledge will be represented (what terms and language will be used), and what interpretations are most acceptable as answers. Objective tests certainly do not provide the "best" evidence of a learner's knowledge just because their results are quantitative.

The purpose of this Toolbox is to offer some simple suggestions about when and how to create objective tests. Stated simply, if you are using objective tests, you might as well make good use of them. This includes making them easy to grade and as student-friendly as possible. Note that this Toolbox is not a primer on the theories of test construction—that is well beyond our purpose.

Why Create Tests?

There may be situations in your teaching when it is appropriate to use comprehensive, paper-and-pencil, objective tests. But the use of such tests may seem to contradict the philosophies we have stated in this book. Here are reasons why some instructors find there are times when tests are a useful evaluation method, even for adult learners.

First, tests sometimes are the best way to give teachers a quick idea of how students are doing. Second, as teachers work through the process of creating a test, they make conscious decisions about what content is worth knowing. When this happens, comprehensive tests serve as guides for designing teaching plans. Third, a comprehensive test helps some students focus on what they are doing in class. If students know that a comprehensive test waits for them sometime soon, most will attend to the activities of the classroom in a more rigorous manner. Finally, when students do well on a comprehensive test, they often feel a real sense of success and accomplishment. The key, for us, was working to make sure that those students who studied hard did well. For many adult students, tests represent the "currency" of an educational experience. Doing well on a homework assignment or a short essay is one thing; however, doing well on a comprehensive test is something quite different. Many learners have told us how surprised and pleased they were that they were learning so much—when they successfully completed tests.

Many of our adult students remember experiences where they have failed tests. Naturally, some test fear remains. When this is the case, comprehensive tests can help re-establish a "success cycle" for learners. If learners begin to have a little success—if they do well on an objective test, they will find out it feels good. We believe this feeling of success can encourage learners to work just a little harder to have more success—because they enjoyed feeling good.

The design of the test should never seek to trick or punish learners for their lack of knowledge, but allow them to show how much they have remembered. And we want to make it clear that with comprehensive tests comes the redundancy of review activities that help students remember the information they will need to successfully answer the test questions. We believe teachers should review and review (in the most enjoyable ways possible) the material they consider most important so that their students will be so ready for the test that anyone who works in class will do well.

Question: Is it better to use an "objective" (closed question) or a "subjective" (open question) test?

Answer: Each type of test has good and bad points. For teachers, making both tests tends to be an equal amount of work. The question is: when do you want to do the work? Objective tests take a lot of time up-front to create them, but they are relatively easy to grade. The good point is that you can save the test (or question pool if you have a good computer) from one year to the next and cut down on your work in following years. An essay test is easier to create, but may take hours to grade. And, it doesn't get easier to grade year after year. You expend the same effort grading a test in year two than you did in year one.

The ability and learning styles of students makes a difference as well. Some adult students have a difficult time putting their thoughts into words especially under the pressure and time limits of a test situation, but may find it easier—more straight forward—responding to objective questions. Others become frustrated by the limited nature of objective test questions, which does not allow them to demonstrate the unique understandings they have constructed in a particular course. They may prefer the freedom of open questions.

How Do I Design and Use Objective Tests?

Following are suggestions, not rules. They vary according to the learners' needs, the course content, and the test situation. Overall, remember that "objective-style" test making is a labour- intensive activity. Prepare to spend a lot of time to develop really effective questions.

1. Use Different Types of Questions for Objective Tests

Following are some descriptions and samples of five different types of questions: fill-in-the-blank, short-answer, multiple-choice, true-false, and matching-style questions.

Fill-in-the-Blank Questions

Fill-in-the-Blank questions provide a sentence where students must know and fill in the appropriate word that completes the sentence. Because choices of words are not provided, it is difficult for students to guess. Fill-in-the-Blank questions are also good because they allow students to answer the question within the context of a larger sentence. Adult students who have a difficult time reading and spelling can have trouble with fill-in questions.

One way to make the questions easier and provide spelling and answer clues is to provide a word pool below the questions for students to choose from. This changes fill-in questions into matching questions.

Avoid . . .

- Avoid using sentences drawn from the course reading material, or students will assume they need to memorize material.

- Avoid ambiguous sentences that could be completed in several different ways:

  Leadership is a process of _____ (communication? control? organizing? leading?).

Do . . .

- Do ask students to supply important information, not incidental words.

- Do place the blank near the end of the question, so the sentence is easier to read and make sense of. For example:

  In England in the late 1700s, people started to invent machinery to do their work, launching the _____ Revolution. (Industrial)

Short-Answer Questions

Short-answer questions can vary from having students write definitions to having them justify or support points from an argument. They give students a structure for answering, but allow more freedom in these answers. Short-answer questions are relatively easy to grade and to design. They require students to create complete responses. Thus they reduce guessing and offer more reliable assessment of learner understanding.

Certain types of short answer questions also can help judge a student's ability to reason or to synthesize information.

Avoid . . .

- Avoid using an open-ended question if you want to determine students' understanding of a particular concept. For example, the following question is a good open-ended question for an essay response, but it would be unfair to grade student responses against one or two pre-determined answers:

  How has email affected the way humans interact with each other?

Do . . .

- Do be very clear and specific in your wording. Use phrases such as these:

  Define the following terms:

A. peer assessment

B. interdependent learning

Name one advantage and one disadvantage of the Apple iPod. Give an example for both the advantage and disadvantage.

■ Try asking students to make a choice and then defend it by providing their reasons. For example:

Choose the number of the statement you agree with most, then write TWO reasons supporting your choice:

1. Kolb's Learning Style Inventory is a good career indicator for adults.

2. Kolb's Learning Style Inventory helps identify introverts and extroverts.

3. Kolb's Learning Style Inventory can help learners understand how they process information.

Multiple-Choice Questions

Multiple-choice questions usually provide a question or statement stem with a number of alternatives from which a student might choose. The questions might be very easy (a simple definition); more difficult, where more than one answer is correct and students have to choose an alternative that includes more than one choice (i.e., both a and c are correct); or very difficult (i.e., where students must infer a great deal from the text). For example:

Easy

In what year did World War II end?

A. 1862

B. 1945

C. 1965

D. 1939

More difficult

Which of the following helped the Japanese people gain a stronger feeling of nationalism?

A. Japan's isolation from the world

B. the success of Japanese sports industries

C. the need to sacrifice personal pleasure to industrialize

D. a and c

E. all of the above

F. none of the above

Most difficult

Which of the following changes in family relationships are brought about by television? (Below the question in the space provided, support any answers you choose.)

A. Families will become more isolated.

B. Families won't stay at home much.

C. Families will become less friendly.

D. Children will live with their families longer.

E. Children will become more difficult for their parents to handle.

Avoid . . .

■ Avoid using an incomplete statement to start the question, because it can be difficult to read. For example:

The year World War II ended in was: a) 1862, b) 1945, c) 1965, d) 1939.

■ Avoid using a negative stem because it can confuse students. For example:

Which was not a cause of the 1839 rebellion?

■ Avoid using ambiguous qualifiers such as "maybe," "often" or "sometimes."

■ Avoid offering two or more responses which are equally correct.

■ Avoid embedding two questions in one.

■ Avoid asking questions about incidental information.

Do . . .

■ Do make up as many responses as you can for each question that are equally plausible.

■ Do try to make each response similar in length and parallel in grammatical structure.

■ Do check questions carefully for clarity and effectiveness. Try them out on colleagues. Try covering all responses to see if the question stands alone and can be answered with a simple statement or word.

■ Do craft questions to test learners' ability to judge and infer. Some instructors give learners a piece of text to read or a graph to interpret. Then the multiple-choice questions ask learners to infer meanings or to solve problems using the information. Such questions may ask learners to judge a best interpretation (but the answer should clearly be the "best" choice, and the instructor needs to be prepared to defend this choice). For example:

Read the poem "Clarendon" below. Then choose the BEST statement to summarize the central theme of the poem:

A. Human beings change most profoundly when they are facing death.

B. Loving relationships are more important than achievements.

C. One never know who one's closest friends are.

D. Men do not enjoy the same quality of relationships as women.

True or False

In True-or-False questions, students are asked to read a statement and indicate whether that statement is either true or false. If students know the information, distinguishing between a true and a false statement is usually easy. If the student does not know the information, the result is the flip of a coin. Often teachers make True-or-False questions more difficult by having students tell why a false statement is false. Otherwise guessing is encouraged.

True-or-False questions are quick to grade. However, it is difficult to write a completely true or absolute statement. Some instructors create negative statements based on the course material, and some build in "tricks" to force students to read questions carefully. For example:

> In 1853, Commodore Matthew Perry became the first person from the Western world to fly into the airport at Tokyo.

In this question, a careless student might see both Matthew Perry and 1853 and miss the fact that he sailed into the harbour and not flew into the airport.

Avoid . . .

- Avoid using generalizations, because they are rarely completely true.
- Avoid negative statements, which are confusing for some students.
- Avoid using very long statements, or statements which contain two ideas.

Do . . .

- Do use statements that are completely true or completely false.
- Do design questions that ask students to distinguish between fact and opinion.
- Do consider presenting students with a graph, chart of statistics, or other piece of text. Then ask them to rate several statements as true or false based on their interpretation of the graph, chart, or text.

Matching Questions

Matching questions work well for asking questions about people, dates, and events, and vocabulary terms and definitions. However, they only test students' recall of information, and can encourage rote memorization if overused. The matching exercise also may be more a search-and-eliminate activity than a demonstration of understanding. Some adult learners may understand the relationship between two items, but be confused by the presentation of these two items in different columns, isolated from meaningful context.

Avoid . . .

- Avoid having lengthy lists of terms (more than 20) as this can confuse the students.
- Avoid asking students to draw lines between the items. This can be confusing, especially in longer lists.
- Avoid giving away the last few matches as freebies. Add extra choices to the list of possible definitions on the right.

Do . . .

- Do put columns all on the same page.
- Do order each line from left to right so that the space is first, the term is second, and the letter and definition to be matched is on the far right. It makes the questions much easier to grade with a key.
- Do make sure that the words and choices are mixed up.
- Do provide very clear instructions. For example:

Match the phrase in Column II with the correct word in Column I. Write the LETTER for the matching phrase in Column II on the line beside each number of Column I.

Column I	Column II
___ 1. Dufay	A. Developed the first system of written notation for music.
___ 2. Leonin	B. Wrote the first known opera.

2. Be Careful to Write Clear Directions

Directions are often taken for granted by teachers who are quite test-wise. But you should not assume that students are as test-wise as you are. For example, we have seen teachers write a question such as "Should the federal government support dictatorships in Middle East?", fully intending that students address the question "Why?" But the teacher did not add the question "Why?" to the end of the first question, and one student simply answered "No."

At the same time, good directions help guide students' time through a test. For example, note the difference between the following directions.

> Question 1: Why has Western influence been important to the growth of Japan?
>
> Question 2: Explain three reasons why Western influence has been important to the growth of Japan.

Directions can encourage students to attend to certain points in the test. For example:

> Read the following statements. If the statement is true, write true in the space to the left of the question number. If it is false, write false in the space to the left of the question number. If the statement is false, give a one-sentence reason why it is false. Be careful. There are some "trick questions" here.

3. Take Tests Yourself Before Giving Them to Students

No teacher should ever give an test without taking it first. Better yet, ask another teacher friend to take it. Teachers often become "Store blind." They get so close to the test that they can't see the problems with it. It is much easier to correct a confusing question before the test than deal with the impact of the confusion later. Don't assume your first attempt at a test is perfect. Essay questions, especially, are prone to problems, and teachers should exhibit care.

4. If You Do Make a Mistake, Give Students the Marks

We recall teachers who have created confusing questions—especially matching questions—where there could be more than one correct answer, depending on how the question is "read" by students. As you grade the test, you may see examples of question problems you did not anticipate. Sometimes you can see, very clearly, that students are reading a question in a correct way—but a way you did not intend nor anticipate.

If this happens, there is no reason to go back over and re-correct every test. Simply add a point to every test paper—admitting the difficulty when you review the test and noting that each paper, whether the student read the question in the way you intended or not, received an additional point. Such a tactic saves time and gives students the feeling that you are being more than fair.

5. Make Objective Tests Easy to Grade

With just a little care, tests can be made much easier to grade. Before you give any test, imagine how you will grade it. (Where will you sit? What will you do? What do you want to guard against?) For short-answer questions, decide exactly what you are looking for in the responses before you start to grade.

For example, in multiple choice, one way to guard against cheating is to ask students to circle the number/letter in the choices and put the number/letter in the space to the left. Consider having students use an answer sheet or card that is separate from the question pages. (Warn students to check their answers very carefully! It's easy to mistakenly skip a question on the answer card.)

6. Avoid Discussing Perceived Differences or Difficulties in Class

When you are grading many tests, you may make errors. Sometimes these errors are simple mistakes in addition. Sometimes you have become unfocused and may have given too few points for essay or short-answer questions.

When we review a test with a group of students, we ask anyone who finds a "problem" to jot it down on a piece of paper which they give us at the end of the class. If the problem is simple addition, they note this. If they believe we have erred in ways that are not fair to their answers, they outline why they believe they should receive more points than they have. (We encourage students to take stands and support these stands. When they write notes about what they perceive to be errors, they are actually attending to program objectives.) We review these notes seriously and add points to the test if we believe they are deserved.

What Are the Benefits of Using Objective-Style Tests?

- Because questions can be marked quickly or scanned electronically, they are useful when evaluating a large group of learners, or when an instructor's time is severely limited.

- Grading of individual students' responses is not biased by the instructor's opinions. There are few interpretive variations affecting the ways different instructors mark the same tests.

- Learner success does not depend on the learner's writing skills. Nor can particularly fluent writers "fudge" their lack of information or understanding.

- Test results provide quantities of data that can be analyzed to determine patterns of students' learning, level of difficulty of the content or questions, clarity of the questions, and follow-up instruction required in particular areas of content.

- Some learners report a satisfying feeling of real accomplishment and mastery when they successfully complete an objective test.

What Are Some Concerns with Using Objective Tests?

- The question design is restrictive, forcing learners to fit their understandings into the test designer's way of describing a concept. The closed questions also do not allow learners to show their own understandings or to explain their rationale for choosing one answer over another. The single-choice correct answer does not reveal learner knowledge that may be close but not identical to the instructor-created response.

- Emphasis is on reading. Learners with poor reading skills are disadvantaged, especially under time limits. Objective tests may demonstrate more the students' inability to read the questions rather than their level of conceptual understanding.

- Some learners may guess at answers, or choose the correct answer without understanding or being able to explain or apply them.

- Objective questions sometimes focus narrowly on learners' ability to memorize information, rather than their ability to apply, interpret, judge, and draw conclusions.

- Questions are time-consuming to produce. Because of this, instructors often re-use questions—which may not always adequately reflect the learning or meet the needs of each new group of students.

- Adults often have difficulty remembering large amounts of information, or recalling and using discrete pieces of information that are isolated from a problem's context. Therefore adults may perform poorly on such tests even when they understand and apply the concepts quite well.

Overall . . .

There are times and places for using objective tests to assess adult learning. Some learners actually prefer them to other modes of assessment. However, good tests are difficult to develop and they are limited in what they reveal about learner understandings. Instructors also need to remember that for many adults tests of any kind may create anxiety and recall negative experiences of failure. Closed-question tests may be particularly frustrating for adults. They see different perspectives and apply knowledge according to context, and have a hard time choosing options according to rigid alternatives. Our recommendation is to use objective tests sparingly and very carefully.

References

Anderson, T. (2004). Teaching in an online learning context. In T. Anderson & F. Elloumi (Eds.). Theory and practice of online learning. Athabasca: Athabasca University. Retrieved April 2008 from http://www.cde.athabascau.ca/online_book

Argyris, C. (1990). Overcoming organizational defences. Needham, MA: Allyn and Bacon.

Beaman, R. (1995). How to end courses with a bang! The teaching professor. Madison: Magna Publications.

Beauchamp, L. & Parsons, J. (1992). Teaching from the inside out. Edmonton: Editions Duval.

Berge, Z. L. (1998). Barriers to online teaching in post-secondary institutions: Can policy fix it? Journal of distance learning administration, 1(2). Retrieved March 19, 2008 from http://www.westga.edu/~distance/Berge12.html

Black, L. C. (1993). Portfolio assessment. In T. W. Banta & Associates (Eds.), Making a difference: Outcomes of a decade of assessment in higher education. San Francisco: Jossey-Bass.

Black, P & Wiliam, D. (1998). Inside the black box: Raising standards through classroom assessment. Phi delta kappan, 80(2), 139-144.

Bloom, B.S. (1965). Taxonomy of educational objectives: The classification of educational goals. New York: David McKay Company, Inc.

Boud, D. (1995). Enhancing learning through self-assessment. London/Philadelphia: Kogan Page.

——. (1991). Implementing student self-assessment. Campbeltown: HERDSA. As cited in Li, L. & Kay, J. (2005), Student self-assessment and learning to think like a computer scientist. School of IT technical report. Sydney: University of Sydney.

Brookfield, S. D. (1990). The skillful teacher: Technique, trust, and responsiveness in the classroom. San Francisco: Jossey-Bass.

——. (1995). Becoming a critically reflective teacher. San Franscisco: Jossey-Bass.

——. (1987). Developing critical thinkers: Challenging adults to explore alternative ways of thinking and acting. San Francisco: Jossey-Bass.

Campbell, J. (1949). The hero with a thousand faces. Princeton: Princeton University Press.

Cervero, R. M. & A. L. Wilson. (1994). Planning responsibly for adult education: A guide to negotiating power and interests. San Francisco: Jossey-Bass.

Covey, S., Merrill, R. & Merrill, R. (1996). First things first: To live, to love, to learn, to leave a legacy. New York: Simon & Schuster.

Davie, L. E. (1997). Program evaluation for adults. In Barer-Stein, T. & Draper, J. A. (Eds.), The craft of teaching adults. Toronto: Culture Concepts.

Elbow, P. (1981). Writing with power. London: Oxford University Press.

Garrison, D.R., Anderson, T., & Archer, W. (2000). Critical thinking in a text-based environment: Computer conferencing in higher education. Internet in higher education, 2(2), 87-105.

Goleman, D. (1998). Working with emotional intelligence. New York: Bantam Books.

Haughey, M. & Anderson, T. (1998). Networked learning: The pedagogy of the internet. Montreal/Toronto: Cheneliere/McGraw-Hill.

Heimlich, J., & Norland, E. (1994). Developing teaching style in adult education. San Francisco: Jossey-Bass.

Jarvis, P. (1992). Learning practical knowledge. New directions for adult and continuing education. 55(1), 89–96.

Joint Committee on Standards for Educational Evaluation. (1994). Program evaluation standards (2nd ed.). Thousand Oaks, CA: Sage Publications.

Kirby, D. & Liner, T. (1982). Inside out: Developmental strategies for teaching writing (2nd ed.). Portsmouth, NH: Heinemann.

Kirkpatrick, D. L. (1982). How to improve performance through appraisal and coaching. New York: AMACOM.

Kolb, D. A. (1984). Experiential learning: Experience as the source of learning and development. Englewood Cliffs, NJ: Prentice-Hall.

Laird, D. (1985). Approaches to training and development (2nd ed.). Reading, MA: Addison-Wesley.

Lave, J., & S. Chaiklin. (1993). Understanding practice: Perspectives in activity and context. New York: Cambridge University Press.

Leslie, L. (1997). Authentic literacy assessment: An ecological approach. New York: Longman.

Luther, M., Cole, E. & Peter G. (Eds.). (1996). Dynamic assessment for instruction: From theory to practice. New York: Captus University Publications.

Marienau, C. (1994). Self-assessment: An essential skill for learning and performance in the workplace. In Proceedings of the 35th annual adult education research conference. Knoxville: University of Tennessee.

Moore, T. (1992). Care of the soul: A guide for cultivating depth and sacredness in everyday life. New York: HarperCollins.

Newman, J. (1991). Interwoven conversations: learning and teaching through critical reflection. Toronto: OISE Press.

Palloff, R.M., Pratt, K., & Stockley, D. (Review). (2001). Building learning communities in cyberspace: effective strategies for the online classroom. The Canadian journal of higher education, 31(3), 175.

The 10 principles: assessment for learning. Qualifications and curriculum authority (Great Britain). Retrieved March 10, 2008, from http://www.qca.org.uk/qca_4336.aspx.

Renner, P. (1993). The art of teaching adults. Vancouver: Training Associates.

Rough, J. (1994, October/November). Measuring training from a new science perspective. Journal for quality and participation, 12-16.

Rourke, L., Anderson, T., Garrison, D. R., & Archer, W. (2001). Assessing social presence in asynchronous text-based computer conferencing. Journal of distance education. Retrieved April 6, 2008 from http://cade.athabascau.ca/vol14.2/rourke_et_al.html

Schön, D. A. (1987). Educating the reflective practitioner: Toward a new design for learning and teaching in the professions. San Francisco: Jossey-Bass.

——. (1983). The reflective practitioner. New York: Basic Books.

Scriven, M. (1991). Evaluation thesaurus. Newbury Park, CA: Sage.

Senge, P., Kleiner, A., Roberts, C., Ross, R., & Smith, B. (1994). The fifth discipline fieldbook: Strategies and tools for building a learning organization. New York: Doubleday.

Senge, P. (1991). The fifth discipline: The art and practice of the learning organization. New York: Doubleday.

Starch, D., & Elliott, E. C. (1912). Reliability of the grading of high school work in English. School review, 21, 442–457.

Stewart, T. A. (1997). Intellectual capital: The new wealth of organizations. New York: Doubleday.

Stiggins, R. J. (2002). Assessment Crisis: The Absence Of Assessment FOR Learning. Phi Delta Kappan, 83(10), 758-65.

Stodel, E., Thompson, T., & MacDonald, C. (2006). Learners' perspectives on what is missing from online learning: interpretations through the community of inquiry framework. The international review of research in open and distance learning. 7 (3). Retrieved April 6, 2008, http://www.irrodl.org/index.php/irrodl/article/viewArticle/325/743.

Tannen, D. (1990). You just don't understand: Women and men in conversation. New York: Ballantine Books.

Tombari, M. L. (1999). Authentic assessment in the classroom: Approaches and practice. Upper Saddle River, NJ: Merrill.

Varela, F. (1989). "Laying Down a Path While Walking." In Thompson, W. (Ed.), Gaia. Boston: Shambhala.

Wagenheim, G. (1994, May). Feedback exchange: Managing group closure. Journal of management education, 18(2), 265–269.

Watkins, K., & Marsick, V. (1993). Sculpting the learning organization. San Francisco: Jossey-Bass.

Wiggins, G., & McTighe, J. (1998). Understanding by design. Alexandria, VA: ASCD.

Index

Use of boldface denotes key term definitions.